Lecture Notes in Computer Science 10473

Commenced Publication in 1973
Founding and Former Series Editors:
Gerhard Goos, Juris Hartmanis, and Jan van Leeuwen

W0193153

More information about this series at http://www.springer.com/series/7409

Haoran Xie · Elvira Popescu
Gerhard Hancke · Baltasar Fernández Manjón (Eds.)

Advances in Web-Based Learning – ICWL 2017

16th International Conference
Cape Town, South Africa, September 20–22, 2017
Proceedings

 Springer

Editors
Haoran Xie
The Education University of Hong Kong
Hong Kong
China

Gerhard Hancke
City University of Hong Kong
Hong Kong
Hong Kong

Elvira Popescu
University of Craiova
Craiova
Romania

Baltasar Fernández Manjón
Department of Software
Complutense University of Madrid
Madrid
Spain

ISSN 0302-9743 ISSN 1611-3349 (electronic)
Lecture Notes in Computer Science
ISBN 978-3-319-66732-4 ISBN 978-3-319-66733-1 (eBook)
DOI 10.1007/978-3-319-66733-1

Library of Congress Control Number: 2017950043

LNCS Sublibrary: SL3 – Information Systems and Applications, incl. Internet/Web, and HCI

Printed on acid-free paper

This Springer imprint is published by Springer Nature
The registered company is Springer International Publishing AG
The registered company address is: Gewerbestrasse 11, 6330 Cham, Switzerland

Preface

ICWL constitutes an annual international conference on Web-based learning, which started in Hong Kong in 2002 and has so far been held in Asia (China, Malaysia, Hong Kong, Taiwan), Australia, and Europe (UK, Germany, Romania, Estonia, Italy). ICWL 2017, the 16th conference in the series, was organized by the Hong Kong Web Society.

This year's conference was located in Cape Town, South Africa. Cape Town, located on the shore of Table Bay, is one of the top tourist destinations in the world. The city has many attractions including Table Mountain, Cape Point, Winelands, Robben Island, and Boulders Beach, home to a penguin colony. In this beautiful city, researchers, scholars, students, and professionals in the field of educational technology from all over the world gathered to share and exchange their state-of-the-art outputs and ideas at this conference.

This year we received 56 submissions from 25 countries worldwide. After a rigorous double-blind review process, 13 papers were selected as full papers, yielding an acceptance rate of 23%. In addition, 9 more short papers and 3 poster papers were selected. These contributions cover the latest findings in various areas, such as: learning models, collaborative learning, serious games, massive open online courses (MOOCS), mobile learning, computer-supported collaborative learning, personalized learning, Web 2.0 and social learning environments, game-based learning, etc.

ICWL 2017 featured a technical program of refereed papers selected by the international Program Committee, keynote addresses, and a doctoral consortium. Furthermore, the conference continued the new initiative, started by ICWL 2016, of holding the "2nd International Symposium on Emerging Technologies for Education" (SETE) at the same location. SETE collected the traditional workshop activities managed by ICWL in the past years, and additionally featured a novel organization in tracks. Workshops and tracks added new and hot topics on technology enhanced learning, providing a better overall conference experience to the ICWL attendees.

Many people contributed to making the conference possible and successful. Firstly, we thank all the authors who considered ICWL for their submissions. We also thank the PC members for their evaluations, which made possible the selection of the accepted papers. For the organization of ICWL 2017, additional thanks go to the organization chair, Gerhard P. Hancke, the Steering Committee representatives, Qing Li and Ralf Klamma, the treasurer, Howard Leung, the publicity chair, Yacine Atif, the Web chair, Bruno Silva, and the joint ICWL-SETE doctoral consortium co-chairs, Zuzana Kubincova and Marco Temperini. We also thank Springer, who kindly offered their sponsorship.

September 2017

Haoran Xie
Elvira Popescu
Gerhard Hancke
Baltasar Fernández Manjón

Organization

Organizing Committee

Conference Co-chairs

Gerhard Hancke   City University of Hong Kong, Hong Kong
Baltasar Fernández Manjón   Universidad Complutense de Madrid, Spain

Technical Program Committee Co-chairs

Haoran Xie   The Education University of Hong Kong, Hong Kong
Elvira Popescu   University of Craiova, Romania

Organization Chair

Gerhard P. Hancke   University of Pretoria, South Africa

Steering Committee Representatives

Qing Li   City University of Hong Kong, Hong Kong
Ralf Klamma   RWTH Aachen University, Germany

Treasurer

Howard Leung   Hong Kong Web Society, Hong Kong

Publicity Chair

Yacine Atif   University of Skovde, Sweden

Web Chair

Bruno Silva   University of Pretoria, South Africa

Joint ICWL-SETE Doctoral Consortium Chairs

Zuzana Kubincova   Comenius University in Bratislava, Slovakia
Marco Temperini   Sapienza University of Rome, Italy

Program Committee

Marie-Helene Abel   HEUDIASYC - Université de Technologie de Compiègne, France
Dimitra Anastasiou   Luxembourg Institute of Science and Technology, Luxembourg
Yacine Atif   University of Skövde, Sweden

Maria Bielikova	Slovak University of Technology in Bratislava, Slovakia
Ig Ibert	Bittencourt Federal University of Alagoas, Brazil
Carlos Vaz de Carvalho	Instituto Superior de Engenharia do Porto, Portugal
Wei Chen	Agricultural Information Institute of CAAS, China
Guangliang Chen	Delft University of Technology, The Netherlands
Dickson Chiu	Faculty of Education, The University of Hong Kong, Hong Kong
Maria-Iuliana	Dascalu Politehnica University of Bucharest, Romania
Giuliana Dettori	Istituto di Tecnologie Didattiche del CNR, Italy
Damiano Distante	Unitelma Sapienza University, Rome, Italy
Giovanni Fulantelli	Istituto Tecnologie Didattiche, CNR, Palermo, Italy
Dragan Gasevic	University of Edinburgh, UK
Rosella Gennari	Free University of Bozen-Bolzano, Italy
Ed Gehringer	North Carolina State University, USA
Denis Gillet	Swiss Federal Institute of Technology in Lausanne (EPFL), Switzerland
Sabine Graf	Athabasca University, Canada
Christian Gütl	Technical University of Graz, Austria
Preben Hansen	Stockholm University, Sweden
Tianyong Hao	Guangdong University of Foreign Studies, China
Eelco Herder	L3S Research Center, Hannover, Germany
Martin Homola	Comenius University, Bratislava, Slovakia
Seiji Isotani	University of São Paulo, Brazil
Malinka Ivanova	Technical University - Sofia, Bulgaria
Mirjana Ivanovic	University of Novi Sad, Serbia
Jelena Jovanovic	University of Belgrade, Serbia
Elisabeth Katzlinger	Johannes Kepler University, Linz, Austria
Ioannis Kazanidis	Technological Educational Institute of Kavala, Greece
Michael Kickmeier-Rust	Graz University of Technology, Austria
Ralf Klamma	RWTH Aachen University, Germany
Tomaz Klobucar	Institut Josef-Stefan, Slovenia
Line Kolås	Nord University, Norway
Milos Kravcik	RWTH Aachen University, Germany
Zuzana Kubincová	Comenius University Bratislava, Slovakia
Amruth Kumar	Ramapo College of New Jersey, USA
Vive Kumar	Athabasca University, Canada
Lam-For Kwok	City University of Hong Kong, Hong Kong
Mart Laanpere	Tallinn University, Estonia
Jean-Marc Labat	Laboratoire d'Informatique de Paris 6, France
Luigi Laura	Sapienza University of Rome, Italy
Elise Lavoué	Université Jean Moulin Lyon 3, France
Howard Leung	City University of Hong Kong, Hong Kong
Frederick Li	University of Durham, UK
Carla Limongelli	Roma Tre University, Italy
George Magoulas	Birkbeck College & University of London, UK

Contents

Social Media and Web 2.0-Based Learning Environments

Assessment and Accessibility in Higher Education

Open Educational Resources and Recommender Systems

Practice and Experience Sharing

Inquiry-Based Learning and Gamification

DojoIBL: Online Inquiry-Based Learning

Angel Suarez[✉], Stefaan Ternier, and Marcus Specht

Welten Institute, Open Universiteit, 6419AT Heerlen, The Netherlands
{angel.suarez,stefaan.ternier,marcus.specht}@ou.nl

Abstract. DojoIBL is a web based platform to support collaborative inquiry-based learning processes. It imitates real-world research processes and organizes inquiry activities into several phases. DojoIBL considers lessons learned from the weSPOT project and offers a cloud-based highly scalable infrastructure that has a strong focus on (mobile) data collection. In this sense, DojoIBL blends formal (desk-top based) learning and informal (mobile) learning. Within the course of 1 year, a design based research methodology was implemented in 10 national and international inquiry projects. Within this period, students were inter-viewed at regular times. Time and task management issues turned out to be critical functionalities and were thus implemented in several iterations.

Keywords: Inquiry-based learning · Cloud-based learning · Community of inquiry

1 Introduction

A learning process has been defined as a sequence of interdependent procedures that aim at transferring new knowledge from the working memory to the long-term memory [5]. Inquiry Based Learning (IBL) builds upon this definition and establishes questions as a starting point for the learning process. Through a combination of formal and informal activities and a continuous exploration based on social interactions students generate new knowledge [3, 11]. IBL has been recognized by policymakers as an efficient vehicle to make students more proficient in STEM (Science, Technology, Engineering and Mathematics) subjects. Additionally, it has been considered essential for scientific innovation and the future knowledge society [1, 6, 15]. The usage of technology in the field of IBL has led to the development of solutions like DojoIBL, an open source implementation that enables flexible structuring of collaborative inquiry processes [13]. DojoIBL is a cloud-based redesign of the weSPOT [12] tool suite that has been conceived to address challenges like scalability, seamlessly and flexible inquiry support, access to open educational resources (OER) and intuitive orchestration support.

2 Inquiry Design

IBL is a complex process and its implementation in real scenarios implies several practical considerations. This manuscript has transformed these considerations into the following design challenges that have been addressed by DojoIBL.

© Springer International Publishing AG 2017
H. Xie et al. (Eds.): ICWL 2017, LNCS 10473, pp. 3–12, 2017.
DOI: 10.1007/978-3-319-66733-1_1

IBL is often based in ill-structured learning tasks that are open ended [4, 10]. So, it requires more support and structure than traditional educational setups. In this informal IBL process, students need freedom to investigate their essential questions and need closer process support and guidance. An essential question is any question that requires a student to develop a plan or to make a decision in order to answer it. Unlike scientists, students do not have a structured mindset with the steps needed to address an essential question. Thus, technology can help to fill this gap and to provide guidance to master applying these inquiry structures. However, there is not a unique inquiry model that supports every essential question. So, tools need flexibility to embrace a very diverse variety of inquiry models. Additionally, designing these flexible inquiry processes from scratch can be challenging for teachers. Following an OER (Open Educational Resource) approach, DojoIBL offers templates for inquiry structures to be reused.

Traditional Learning Management Systems (LMS) work with courses. When students enroll in a course, they usually participate in a shared space in which everyone sees each other's contributions. To enable independent group work within a course, LMSs use groups. In the context of IBL, collaborative group work has been proven to have positive influence of support on task and team regulation [9]. So, it is especially relevant to allow teachers to organize and to regulate groups within an inquiry structure. DojoIBL makes a clear distinction between, the inquiry structure –the equivalent of a course in a LMS– and the runtime –that refers to the space in which students work together–. This differentiation also facilitates the reusability of an inquiry structure. If a teacher wants to reuse only an inquiry structure with another group of students, there is no need to copy, clone or start a new inquiry from scratch. DojoIBL handles this situation very intuitively.

From a technical point of view, the role of technology bridging the gap between formal and informal learning is a key feature. IBL, as a combination of formal and informal activities, requires contextual support. In IBL students are often distributed across different places. Therefore, tools need to bring students together providing a shared space to exchange e.g. instant messages or data collected. An additional aspect when enabling a digital shared space for collaboration is scalability. Inquiry processes often have periods of high volume of data traffic, especially supporting in-field inquiry that requires sharing large amount of multimedia data files and simultaneous connections to the server. To address these challenges, DojoIBL provides a cloud-based scalable solution that bases its front-end in HTML5. The first characteristic makes DojoIBL to scale up with an increasing number of users. The second one enables run across different kinds of devices including laptops or mobile devices. This, in turn, can support a large number of students exchanging information in a shared space while working in their collaborative inquiry projects.

2.1 Flexible Inquiry Support

An inquiry is a process with the aim to solve a problem, understand a phenomenon or to create knowledge. Scientific inquiry in empirical sciences answers the question of how phenomena are related. It is about cause-consequence relations, which can be tested in experiments. Recent literature [8] synthesized the most common inquiry cycles resulting in a framework that informs designers to model inquiry learning activities e.g. [16]

suggest an inquiry cycle consisting of 5 steps: (1) ask, (2) investigate, (3) create, (4) discuss and (5) reflect. [2] present a 5-step variation: (1) question, (2) predict, (3) experiment, (4) model and (5) apply, [7] presents a slightly different 6-step model: Inquisition-acquisition-supposition-implementation-summation-exhibition. Similarly, the weSPOT project has defined an IBL-model that consists of six –optional- steps. One the biggest challenges for teachers is to use these models in practice to create inquiry based learning lessons. They need to shift from teaching content into directing kids to find their own learning paths. Thus, they need inquiry structures/models for students to let them experience what inquiry based learning is about.

Tafoya [14] suggested four kinds of inquiry-based learning differentiating student autonomy. The first level is a confirmation inquiry in which students are provided both with the structure of the inquiry as well as the answers. This is useful to become familiar and to have a first experience with an inquiry process. The fourth (most challenging level for students) is an open inquiry. Here students act like scientists, deriving a question, designing the operationalization and carrying out the investigation.

There is quite a startup cost involved for a teacher to create a first inquiry structure. An experienced teacher wants maximum flexibility and the possibility to define custom phases and activities. A novice will want to start with an existing inquiry structure. DojoIBL provides both options. It enables teachers to create an inquiry from scratch (Fig. 1a) or a user can select an inquiry model that is available in literature (Fig. 1b and c). In this sense the tool takes into account lessons learned from Tafoya [14]. A novice teacher can choose an existing -proven- inquiry structure and explore the demo activities that are offered. A more experienced teacher can create a custom structure and has full control over phases and types of activities that are to be conducted within a phase.

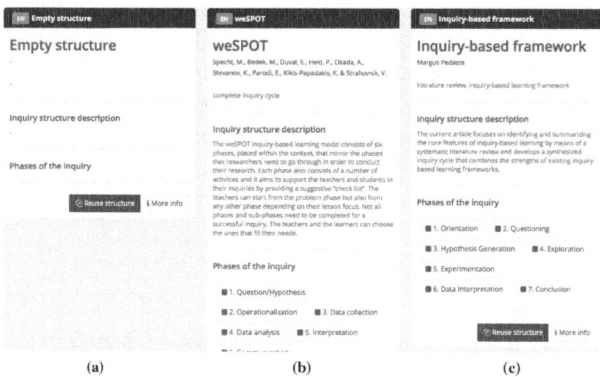

Fig. 1. List of inquiry templates available. Each template represents an existing inquiry model in the literature

2.2 Orchestrating Inquiry Group Work

DojoIBL makes a clear distinction between the inquiry model/structure, discussed in Sect. 2.1, and the runtime data that is produced by the learner. An inquiry structure can allocate various independent groups of students working with their own inquiry space. Each inquiry group share the inquiry structure (model), but participants in those groups can communicate (Fig. 2: the chat is in the right side) and work independently from other groups.

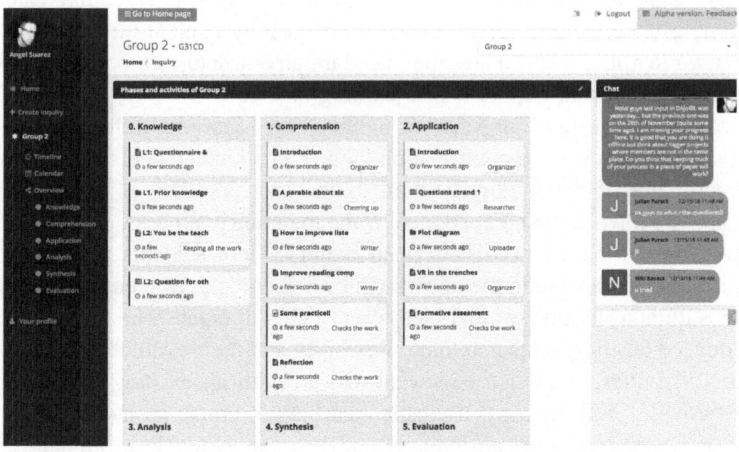

Fig. 2. Students' view of an inquiry. Chat on the right. Inquiry structure on the center.

The students' view has five screens; three (inquiry view, phase view and activity view) to visualize the structure and the content of an inquiry, the timeline view (Sect. 2.3) and the calendar view (Sect. 2.4). The inquiry view (Fig. 2) shows the whole inquiry structure. Each grey block corresponds to a phase which is formed by inquiry activities. An inquiry activity is an extensible object in the DojoIBL framework. While, default activities are rich text, discussion, data collection and mind mapping activities, new type of activities can be easily created by the developers extending the activity object in the DojoIBL framework. Inquiry activities are authored by the teacher in order to guide learners through inquiry process. Often, they have a colored border that determines which role (a learner with a responsibility) is in charge of the given activity.

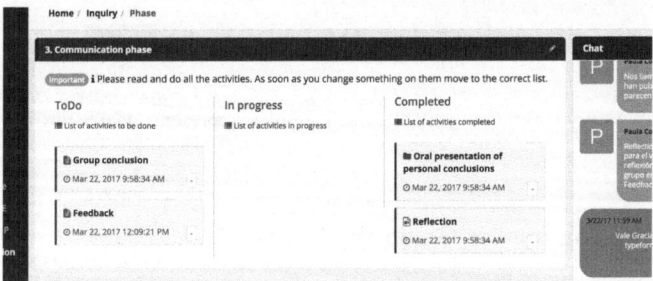

Fig. 3. Phase view of an inquiry. It provides three columns to monitor the status of the activity.

The second screen (Fig. 3) is the phase view. It is organized in three columns: to-do, in progress and completed. Students can drag and drop activities in between these columns to set the status of the activities. Motivating students to reflect upon the status of an activity is important for both student and teacher. The teacher gets an indication of progress students have made. A student group receives insight on their productivity and can reflect on what remains to be done.

2.3   Students' Awareness

DojoIBL builds upon a powerful notification system that sends server generated notifications to the desktop client, but also to Android and iOS devices. Notifications are broadcasted for various types of events. For instance, when a teacher alters or creates an activity, or when a student sends a new message a notification is sent. Once the notification arrives, it is visible for 2 s in right upper corner. When the user opens the notification, the corresponding information item (e.g. the chat) is opened.

The timeline (Fig. 4) keeps the user informed of what is going on in the inquiry. When a user is not online, some notifications will not be received (e.g. when a user comments on an activity). Rather than having the user to check all activities for updates, the timeline lists progress for all activities.

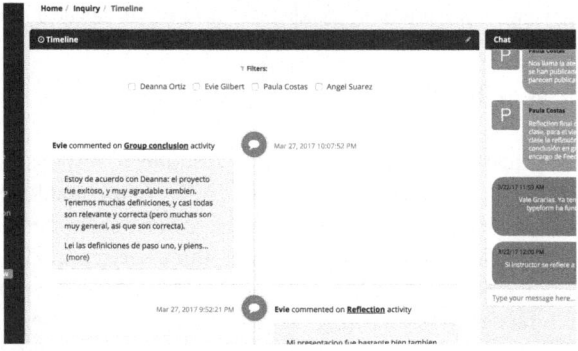

Fig. 4. Timeline of the inquiry with recent contributions. There is one per inquiry group.

Timeline entries are organized by date, and thus make easy overview of recent contributions possible. Clicking on an entry brings the user to the corresponding activity and provides more context information. For instance, it shows the message within the context of other messages in an activity.

Students and respondents indicated that although this is helpful, they would like the notification system to integrate with their mailbox. Future implementations will consider a configuration option to receive either an email each time something happens, a daily digest or no notifications at all.

2.4   Time Management

During interventions with experts and teachers, time management was often pointed out as a crucial functionality. The DojoIBL calendar (Fig. 5) has been developed as a solution for displaying activity deadlines as a visual indicator for tasks that lie ahead. The deadlines are defined at the level of inquiry group, so each inquiry group manages its time independently from the other groups. This enables better time management for groups and facilitates more self-regulated processes.

Fig. 5.   Calendar view with the activity deadlines. There is one calendar per inquiry group.

3   The DojoIBL Cloud Based Architecture

In a traditional physical deployment setting, an institute is responsible for acquiring software and hardware to implement e.g. an LMS. With cloud computing, these resources are made available through a network. Hardware, software and data are made available on demand. Cloud applications come in three service models. Software as a service (SaaS) cloud applications offer an application to the customer. The cloud based service provider offers this service (e.g. email, project management, customer relationship, …) to a customer that can often configure the software to his needs. Platform as a service (PaaS) often standardised services (e.g. access management, data storage, database management…) The service provider maintains the framework and infrastructure but often offers facilities for development in languages like Python,.NET or Java. PaaS customers do not get direct access to the operating system but operate with the definition of the platform. Infrastructure as a service (IaaS) introduces most flexibility but comes with more maintenance for the customer. Infrastructure such servers, network and data storage is offered to the customer that has complete freedom in how to use the hardware.

DojoIBL has been developed to run using PaaS services and offers its functionality as SaaS cloud application. Building on a PaaS service comes with the advantage of not having access to the operating system, which lowers administrative burdens. The PaaS service offers unlimited access to both processing power and information storage. As more users use the system simultaneously, the system can allocate more servlet containers. The database is implemented as a schemaless NoSQL store that provides scalable retrieval and storage of data.

Figure 6 shows a simplified overview of the DojoIBL architecture. Application layer components have been developed either in AngularJS for web browsers or in Ionic for mobile devices. The front-end applications communicate with a REST based web service stack that is offered by the DojoIBL engine. All components in the business logic layer rely on third party services offered either by the PaaS system or by external providers. The mobile notification component for instance relies on external providers such as Google Cloud Messaging (GCM) to broadcast notification to Android devices, while Apple Push Notifications (APN) sends notifications to iOS devices.

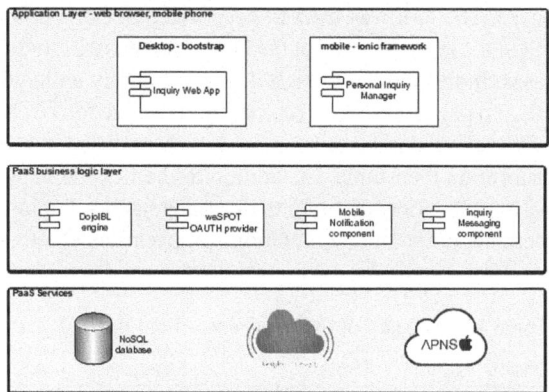

Fig. 6. Simplified DojoIBL architecture

The NoSQL database makes inquiries, groups and other objects persistent. The DojoIBL class diagram relates the most important classes that are required by the different components. After authentication by weSPOT identity provider, user details are represented by an Account object. Every user can create an arbitrary amount of Inquiries or can participate as a student in an Inquiry Group. The inquiry messaging component manages a chat. Through a Thread, a chat is bound to an Inquiry Group. Within this group, users can post an arbitrary number of messages. The messaging component relies on the notification component to broadcast new messages to various devices.

4 DojoIBL Usage

During the last year, the DojoIBL platform has been used in different types of collaborative IBL processes. During this period, a design based research approach was set up with several trials at Dutch and European level involving almost 200 participants. Table 1 shows an overview of the pilots conducted between June of 2016 and March

2017. The structures created for the pilots varied from 2 up to 7 phases with a different number of activities per phase. Often these pilots went also beyond the IBL approach and were characterized as group work. This shows the flexibility of DojoIBL to offer support in different contexts. For example, 12 students from the MP4 (Middle Program Year school) course at the International School of Eindhoven, carried out an investigation about World War 1 using the levels of Bloom's taxonomy as phases (6 levels = 6 phases). The goal of the inquiry was to learn more about reading and listening comprehension skills through inquiry activities related to the WW1. Within each phase -from Knowledge to Evaluation- students acquired understanding about their evaluation criteria for the inquiry, and they finished the inquiry applying the criteria in the context of WW1 e.g. reading and listening fragments from soldiers in the trenches. In another trial at the Agora school, DojoIBL was used to conduct an inquiry challenge to design the logo of DojoIBL. In this case the process was divided in two phases: the design and the implementation phase. The tool was used to keep track of the decisions made and the improvements done in the logo. In a trial at the Open Universiteit, students carried out an inquiry with 7 phases. In this case, although it was not purely an inquiry, the 7 participants used DojoIBL as a personal space to discuss and receive feedback about their PhD. Each phase was assigned to one participant, and each participant was responsible for facilitating a brainstorm on their topic. In addition to the flexible inquiry structure support, Table 1 shows a great variety of group work arrangements. For instance, continuing with examples described, different configurations of groups can be found. The first two

Table 1. Summary of the pilots carried out the first year.

Organization – duration – topic	Users	Structure	Message - comments
Open University – 2 weeks Internal organization	19 researchers (4 groups)	Phases: 5 Activities: 45	M: 512 – C: 407
Int. School Eindhoven – 1week Ancient Rome	34 11yo-students (18 groups)	Phases: 4 Activities: 7	M: 206 – C: 39
Int. School Eindhoven – 4 months Spanish Satirical Magazines	2 17yo-students	Phases: 4 Activities: 25	M: 182 – C: 282
Int. School Eindhoven – 3 months World War 1	12 13yo-students (2 groups)	Phases: 6 Activities: 28	M: 185 – C: 59
Int. School Eindhoven – 2 months Spanish Language Learning	28 9yo-students (12 groups)	Phases: 3 Activities: 18	M: 949 – C: 314
Open University – 3 months 'PhDs Round Table'	7 researchers	Phases: 7 Activities: 12	M: 173 – C: 42
Workshop with Teachers – 1 day DojoIBL Demo	40 teachers	Phases: 6 Activities: 20	M: 2 – C: 3
Agora School – 1week Design DojoIBL Logo	4 13yo-students	Phases: 2 Activities: 4	M: 12 – C: 14
Escola Sadako – Planned International Exchange	40 14-yo students	Phases: 3 Activities: 12	M: 0 – C: 0
Agora School – Planned International Exchange	12 14yo-students	Phases: 6 Activities: 10	M: 0 – C: 0
Total	**199**		

trials –at the school in Eindhoven and Agora– only have one group defined, while the third trial has two groups of 6 students each. In this case, they follow the same Bloom's taxonomy structure but they worked independently at a different pace. Ultimately, these examples illustrate the flexibility of DojoIBL supporting very diverse inquiry processes.

In order to get more insights on the user experiences in DojoIBL, and to assess its effectiveness in collaborative settings, three questionnaires and semi-structured interviews were distributed during schools' and university's trials. At the University, experts in IBL showed a great degree of acceptance: UX scores were high. Moreover, the experts' feedback led to significant improvements in the DojoIBL interface – implementing a better inquiry structure overview– that were discussed in the chapter 2.2 of this manuscript. In the school context, preliminary results about the group efficiency showed high scores in the 'coordinating' and 'trust' scales, while the 'personal understanding' and 'adapting' scales did not score so well. Since there was no experimental group and the population was limited, interpretations have been taken cautiously. Nevertheless, qualitative data from the semi-structured interviews with students confirmed the general positive acceptance and the adequate support that DojoIBL provides for the collaborative inquiry process.

5   Conclusion

Inquiry based learning (IBL) has been suggested as an efficient approach for STEM subject teaching, however it is a complex endeavor for teachers and students to implement in real settings.

This manuscript has collected results in the field of IBL and has transformed them into design challenges that have been addressed in DojoIBL. As a result, a flexible cloud based solution with special focus on process structure, simplicity, awareness and time management has been implemented. The design based research approach took place in close collaboration with school stakeholders. After 10 Dutch and European trials with 200 students including teachers, students and researchers, DojoIBL has finally reached a stable phase.

All in all, the retrospective evaluation of DojoIBL after one year of work is promising. The users' feedback confirmed that DojoIBL could assist teachers and researchers to shape new effective collaborative inquiry structures in which students generate more individual and collective meaning. This, together with the non-project basis maintenance culture, has led DojoIBL to a sustainable model that encourages the team to strive for a scaling up phase.

References

1. Ally, M. (ed.): Mobile learning - Transforming the delivery of education and training. AU Press, Edmonton (2009)
2. Bruce, C., Bishop, P.: Using the web to support inquiry-based literacy development. J. Adolesc. Adult Literacy **45**(8), 706–714 (2002)

3. Garrison, D.R., et al.: Critical inquiry in a text-based environment: computer conferencing in higher education. Internet High. Educ. **2**(2–3), 87–105 (1999)
4. De Jong, F., et al.: Regulative processes in individual, 3D and computer supported cooperative learning contexts. Comput. Hum. Behav. **21**(4), 645–670 (2005)
5. Kirschner, P.A., et al.: Why minimal guidance during instruction does not work: an analysis of the failure of constructivist, discovery, problem-based, experiential, and inquiry-based teaching. Educ. Psychol. **41**(2), 75–86 (2006)
6. Kuenzi, J.J.: Mathematics (STEM) Education : Background, Federal Policy, and Legislative Action (2008)
7. Llewellyn, D.: Teaching high school science through inquiry: A case study approach. Corwin Press, Thousand Oaks (2005)
8. Pedaste, M., et al.: Phases of inquiry-based learning: definitions and the inquiry cycle. Educ. Res. Rev. **14**, 47–61 (2015)
9. Saab, N., et al.: Support of the collaborative inquiry learning process: influence of support on task and team regulation. Metacognition Learn. **7**(1), 7–23 (2012)
10. Salovaara, H.: An exploration of students' strategy use in inquiry-based computer-supported collaborative learning. J. Comput. Assist. Learn. **21**(1), 39–52 (2005)
11. Scardamalia, M., Bereiter, C.: Higher levels of agency for children in knowledge building: a challenge for the design of new knowledge media. J. Learn. Sci. **1**(1), 37–68 (1991)
12. Specht, M., et al.: weSPOT: inquiry based learning meets learning analytics (2013)
13. Suárez, Á., Ternier, S., Prinsen, F., Specht, M.: Nurturing communities of inquiry: a formative study of the DojoIBL platform. In: Verbert, K., Sharples, M., Klobučar, T. (eds.) EC-TEL 2016. LNCS, vol. 9891, pp. 292–305. Springer, Cham (2016). doi:10.1007/978-3-319-45153-4_22
14. Tafoya, E., et al.: Assessing inquiry potential: a tool for curriculum decision makers. Sch. Sci. Math. **80**(1), 43–48 (1980)
15. Tienken, C.H.: Conclusions from PISA and TIMSS testing. Kappa Delta Pi Rec. **49**(2), 56–58 (2013)
16. White, B.Y., Frederiksen, J.R.: Inquiry, modeling, and metacognition: making science accessible to all students. Cogn. Instr. **16**(1), 3–118 (1998)

Codebreakers: Designing and Developing a Serious Game for the Teaching of Information Theory

Jacob Greeff[1]($\boxtimes$), Reolyn Heymann[2], Murray Heymann[2], and Carl Heymann[2]

[1] TELIT-SA, Faculty of Economic Science and Information Technology, North-West University, Vaal Triangle Campus, Vanderbijlpark, South Africa
japie.greeff@nwu.ac.za
[2] Department of Electrical and Electronic Engineering Science, Faculty of Engineering and the Built Environment, University of Johannesburg, Johannesburg, South Africa
rheymann@uj.ac.za, heymann.murray@gmail.com, ch.heymann@gmail.com

Abstract. This paper reports the conceptualization, design, and development of the first and second prototype of a serious game for the teaching of the basics of Information Theory. Using the steps for a needs and context analysis, the researchers, lecturer and game developers participated in a focused group discussion to conceptualize the context and content for the game. Based on the design concepts found through the literature review, the team chose to follow a design research approach to create the academic intervention. The team used known game attributes and design principles, as well as feedback from guided evaluations, to create the first two prototypes of the game Codebreakers which is currently being used at the University of Johannesburg. As described in the design research approach, the team used an iterative process to develop the prototypes, with the final goal being to reach a point where the academic intervention can be generalized to other contexts.

Keywords: Serious games · Engineering education · Self-determination theory

1 Background

As it is a final year module, Telecommunications can be very difficult for students to grasp the finer details of and in this context the academic staff sought to create a technology driven intervention to offer students an additional means of practicing their problem-solving skills. The specific intervention chosen was in the form of a serious game called Codebreakers. As the study was undertaken specifically to create an artifact to be used in the classroom, an educational design research approach (EDR), and more specifically a developmental studies approach [1] was chosen.

Behnke [2] explored the concept of applying the lens of self-determination theory to analyse the application of serious games and gamification interventions to the context of computer science education, and this same approach is followed in the

H. Xie et al. (Eds.): ICWL 2017, LNCS 10473, pp. 13–22, 2017.
DOI: 10.1007/978-3-319-66733-1_2

creation of the Codebreakers serious game. The application of games based interventions for the teaching of university level courses in the South African context is not without president as can be seen by previous work done by Leendertz, Fitchart and Booth [3].

With this concept in mind, an initial prototype of a game based intervention was created, and evaluated by the lecturer (as content specialist), a previous student, a post graduate student and a game developer. From this, a number of insights were gained, and fed into the creation of a second prototype, this time as a full game. This full prototype was again evaluated and then field trialed in the 1st semester of 2017 in the module with 91 students. This paper reports on the process of conducting the initial needs analysis and development of the first and second prototypes. It should be noted that this project is in the second phase of EDR and as described in [1, 4], this means that the intervention should be fit for purpose in the specific context it is being applied to, but may not be ready for generalization to other contexts just yet.

2 Literature Review

2.1 Serious Games

Alvarez & Djaouti proposed the following formal definition for serious games:

> "Computer application, for which the original intention is to combine with consistency, both serious (Serious) aspects such as non-exhaustive and non-exclusive, teaching, learning, communication, or the information, with playful interaction from the video game (Game)." [5]

The above definition is used for the purpose of this article, but it is important to note as pointed out by Ulicsak that there is currently no universally accepted formal definition for serious games in the current literature [6]. It is sufficient however to view serious games as full games that are not purposefully developed only for their entertainment value. This concept does highlight the fact that developers of serious games need to focus on both the traditional fun aspects of games, as well as to ensure that the serious content they have to convey is brought forth clearly. It is for this reason then that Derryberry proposes that serious games development is a "team sport" involving members from the game design community, subject matter experts and students of the material that is representative of the serious aspect of the game being developed [7].

A distinction is made at this point between Serious Games and Gamification of university courses. The differences between the two used for the purpose of this article are put forth by Deterding, Dixon, Khaled and Nacke [8] with the main difference between the two concepts being that a serious game is a "whole" game, whereas a gamified system is one that only uses some game elements in its design. Game elements in this context can mean any aspects of a game that can be isolated and applied separately. With this in mind, the essential characteristics or dimensions of effective instructional games evaluated are the ones put forth by Garris, Ahlers and Driskell as: (i) Fantasy, (ii) Rules/Goals, (iii) Sensory Stimuli, (iv) Challenge, (v) Mystery and (vi) Control [9].

2.2   Self-determination Theory

If the goal of a serious game is to allow students to explore some material in the context of a game, then students need to feel motivated to do so. In terms of motivation, there is a distinction made in the literature between intrinsic motivation (doing something for the satisfaction it brings) and extrinsic motivation (doing something to attain some external outcome) [10]. Self-determination Theory puts forth 3 main needs that people need to fulfill in order to feel self-motivated to do some task namely (i) Competence or gaining mastery over some challenge over time, (ii) Relatedness or social interaction with other people, and (iii) Autonomy or the ability to make choices and have control. In terms of game development, Behnke described how different game elements can be categorized into these 3 needs [2]. The educational context brings a unique benefit as the above needs can be addressed by the game to attempt to gain intrinsic motivation from students, but as there is also the extrinsic need to do better in the course (as represented by the course grade) so both motivations can be addressed.

3   Research Design and Methodology

3.1   Educational Design Research and Development Studies

Akker, Plomp and Nieveen define Educational Design Research (EDR) as follows:

> *"to design and develop an intervention (such as programs, teaching-learning strategies and materials, products and systems) as a solution to a complex educational problem as well as to advance our knowledge about the characteristics of these interventions and the processes to design and develop them, or alternatively to design and develop educational interventions (about for example, learning processes, learning environments and the like) with the purpose to develop or validate theories."* [1]

The core of the EDR process is therefor to not only generate research documentation to guide the creation of educational interventions, but rather to document the process of creation of these interventions. Within EDR, there are two distinct approaches that can be taken namely Validation studies (creating artifacts with the goal of validating a theory) and Development studies (the creation of educational intervention artifacts). For the purposes of this study the latter focus is of most relevance.

One of the characteristics of an EDR study is that there are a number of research cycles undertaken within a number of defined phases throughout the course of the study as can be seen in [1]. The flow of this specific study is described in Fig. 1.

As can be seen from Fig. 1, the study is split up into 3 phases namely (i) The preliminary research phase (Needs and context analysis), (ii) the design, development and test phase and (iii) the semi summative evaluation phase. Each of these phases are then made up of a number of research cycles. The steps indicated in Fig. 1 for the research cycle are defined by Plomp in [1]. The design and prototyping of the software artifact in this study is done through an Agile development methodology. In this article, the first three cycles of the study are explored.

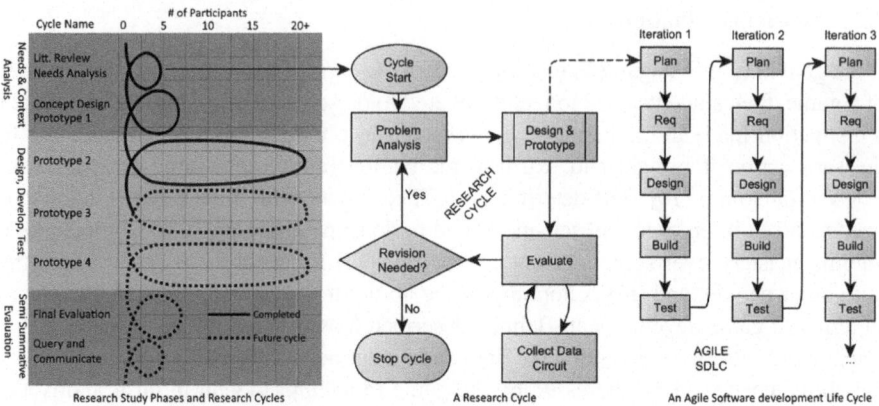

Fig. 1. The design research approach followed

3.2   Measuring Success

In EDR, as an iterative process is followed, it becomes difficult to define when the study has effectively "completed". In order to overcome this problem, the concept of quality evaluation was put forward by Nieveen [11] such that the artifact is evaluated at the end of each cycle to measure how "fit for purpose" it is. The criteria that the artifact is measured against are: (i) Relevance (is it based on state of the art knowledge?), (ii) Consistency (Is it logically designed?), (iii) Practicality (Is it fit for purpose?) and (iv) Effectiveness (Does it result in the required outcome?).

These criteria are measured to different extents depending on the phase of the research being done as follows [1]: (i) Preliminary research phase (content relevance and consistency focus), (ii) Development phase (initially a consistency and practicality focus with a later shift to effectiveness) and (iii) Assessment phase (practicality and effectiveness focus). Tessmer presents evaluations that can be done in an EDR study, and ranks them by how formal and resistant to change each of the evaluations are in [12].

4   Preliminary Research Phase

Phase 1 of the study involved the literature review (which is also part of each cycle in an ongoing body of work), as well as the needs and context analysis. The steps required for a needs and context analysis are put forth by McKillip as [13]: (i) identifying the audience and purpose for the analysis, (ii) describing the target population and service environment, (iii) identifying the needs, (iv) assessing the needs and (v) communicating and collating the results. This section describes the outcome of the initial needs analysis done at the start of the study.

4.1 Needs Analysis

Identifying the audience and purpose for the analysis. As stated previously, the audience for this specific game would be final year engineering students. As information theory is not an elective module, and one in which students occasionally struggle due to the fact that a number of the theories are difficult to put into practice immediately due to its more mathematical nature, it was decided that it would be an ideal test bed for the creation of a serious game. Students at this level are expected to have a high level of skill when it comes to applying more abstract ideas to problem solving and be very familiar with digital technology (even if they are not fundamentally "gamers"), so the audience seemed like a good candidate for this style of intervention.

Describing the target population and service environment. As stated previously, students in this population already have a high level of familiarity with digital technology and as such no problems were foreseen in getting students to understand the game or how to play it. With this in mind, the knowledge, skills, values and attitudes that are required of the students to successfully gain the knowledge were reflected upon by the research team.

As the final goal of the research team is to validate the use of serious games in the greater context of the university, there is a certain level of sensitivity required to the problem of access and platform independence. as not all students will have access to a computer at home and library workstations may not be appropriate for the installing of games. As such, HTML5 compliant game engines were explored from the start of the project as they allow for the greatest level of access, and when responsive design principles are followed will give a similar experience across mobile, tablet or desktop environments. Access would not be limited to specific times or locations to students so that they have the ability to choose when, where and how often they wish to play. All that would be required is some way to gain internet connectivity to access the game.

Identifying the needs. The main need of the students in this specific module was to have some way of practicing solving problems once the problem-solving techniques are understood. In terms of which specific problems would be addressed, the following sections of the syllabus were proposed as being good candidates: (i) Probability theory and Boolean algebra, (ii) Error-Correcting Block codes (Hamming code), (iii) Source coding (Shannon-Fano and Huffman algorithms), (iv) Markov chains and (v) Channel capacity.

Assessing the needs. Once the areas to be addressed were evaluated by the team, they were prioritized and used as input into the initial conceptual design to validate whether the concepts in the syllabus could be effectively translated into game mechanics. This was done in collaboration with a student who had completed the course, and their knowledge and skill levels was used as a gauge. For the initial conceptual design, Hamming codes (as a specific block code) was used to evaluate whether a full game system would be worth developing (see Sect. 4.2).

Communicating and collating the results. With the above initial analysis completed, the researchers put together conceptually which areas they would like to address specifically with the serious game intervention, and specifically how they would approach the problems of addressing the students' knowledge and skills needs. This was done specifically by creating the conceptual design, discussing the overall strategy with a leader in the engineering education focus group in the department as well as with fellow lecturers as to how the process would be followed. After very positive feedback all around, the go-ahead was given to create the initial conceptual prototype.

4.2   Conceptual Prototype

As the subject matter lent itself well to encoding and decoding of information, the idea of covert operations, spies and codebreaking came to the fore as an appropriate concept for a game. The conceptual prototype was created in Gamemaker: Studio with pixel art sourced either online from open source projects or created by the research team. Using the film "Casablanca" [14] as inspiration, a conceptual prototype was built where the player controls Ilsa, and attempts to rescue Rick from a Nazi jail cell using Hamming code to unlock the jail cell doors as can be seen in Fig. 2.

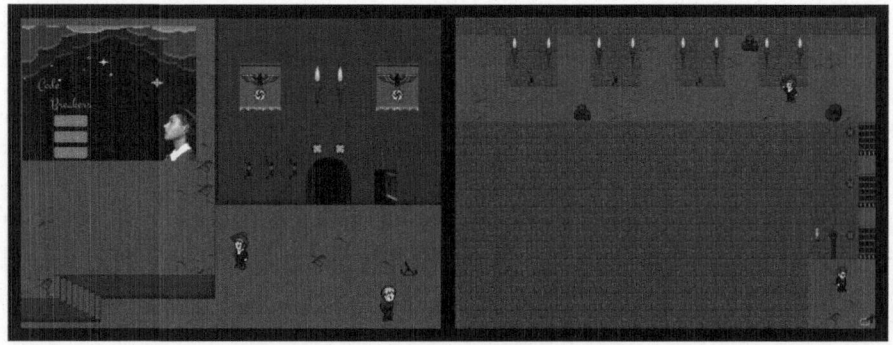

Fig. 2. Codebreakers, featuring Ilsa, Rick and Hamming code

Although showing that the proposed mechanics for the game would work, feedback received was that the overall storyline should not be used. The reason for this is that although Casablanca has been part of the western consciousness for a very long time, this context would not translate well into the South African context. Additionally, although used as the stereotypical "bad guys", the Nazi symbolism ran the risk of making students feel uncomfortable.

5   Development Phase

Following the feedback received on the conceptual prototype put forward, a second prototype game was developed, this time as a full game design. The attributes of the game are described using the seven attributes of games described by Derryberry [7]. The first full field trial of the system was conducted during the first semester of 2017.

Final results will be published in a subsequent paper. The game was developed in JavaScript using the Phaser.io game engine. Artwork used was either purchased from the itch.io asset store, or created by the team specifically for this version of the game.

5.1   Backstory and Storyline

The game, maintaining the name "Codebreakers", has the player exploring a castle and then being trapped in a prison cell by the villainous, Dr. H, Master of Codes. They need to travel the world and break all the codes before they will be set free.

Game mechanics and rules of the game   As can be seen in Fig. 3, the primary game interaction is based on a retro JRPG style of gameplay where players are free to move throughout the over world of the castle (1) and enter the dungeon to select mini games (2). Puzzles are randomly chosen from a selection of appropriately difficult versions of each of the problems being attempted. The remaining sections marked in Fig. 3 are:

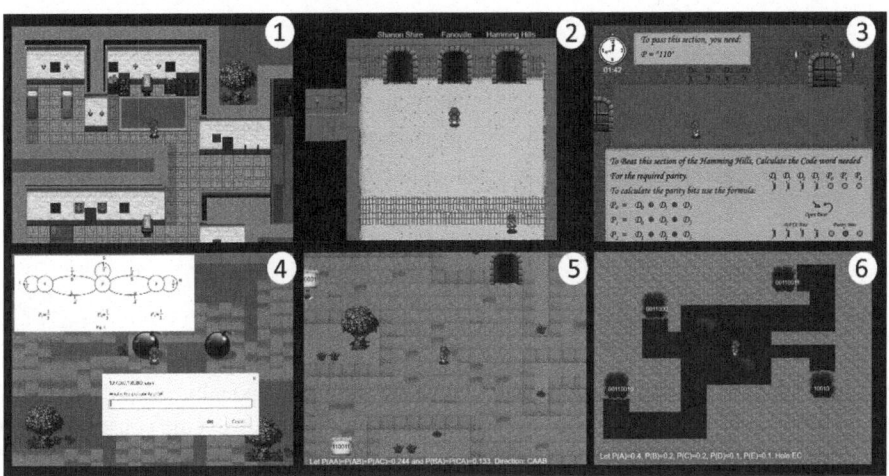

Fig. 3. Full game overview showing different worlds and puzzles

- In the Hamming Hills (3), players manipulate levers to open doors to escape a prison. The lever state required is based on the Hamming code problem stated.
- In the Shannon Shire (4), players move through a maze that has bombs blocking their path. When touched, bombs are disarmed by indicating the probability of a specific state change on the supplied Markov diagram.
- In Fano Forest (5), players navigate through a forest by following signs that are marked with the source encoded value represented by the probabilities at the bottom of the screen (using standard source encoding).
- In Huffman holes (6), similar to (5) students use the Huffman (or greedy) algorithm to create the source encoding which shows the correct path through caves.

Every time a player enters one of the above sections, their start time is logged and if successfully completed the end time is logged. Unsuccessful attempts are logged by indicating a *null* as the completion time.

5.2   Immersive Graphical Environment

The game is designed with a retro JRPG look that was chosen due to the current popularity of games of this nature, access to artwork assets, artwork skills available in the development team and the accessibility of the style. Feedback for this was very positive, and subsequent iterations will continue in this direction.

5.3   Interactivity

The game allows players to move freely through the game world and if they feel they don't want to complete a specific puzzle they are free to leave back to the selection screen and choose either a different one of the same nature, or one of the other game worlds. This level of autonomy is added to ensure players don't get overly frustrated and to increase the level of flow.

5.4   Challenge or Competition

For all of the above-mentioned puzzles, the relative ranking of students is based on the time it takes for them to traverse through each of the worlds. Scores are shown on a leaderboard to allow students to compete but each world has its own leaderboard meaning that students aren't forced to complete all worlds in order to compete.

5.5   Risks and Consequences

Students are free to participate as they choose as there is no penalty for only partially playing or even for not playing at all. Additionally, the game lowers the consequence of failure, as although the player can fail to complete a puzzle, there is no cost associated with this and they are free to try again. The level of immediate feedback and re-usability is one of the best characteristics of the serious game style intervention.

6   Results

6.1   Research Activities Overview

It is important to note that in keeping with the concepts of game design students were given a choice as to whether they would participate or not. Table 1 shows the number of participants and analysis techniques used. For the current field test, the research team of 4 members are the content expert, game design expert, programming expert and student are participating with the current class of 91 students to trail the suitability of the game in the first set of outcomes for the module. As of the writing of this paper more than 300 game world attempts have been recorded during the field trial.

Table 1. Research activities

Phase	Cycle	Circuit	Strategy						Participants		#
			WT	ME	OT	DS	ER	FT	Users	Experts	
Needs and content analysis	Literature review	1	×				×		0	2	2
	Conceptual design	2				×	×		0	2	2
	Conceptual Prototype	3			×	×	×		0	2	2
		4		×		×	×		2	3	5
Design and development	2nd prototype	5				×			2	4	6
		6				×	×		0	4	4
		7		×	×	×	×		0	4	4
		8[a]	×					×	88	4	92

Where WT = Walk Through, ME = Micro Evaluation, TO = Try Out, DS = Design Session, ER = Expert Review, FT = Field Trail, [a]Currently in progress.

7 Conclusion

The required outcome of the first two research cycles was to conceptualize, design and develop a game for final year students doing a Telecommunications module giving students an additional tool to practice the skills they have learned in the coursework. From the needs analysis the researchers, designers and developers were able to conceptualize a full game world as well as a series of mini games using the module's syllabus. Students shared that their experience of the game was very positive, and will be given an opportunity to help design the following iteration. The theme from the game grew from the source material, and will continue to do so. Following iterations will focus on expanding the current narrative, adding in additional mini games to cover the full syllabus and integrating the back end of the game system to the university's learning management system. A literature review was done to ensure a high level of quality and sufficiently place the work in the proper context, and this process will continue with future iterations to ensure game is as suitable as possible. During the first semester of 2017 students in the module were playing the game both inside and outside of the classroom. The lecturers, researchers and designers are continually collecting quantitative and qualitative data to evaluate the usability of the mini games conceptualized for the game through the course of the field trial, and will continue to collect feedback from all stakeholders to guide the creation of future iterations through questionnaires, contact sessions and workshops.

As this is a EDR process that is being followed, the initial prototypes of the game will be very context specific, but the goal of the research team is to continue to thoughtfully reflect on this, and identify areas that can be generalized to other contexts.

References

1. van den Akker, J.J.H., Plomp, T., Nieveen, N.M.: Educational Design Research. SLO, Enschede (2013)
2. Behnke, K.A.: Gamification in Introductory Computer Science, in ATLAS Institute, University of Colorado Boulder (2015)
3. Leendertz, V., Lizanne, F., Martin, B.: Survive with Vuvu in the Vaal: conceptualizing, designing and developing a Serious Game for first year statistics students at the Vaal Triangle Campus, in EdMedia 2015, Montreal, Quebec, Canada. pp. 328–338 (2015)
4. McKenney, S., van der Akker, J.J.H.: Computer-based support for curriculum designers: a case of developmental research. Educ. Technol. Res. Dev. 53(2), 41–66 (2005)
5. Alvarez, J., Djaouti, D.: An introduction to Serious game definitions and concepts. In: Proceedings of the Serious Games & Simulation for Risks Management Workshop 2011, Paris. pp. 11–15 (2011)
6. Ulicsak, M.: Games in Education: Serious Games, a Futurelab literature review. Futurelab, United Kingdom (2010)
7. Derryberry, A.: Serious games: online games for learning. Adobe, San Jose (2007)
8. Deterding, S., et al.: Gamification: Toward a Definition. In: CHI 2011, Vancouver, BC, Canada, pp. 1–4 (2011)
9. Garris, R., Ahlers, R., Driskell, J.E.: Games, motivation, and learning: a research and practice model. Simul. Gaming 33(4), 441–467 (2002)
10. Ryan, R., Deci, E.: Self-determination theory and the facilitation of intrinsic motivation. Soc. Dev. Well-Being Am. Psychol. 55(1), 68–78 (2000)
11. Nieveen, N.: Prototyping to reach product quality. In: van den Akker, J., Branch, R.M., Gustafson, K., Nieveen, N., Plomp, T. (eds.) Design Approaches and Tools in Education and Training, pp. 125–137. Springer, Dordrecht (1999). doi:10.1007/978-94-011-4255-7_10
12. Tessmer, M.: Planning and conducting formative evaluations. Kogan Page, London (1993)
13. McKillip, J.: Need Analysis, in Handbook of Applied Social Research Methods. SAGE, Thousand Oaks (1998)
14. Curtiz, M.: Casablanca, 102 min. Warner Bros, United States (1942)

Design and Evaluation of a Smart Device Science Lesson to Improve Students' Inquiry Skills

Leo A. Siiman[1(✉)], Margus Pedaste[1], Mario Mäeots[1], Äli Leijen[1], Miia Rannikmäe[1], Zacharias C. Zacharia[2], and Ton de Jong[3]

[1] University of Tartu, Tartu, Estonia
leo.siiman@ut.ee
[2] University of Cyprus, Nicosia, Cyprus
[3] University of Twente, Twente, The Netherlands

Abstract. The prevalence of smart devices among young people is undeniably large, but concerns that they distract learning may be limiting their use in schools. In this study we demonstrate how tablet computers can be used effectively for teaching science. A digital biology lesson was designed in the Go-Lab environment and tested with 28 students (16–18 years old). Among the multiple tasks in the lesson, students had to search the internet for information, share digital data, formulate research questions and hypotheses using Go-Lab inquiry apps and interact with a virtual laboratory. Two conditions which differed only in the level of scaffolding provided by inquiry apps were studied. Results from pre- to posttest scores showed a statistically significant improvement in inquiry skills for students in both conditions. Overall, the findings suggest that an effective way to apply smart devices in science lessons is with digital materials that engage students in inquiry-based learning.

Keywords: Inquiry learning · Smart technology · Virtual laboratory · Inquiry cycle · Instructional design · Digital competence

1 Introduction

The prevalence of smart devices among young people today is undeniably large, but concerns that they distract learning may be limiting their use in schools. A survey of teacher views conducted with more than 2,000 middle and high school U.S. teachers found that 87% of respondents believed digital technologies were creating "an easily distracted generation with short attention spans," and 64% said digital technologies did "more to distract students than to help them academically." [1]. Nevertheless, the mobility of smart devices such as smartphones and tablets, their increasingly powerful computing capabilities and Wi-Fi access to the internet offer vast potential for learning—provided that meaningful classwork activities are created to engage the attention of students. Additionally, the responsible and educational use of smart devices in schools can support the development of students' digital competence, a general competence described, for example, by the DigComp framework as a set of knowledge, attitudes and skills needed by citizens to use digital technologies to achieve goals related to work,

© Springer International Publishing AG 2017
H. Xie et al. (Eds.): ICWL 2017, LNCS 10473, pp. 23–32, 2017.
DOI: 10.1007/978-3-319-66733-1_3

employability, learning, leisure, inclusion and/or participation in society [2]. However, a recent pilot survey of 6th and 9th grade Estonian students showed that although a majority may use smart devices very frequently for digitally competent activities, such as searching for information on the internet or communicating with others in digital environments, these activities occur primarily in contexts not related to school learning [3].

Especially important nowadays is to engage young people in science and mathematics. Success in today's technology-driven knowledge economy increasingly requires the types of skills students learn by studying these subjects. However, studies show that students in Europe [4], including Estonia [5], have low motivation towards learning science and mathematics. Changes in science instruction, along with new digital learning opportunities may offer better approaches to fostering positive attitudes among young people towards science and mathematics.

In the United States, the report *A Framework for K–12 Science Education*, describes a new approach to science instruction where more emphasis is placed on helping students engage in thinking and solving problems the way scientists do, and supporting students to better see how science is relevant to their lives [6]. More specifically, the framework advocates integrating three dimensions: (1) the *practices* by which scientists and engineers do their work; (2) the *crosscutting concepts* that apply across science disciplines; and (3) the *core ideas* in the disciplines. An emphasis on students actually "doing" the practices of science and engineering is further elaborated in the framework with eight key practices: (1) asking questions for science and defining problems for engineering; (2) developing and using models; (3) planning and carrying out investigations; (4) analyzing and interpreting data; (5) using mathematics and computational thinking; (6) constructing explanations for science and designing solutions for engineering; (7) engaging in argument from evidence; and (8) obtaining, evaluating, and communicating information. These practices describe various inquiry skills that scientists and engineers apply when solving problems. Opportunities for young people to directly experience and apply these practices form the foundation of inquiry-based science education. A meta-analysis of active learning approaches in science education, overwhelmingly inquiry-based learning approaches, shows that such teaching methods are much more effective than traditional teaching approaches such as lecturing [7].

In Estonia, the importance of inquiry-based learning in science education has been recognized since 2011 in the National Curriculum at both the basic and secondary school levels. More recently, revised national science exams for 4th and 7th grade Estonian students now specifically assess inquiry skills such as formulating research questions and/or hypotheses; analyzing natural objects, phenomena and processes and explaining the cause-and-effect connections between them; planning experiments; and drawing conclusions from scientific data [8].

Research shows that inquiry-based learning can be enhanced through the use of computer simulations [9, 10]. Numerous interactive computer simulations for teaching and learning science can be found for free on the internet (see e.g., The PhET project at https://phet.colorado.edu). Interactive science simulations, such as virtual laboratories, offer the opportunity for students to learn by manipulating variables to discover cause-and-effect relationships, much like scientists might do when investigating unknown phenomena for the first time. However, students often struggle with inquiry tasks and consequently the effectiveness of technology-enhanced inquiry learning requires inquiry processes to be structured and scaffolded [9].

The Go-Lab (Global Online Science Labs for Inquiry Learning at School) environment is an online open educational resource that allows interactive science simulations to be integrated in structured and scaffolded digital learning spaces [11]. After a simulation is integrated in a Go-Lab learning space the space can be further enhanced by adding text, embedding multimedia content (images, videos, HTML5 elements), and adding Go-Lab learning applications (apps). All of these resources together constitute what is called an inquiry learning space (ILS). An ILS contains all the resources and tasks to engage students in inquiry-based learning.

The usual lesson plan of a Go-Lab ILS is based on the inquiry cycle framework of Pedaste et al. (2015) in which five general inquiry phases are identified: orientation, conceptualization, investigation, conclusion and discussion [12]. In each of these inquiry phases it is possible to provide students with guidance to address difficulties they may have with completing specific inquiry processes [13]. The conceptualization inquiry phase, in which students state theory-based questions and/or hypotheses, can be especially difficult for students.

In this study we designed a Go-Lab ILS for students to complete in their regular classroom while using their school's tablet computers. The learning effects of two conditions of scaffolding in the conceptualization inquiry phase were studied. The aim of the study was to evaluate the effectiveness of the ILS during classroom implementation in terms of changes in students' inquiry skills. In particular, the main research question was, "How to design an inquiry lesson in a technology-enhanced learning environment featuring virtual experiments and working on smart devices to facilitate the improvement of students' inquiry skills?"

2 Method

A biology teacher from a public secondary school in Estonia agreed to implement the Go-Lab intervention in his class during a regular 75 min lesson. A total of 28 students (6 boys, 22 girls) having a mean age of 17.0 ($SD = .74$) participated in the intervention. Students used their school's tablet computers (including a keyboard dock) and worked in groups of 3 to 5 persons to complete the digital lesson. A researcher was present to make observations as well as answer (technical) questions if necessary.

A virtual laboratory from the Virtual Biology Lab Project called *Sexual Selection in Guppies* (see http://virtualbiologylab.org/selection/) was selected as the computer simulation of interest. This simulation allows students to recreate the classic experiments performed by the biologist John Endler when he first investigated the balance of natural and sexual selection in guppy fish in the 1970s. Originally this virtual laboratory was created as a Java applet, but in order to make it compatible with smart devices, we created a new HTML5 version of it for use in this study (see Fig. 1 for a visual comparison of the two simulations).

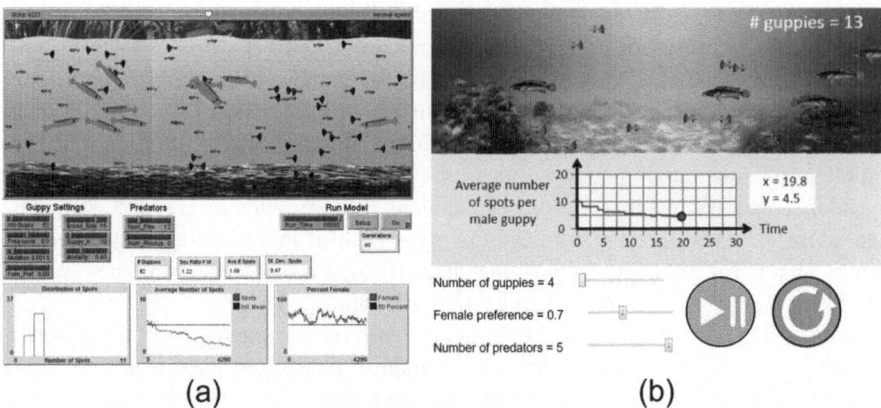

Fig. 1. Screenshots of the Sexual Selection in Guppies virtual laboratory: (a) the original Java applet version at http://virtualbiologylab.org/selection, (b) the redesigned smart device compatible version (http://leosiiman.neocities.org/guppy/GuppyLab.html).

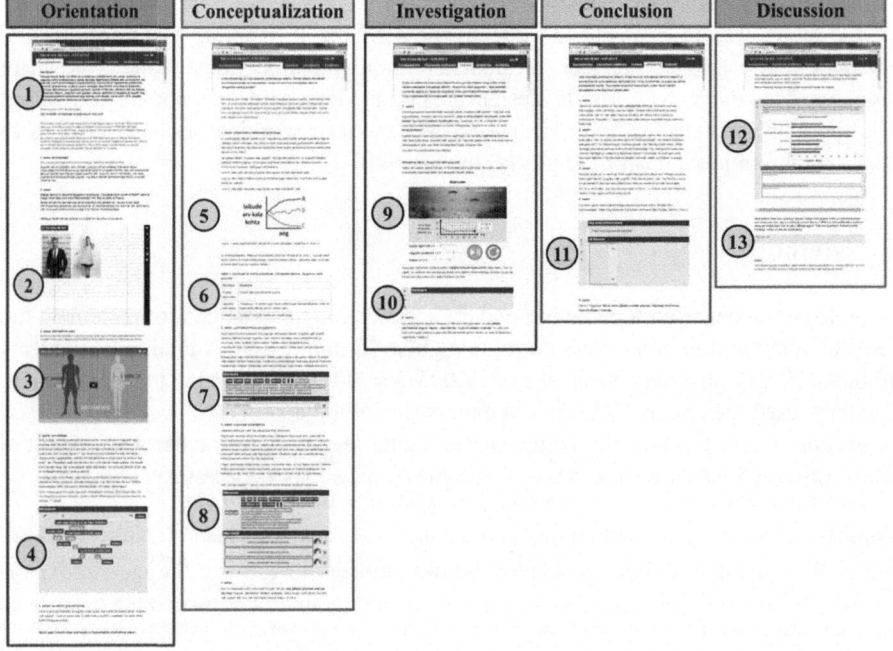

Fig. 2. Zoomed out screenshots of the five inquiry phases for the Go-Lab ILS *Is it good to be beautiful?* A detailed descriptions of the content in each of these phases is given in Table 1. Notable design elements that form the structure of the ILS include: (1) text, (2) Padlet wall, (3) YouTube video, (4) Concept Mapper app, (5) image, (6) table, (7) Question Scratchpad app, (8) Hypothesis Scratchpad app, (9) virtual laboratory, (10) Observation Tool app, (11) Conclusion Tool app, (12) Reflection Tool app, and (13) Input Box app.

Table 1. Sequence of tasks and their descriptions in the Go-Lab ILS *Is it good to be beautiful?* (http://www.golabz.eu/spaces/it-good-be-beautiful).

Inquiry phase	Task sequence	Task description
Orientation	Read about the objectives of the lesson	Students are introduced to the inquiry lesson. They are informed that in this phase they will gather background material to create a concept map. A puzzling question is asked to spark the curiosity of students: "Is it always good for a person or an animal to look beautiful?"
	Get familiar with key terminology	Relevant terminology (*natural* and *sexual selection*) is briefly defined and links to more exact definitions on the internet is provided
	Use the Padlet app to share digital information	Students are instructed to contribute to a classroom discussion by adding a picture of a person they think is beautiful to a virtual "wall" (on Padlet.com)
	Watch a short video	Students watch a 3 ½ min long YouTube video about 'Why Sexy is Sexy'
	Create a concept map	Students are instructed to think about the characteristics of their ideal spouse and complete a partially filled-in concept map using the Concept Mapper app. For each characteristic they need to identify both positive and negative concepts (e.g., a sexy body arouses me; a sexy body suggests my potential spouse spends too much time exercising and not enough time studying)
	Read additional material	Students are instructed to read about guppy fish and then move on to the conceptualization inquiry phase
Conceptualization	Read about the aims of the conceptualization phase	It is explained to students that in this phase they will formulate research questions and hypotheses that will be tested using a virtual laboratory. They are introduced to a study made by biologist John Endler when he investigated the balance of natural and sexual selection in guppy fish in the 1970s
	Visualize the dependent variable from a figure	A figure is used to illustrate how the dependent variable (i.e. average number of spots per male guppy) can vary with time in different ways depending on the influence of independent variables in the environment
	Visualize independent variables from a table	A table is used to list the independent variables that can be changed in the virtual laboratory (i.e. initial number of guppies, female preference for spotted guppies, number of predators in the environment)

(*continued*)

Table 1. (*continued*)

Inquiry phase	Task sequence	Task description
	Formulate research question(s)	Students are instructed to formulate research question(s) using the Question Scratchpad app
	Formulate hypotheses	Students are instructed to generate hypotheses using the Hypothesis Scratchpad app and then move on to the investigation inquiry phase
Investigation	Read about the aims of the investigation phase	It is explained to students that the main goal of the investigation phase is to collect evidence that can be used to confirm or reject their hypotheses
	Interact with the virtual lab to perform experiments	Students are instructed to perform experiments with the virtual laboratory. The lab allows students to vary three independent variables and observe the effects visually on a graph showing how the dependent variable changes with time
	Record observations	Students are instructed to record their observations using the Observation Tool app. Students are reminded to make as many experiments as needed to address their hypotheses, and once finished proceed to the Conclusion inquiry phase
Conclusion	Read about the aims of the conclusion phase	Students are instructed to draw conclusions in this phase based on the evidence they previously collected
	Draw conclusion(s)	Students are instructed to use the Conclusion Tool app to make conclusions(s). The app allows them to see their research questions and hypotheses made in the conceptualization inquiry phase and their observations made in the investigation phase
Discussion	Read about the aims of the discussion phase	It is explained to students that reflection is an important learning strategy for improving their future performance in inquiry and that communicating knowledge is an important part of how scientists work
	Reflect on inquiry experience	Students are instructed to use the Reflection Tool app to look at their time spent in each inquiry phase and reflect on two questions: (1) Which inquiry phase was the most difficult for you and why?; and, (2) What would you do differently the next time you conduct an inquiry investigation?
	Answer the question 'Is it good to be beautiful?'	The Input Box app is used to ask a final open response question: Is it good to be beautiful?
	Read optional reference material	An internet link to the original research article published by John Endler is provided

The virtual laboratory was integrated into the Go-Lab learning environment via creation of an ILS called *Is it good to be beautiful?* Our study used an Estonian language ILS but an equivalent English language version can be found at http://www.golabz.eu/spaces/it-good-be-beautiful. The ILS was designed following the inquiry-based learning framework of Pedaste et al. (2015) to include the five general inquiry phases [12]. The phases can be individually navigated using "tabbed" browsing on smart devices. Figure 2 shows zoomed out screenshots of the five inquiry phases and notable design elements. Table 1 provides a detailed description of the lesson plan used for this ILS.

The Go-Lab intervention included two conditions: one condition where inquiry apps (Question Scratchpad and Hypothesis Scratchpad) in the conceptualization phase of the ILS displayed predefined terms to help students formulate research questions and hypotheses, and the other condition where the inquiry apps did not display these terms. The predefined terms condition explicitly listed independent and dependent variables relevant to the virtual laboratory. Students were randomly assigned to one of the two conditions.

Assessment of inquiry skills was performed using paper-based tests administered a few days before and after the Go-Lab intervention. Items measuring *identifying variables* and *identifying and stating hypotheses* from the Test of the Integrated Science Process Skills (TIPS) and the TIPS II test were used [14, 15]. TIPS was used as the pretest and TIPS II as the posttest. Students were allotted about twenty minutes to complete the 21 multiple choice items in each test.

3   Results and Discussion

The results of the inquiry skills pre- and posttests are presented in Table 2. A Wilcoxon signed-rank test was conducted to check for differences in pre- to posttest scores. The test showed significant increases in scores for students in the *with* predefined terms condition ($Z = -3.516$, $p < 0.05$), as well as for students in the *without* condition ($Z = -3.059$, $p < 0.05$).

Table 2. Descriptive statistics of the inquiry skills pre- and posttest scores for students in the conditions with and without predefined terms in the Question and Hypothesis Scratchpad apps.

Inquiry skills test score	With ($N = 16$)		Without($N = 12$)	
	Mean	Std. Dev.	Mean	Std. Dev
Pretest score	12.38	2.53	12.00	2.73
Posttest score	13.75	2.21	13.08	1.08
Gain score	*1.37*	*2.73*	*1.08*	*3.23*

One explanation why students' inquiry skills improved in both conditions is that students aged 16 to 19 are already familiar with stating research questions and hypotheses, and including predefined terms as additional scaffolding support is unnecessary. Alternatively, it may be that the overall ILS design provided enough support for students to identify the key independent and dependent variables when formulating their research questions and hypotheses. Either way it is important to emphasize that the content of the digital lesson was not directly related to the content assessed by the inquiry skills tests. For example, a representative test item in TIPS II reads as follows:

Some students are considering variables that might affect the time it takes for sugar to dissolve in water. They identify the temperature of the water, the amount of sugar and the amount of water as variables to consider. What is a hypothesis the students could test about the time it takes for sugar to dissolve in water?

1. *If the amount of sugar is larger, then more water is required to dissolve it.*
2. *If the water is colder, then it has to be stirred faster to dissolve.*
3. *If the water is warmer, then more sugar will dissolve.*
4. *If the water is warmer, then it takes the sugar more time to dissolve.*

As the above example helps illustrate, the inquiry skills items are domain-general and do not evoke subject-specific knowledge. Instead they aim at assessing students' comprehension of a set of practices (i.e. identifying and stating hypotheses, identifying variables) needed to engage successfully in scientific inquiry.

From researcher observations made during the intervention, students appeared to be engaged with the inquiry tasks and progressed in a timely manner through each of the inquiry phases. These observations were made in part using the "teacher" view in the Go-Lab platform, which allows an ILS author to view the work done by individual users who have accessed that ILS. More advanced functionality, such as Go-Lab learning analytics apps, allow ILS authors to view exactly how much time users spent in an inquiry phase and the number of actions they made using Go-Lab inquiry apps.

On the whole, it appeared that the five general inquiry phases helped structure learning for students and kept them engaged with an assortment of tasks associated with scientific inquiry practices. This Go-Lab inquiry cycle framework is similar to how the WISE web-based inquiry science environment applies the knowledge integration framework [16] to structure its learning tasks, and which also has shown to be effective in inquiry-based science lessons [17]. However, the reliance of many WISE units on Flash (.swf) and Java (.jar) objects does not make it a suitable for use with smart devices. In contrast, the prominent use of HTML5 components in the Go-Lab environment makes it quite compatible with smart devices. Moreover, the modular design of inquiry tasks in five different inquiry phases and scaffolded with various inquiry apps can help facilitate navigation and learning for smart device users. Overall, the Go-Lab Platform provides a new and useful environment for educators to design smart device compatible learning experiences to improve students' inquiry skills.

4 Conclusion

In summary, this study demonstrated an example of smart device use in the science classroom by which students improved their inquiry skills. A digital lesson created in the Go-Lab environment consisting of five inquiry phases appeared to engage students in the scientific reasoning processes necessary for successful inquiry learning. Future research could benefit from also studying if, in addition to better academic outcomes, students exhibit more positive attitudes towards science after engaging in inquiry learning using smart devices.

Acknowledgements. This study was partially funded by the Estonian Research Council through the institutional research funding project "Smart technologies and digital literacy in promoting a change of learning" (Grant Agreement No. IUT34-6). This study was also partially funded by the European Union in the context of the Go-Lab project (Grant Agreement No. 317601) under the Information and Communication Technologies (ICT) theme of the 7th Framework Programme for R&D (FP7). This document does not represent the opinion of the European Union, and the European Union is not responsible for any use that might be made of its content.

References

1. Purcell, K., Rainie, L., Heaps, A., Buchanan, J., Friedrich, L., Jacklin, A., Chen, C., Zickuhr, K.: How Teens Do Research in the Digital World. Pew Internet and American Life Project, 1 November 2012. http://www.pewinternet.org/2012/11/01/how-teens-do-research-in-the-digital-world/
2. Ferrari, A.: DIGCOMP: A Framework for Developing and Understanding Digital Competence in Europe. Publications Office of the European Union, Luxembourg (2013)
3. Siiman, L.A., Mäeots, M., Pedaste, M., Simons, R.-J., Leijen, Ä., Rannikmäe, M., Võsu, K., Timm, M.: An instrument for measuring students' perceived digital competence according to the DIGCOMP framework. In: Zaphiris, P., Ioannou, A. (eds.) LCT 2016. LNCS, vol. 9753, pp. 233–244. Springer, Cham (2016). doi:10.1007/978-3-319-39483-1_22
4. Sjøberg, S., Schreiner, C.: The ROSE project. An overview and key findings (2010). http://roseproject.no/network/countries/norway/eng/nor-Sjoberg-Schreiner-overview-2010.pdf
5. Teppo, M., Rannikmäe, M.: Paradigm shift for teachers: more relevant science teaching. In: Holbrook, J., Rannikmäe, M., Reiska, P., Ilsley, P. (eds.) The Need for a Paradigm Shift in Science Education for Post-Soviet Societies: Research and Practice (Estonian Example), pp. 25–46. Peter Lang GmbH, Frankfurt (2008)
6. National Research Council: A framework for K-12 science education: practices, crosscutting concepts, and core ideas. The National Academies Press, Washington, DC (2012)
7. Freeman, S., Eddy, S.L., McDonough, M., Smith, M.K., Okoroafor, N., Jordt, H., Wenderoth, M.P.: Active learning increases student performance in science, engineering, and mathematics. Proc. Natl. Acad. Sci. U.S.A. **111**, 8410–8415 (2014)
8. Pedaste, M.: Uudne lähenemine loodusainete tasemetöödes [A new approach for the natural sciences state examinations]. Õpetajate Leht, 21 April 2017. http://opleht.ee/2017/04/uudne-lahenemine-loodusainete-tasemetoodes/
9. de Jong, T.: Computer simulations – technological advances in inquiry learning. Science **312**, 532–533 (2006)
10. Zacharia, Z.C., de Jong, T.: The effects on students' conceptual understanding of electric circuits of introducing virtual manipulatives within a physical manipulatives-oriented curriculum. Cogn. Instr. **32**(2), 101–158 (2014)
11. de Jong, T., Sotiriou, S., Gillet, D.: Innovations in STEM education: the go-lab federation of online labs. Smart Learn. Environ. **1**(1), 1–16 (2014)
12. Pedaste, M., Mäeots, M., Siiman, L.A., de Jong, T., van Riesen, S.A.N., Kamp, E.T., Tsourlidaki, E.: Phases of inquiry-based learning: definitions and the inquiry cycle. Educ. Res. Rev. **14**, 47–61 (2015)

13. Zacharia, Z.C., Manoli, C., Xenofontos, N., de Jong, T., Pedaste, M., van Riesen, S., Tsourlidaki, E.: Identifying potential types of guidance for supporting student inquiry when using virtual and remote labs: a literature review. Educ. Tech. Res. Dev. **63**, 257–302 (2015)
14. Dillashaw, F.G., Okey, J.R.: Test of the integrated science process skills for secondary science students. Sci. Educ. **64**, 601–608 (1980)
15. Burns, J.C., Okey, J.R., Wise, K.C.: Development of an integrated process skill test: Tips II. J. Res. Sci. Teach. **22**, 169–177 (1985)
16. Linn, M.C.: The knowledge integration perspective on learning and instruction. In: Keith Sawyer, R. (ed.) The Cambridge Handbook of the Learning Sciences, pp. 243–264. Cambridge University Press, New York (2006)
17. Chiu, J.L., Linn, M.C.: Supporting knowledge integration in chemistry with a visualization-enhanced inquiry unit. J. Sci. Educ. Technol. **23**, 37–58 (2014)

WeiboFinder: A Topic-Based Chinese Word Finding and Learning System

Wenhao Chen[1(✉)], Yi Cai[2], Kinkeung Lai[3], Li Yao[4], Jun Zhang[5], Jingjing Li[6], and Xingdong Jia[7]

[1] Department of Management Science, City University of Hong Kong, Kowloon Tong, Hong Kong
wenhachen2-c@my.cityu.edu.hk
[2] School of Software Engineering, South China University of Technology, Guangzhou, China
ycai@scut.edu.cn
[3] International Business School, Shaanxi Normal University, Xi'an, China
mskklai@outlook.com
[4] College of Information Science and Technology, Beijing Normal University, Beijing, China
yaoli@bnu.edu.cn
[5] School of Computer Science, South China University of Technology, Guangzhou, China
junzhang@ieee.org
[6] South China Normal University, Guangzhou, China
jingjing.li1124@gmail.com
[7] Shenzhen Polytechnic, Shenzhen, China
jiaxingdong@szpt.edu.cn

Abstract. With the explosive growth of user-generated data in social media websites such as Twitter and Weibo, a lot of research has been conducted on using user-generated data for web-based learning. Finding users' desired data in an effective way is critical for language learners. Social media websites provide diversified data for language learners and some new words such as cyberspeak could only be learned in these online communities. In this paper, we present a system called WeiboFinder to suggest topic-based words and documents related to a target word for Chinese learners. All the words and documents are from the Chinese social media website: Weibo. Weibo is one of the largest microblog social meida websites in China which has similar functions as Twitter. The experimental results show that the proposed method is effective and better than other methods. The topics from our method are more interpretable and topic-based words are useful for Chinese learners.

Keywords: Social media · Chinese learning · Topic modeling · Semantic computing · Text mining

© Springer International Publishing AG 2017
H. Xie et al. (Eds.): ICWL 2017, LNCS 10473, pp. 33–42, 2017.
DOI: 10.1007/978-3-319-66733-1_4

1 Introduction

Over the past several years, as the development of Internet, social media websites such as Twitter and Weibo have received much attention due to their enormous users and user-generated content. In China, Weibo is one of the largest microblog social meida websites and the platform is similar as Twitter. A lot of users post their opinions about different topics in Weibo every day. Most of the posts are written in Chinese. A lot of research has been done to explore the benefits of using social media in education and web-based learning [6]. Faizi et al. [7] claim that social media is an optimal virtual environment for learning foreign languages. Xie et al. use social media to generate incidental word learning task [22]. Incidental word learning and intentional learning are the two main approaches to word learning [11]. Comparing to intentional learning or traditional learning via text books, incidental word learning motivates learners better and provides richer contexts [22]. In this paper, we provide a system called WeiboFinder to help Chinese learners to find different aspects about a Chinese word and each aspect has a list of related words which provide a source for the incidental word learning task. For example, if a student want to learn some Chinese words about Chinese finance market, Weibofinder can generate a list of incident words for learning such as "Industry Sector", "Interest rate cut", "Index" and "Circuit breaker" about the word "Shanghai Stock Exchange Composite Index".

Social media websites in general include a rich variety of data sources. Nowadays the task of identifying high-quality user-generated content in social media sites becomes increasingly important [1]. How to generate high quality information and learning materials about a keyword for language learners from social media websites is the question we want to discuss in this paper. To extract the aspects of the keyword in addition with relevant words and materials, we use the topic modeling method LDA. It will generate topics with relevant words, and the relevancy between documents and topics. Recently, topic modeling methods such as LDA have gained attention [12] because they can help to identify expressions that describe concepts. Standard topic modeling method such as LDA has limitations. Mimno et al. [17] found that the topic generated by LDA sometimes is not interpretable and has no meaning. The reason is that some common words are included in different topics. As a result, a lot of research has been conducted to enhance the topic modeling ability of LDA by including term weights in the model. Wilson et al. [21] proposed a model WLDA using term weighting schemes to weight terms in LDA. Term weighting schemes are widely used to measure the importance of words in documents. Based on Wilson's work, Yang et al. [13] defined the common words in different topics as topic-indiscriminate words and present a TWLDA model based on the WLDA model.

In this paper, we extend the work presented in [13] and use TWLDA to build up a Chinese word finding and learning system called WeiboFinder for Chinese Learners. The characteristics and contribution of our work is as follows: (a) To build up the system, we provide a method to enhance the Chinese segmentation ability of traditional tools using association rule. (b) We propose a novel Chinese word finding and learning system called WeiboFinder based on Weibo posts in which students could input the keyword that they are interested in and the system will return the relevant words and posts for them to read. (c) The results of using different term weighting scheme in TWLDA are discussed and we use an entropy-based method to determine the topic discriminating power of words. To demonstrate the effectiveness of the proposed method, we conducted experiments comparing the performance of our method with other LDA models. The results show that the proposed method outperforms other methods. The topics extracted through our method are in line with students' understanding and could be used to learn the target word and extend the study in relevant areas.

2   Related Work

2.1   Social Media Learning

In recent years, social media websites, such as Facebook, Twitter and Weibo become more and more popular. Large volume of information is published by online users in these websites. Social media in general provides diversified data for different tasks. Through analyzing the blog content, Liang et al. [15] indicated that a company can get the first hand knowledge or feedback from its clients. In terms of language learning, [22] used the social media data to generate topic-based profile about a learner and recommend learning task based on the profile. A lot of research has been conducted to discuss the social media based e-learning [14,25]. Zou et al. [24] proposed a method to predict the pre-knowledge on vocabulary for language learners. As Chinese is quite different with English and it is more complicated in terms of segmentation, the number of research on Chinese social media mining is limited. In previous research, Gao et al. [9] indicated the difference between Sina Weibo and Twitter. Yang et al. [23] have proposed a classifier to automatically detect the rumors from a mixed set of information from the posts in Sina Weibo. For sentiment analysis, Rui et al. found out that the correlation of anger among users is significantly higher than that of joy in Sina Weibo [8]. There are also researches about multi-lingual sentiment analysis, K. Ahmad et al. [2] developed a local grammar approach which works equally on English, Chinese (Sino-Asiatic) and Arabic (Semitic). Liu et al. [16] proposed a topic-sensitive probabilistic model using LDA to find experts for questions in Zhihu.

2.2   Topic Modeling

Topic modeling method such as LDA is a frequently used text-mining tool for discovering aspects in a text body. Although LDA is widely used, it has the limitation that some topics generated will mix general words which make the topics uninterpretable. To enhance the ability of standard LDA in generating unmixed topics, Andrezejewski et al. [3] designed a new model called DF-LDA which takes domain knowledge given by users into consideration. Similar as Andrezjewski, other research use expert domain knowledge [5] and seed words [4] to guide LDA. The method proposed in this paper is based on previous research on Term Weighting LDA. Wilson et al. [21] claimed that LDA should involve weights of words in the model. Words which scatter across more documents are less important and should has a lower weight. Yang et al. proposed a TWLDA algorithm based on the discussion of the topic discriminating power of words [13].

3 The Proposed Model

3.1 Chinese Segmentation

Unlike English, there is no space between Chinese words in a Chinese sentence. The first step of Chinese text mining task is Chinese words segmentation [19]. In our research, we first use two famous tools for Chinese segmentation: Jieba and Standford CoreNLP. Jieba uses the dynamic programming to find out the most probable combination and hidden markov model to detect new words. Similar as Jieba, Stanford CoreNLP is designed by the Stanford Natural Language Processing Group for text analysis. In our experiments, we find out that some specific words in Weibo cannot be identified through these 2 methods. As a result, we use association rule mining to improve the segmentation result [10] and find out frequent Chinese phrases. Let $C = \{c_1, \ldots, c_n\}$ be a set of Chinese items, and D be a set of transactions. Each transaction consists of a subset of items in C. The problem of mining association rules is to generate all association rules in D that have support and confidence level greater than the minimum requirement. As the result shown in Fig. 1, the Chinese phrase with the meaning "Hong Kong and Shenzhen Stock Connect" can only be found by our method. Although our method has better performance in terms of new word detection. It is possible that some redundant words are generated as well. To pruning the redundancy, p-support [10] is used. P-support of a word w is the number of the sentences including the word and these sentences don't contain any superset word phrase of w. If a word has a p-support lower than the minimum requirement which we set to 3 and it is a subset of other word phrases, it will be pruned.

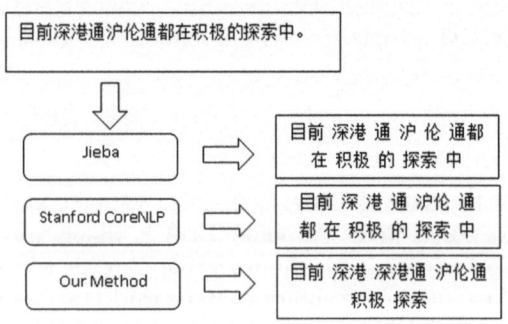

Fig. 1. Chinese segmentation results comparison.

3.2   System Framework

In previous research, Yang et al. [13] indicated that words have different topic discriminating power which denote the ability of a word to discriminate different topics. To eliminate the impact of topic-indiscriminate words, the number of these words should be reduced in the LDA model. Wang et al. [20] compare bdc with other state-of-the-art term weighting schemes and find out bdc outperforms others in text categorization tasks. Topic-indiscriminating words will be considered as unimportant and get relatively low weight. In this paper, inspired by previous research on TWLDA, we propose a Chinese topic words finding and learning system using TWLDA.

As the topics are unknown in the beginning, we need to first get the initial topic words based on standard LDA and then word weights could be calculated using different term weighting schemes. Our method will first execute standard LDA in the dataset and term weights are calculated based on the result. The term weights in our method are calculated as follows:

$$bdc(t) = 1 + \frac{\sum_{i=1}^{k} \frac{p(t|c_i)}{\sum_{i=1}^{k} p(t|c_i)} \log \frac{p(t|c_i)}{\sum_{i=1}^{k} p(t|c_i)}}{\log(k)} \tag{1}$$

Where k is the number of topics. $bdc(t)$ is the weight of term t. $p(t|c_i)$ is the proportion of the term t in its relevant topic c_i.

The framework of our system is shown in Fig. 2. Firstly, the Weibo posts including the input word are extracted and subject to the pre-processing mechanism. After the process of segmentation, stemming and words pruning, each post is transformed to a list of Chinese words. Then we could use the TWLDA model to generate relevant topics about the word students want to learn. The TWLDA model has 5 steps. In the first step, as shown in Fig. 2, LDA is executed in the data set and we can get the initial information about the topics. After that, based on the result of step 1, *bdc* term weighting scheme is applied to calculate the word weights. Different term weighting schemes can be used in this step. In step 3, the number of words is diminished proportionally according to weights of words. Step 4 is to execute the LDA again, using the discounted values calculated in step 3. Conditional probability of word t in document m under topic k is calculated as Eq. 2 which is same as standard LDA. The difference is that the counting variables are replaced with the discounted values. The word t will have less probability to be assigned in topic k if the weight of word t is lower. Finally, in step 5, topics about the input Chinese word could be generated from the result. Each topic will have a list of relevant words. Based on the ranking of words, the top 20 words of a topic are defined as expressions that describe an aspect of the input word. These topics and related words could help Chinese learners to extend their study in Chinese learning as a lot of incidental words are generated. In addition, documents related to each topic will be recommended to Chinese learners for reading. Based on the relevancy, top 20 documents about a topic are suggested for study.

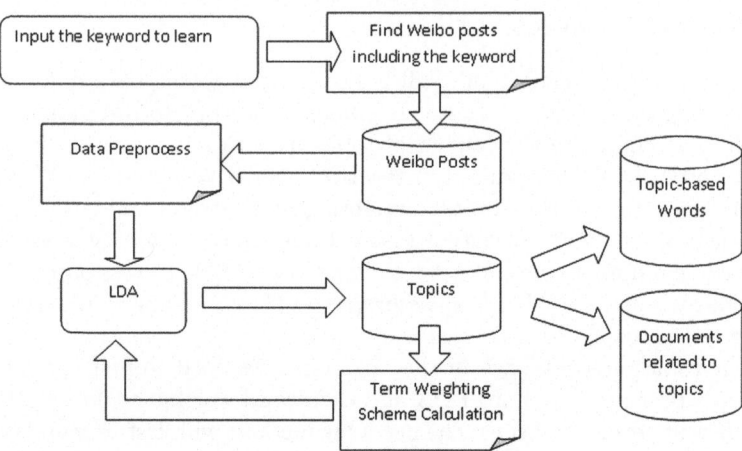

Fig. 2. Framework of WeiboFinder.

$$p(z_i = k | \overrightarrow{z}_{k,\neg i}, \overrightarrow{\omega}, \overrightarrow{\alpha}, \overrightarrow{\beta}) = \frac{n_{m,\neg i}^k + \alpha_k}{\sum_{k=1}^{k=K} (n_{m,\neg i}^k + \alpha_t)} \frac{n_{k,\neg i}^t + \beta_k}{\sum_{t=1}^{t=V} (n_{k,\neg i}^t + \beta_t)} \quad (2)$$

4   Experiments

In this section, we describe experiments conducted to evaluate the performance of our system. In our experiments, we use topic coherence and precision to evaluate the result. 20 students are invited to analyze whether the topics and related words are inline with their understanding and useful for the study of Chinese.

4.1   Data Set and Experiment Setup

The datasets used in our experiments are the collections of Weibo posts in different periods. Weibo is one of the most famous social media websites in China which has similar functions as Twitter. Considering the scenario that students input a Chinese word: "Shanghai Stock Exchange Composite Index", the posts including this word will be automatically crawled from Weibo. The posts are divided into 3 datasets based on the posting time which are 2015 dataset (6112 posts), 2016 dataset (7579 posts), 2017 dataset (2186 posts).

For all models, we take a single sample as posterior inference after 2500 iterations of Gibbs sampling. The aspect number K was set to 20. As small change of α and β will not have big impact, we set $\alpha = 1$ and $\beta = 0.1$ as the setting in (Chen et al. [5]). For the term weighting LDA, the iterations of preceding LDA model are set to 1000 which is the same as the setting in (Yang et al. [13]).

4.2   Experiment Result

Topic coherence is used to evaluate the performance of different LDA models. Higher topic coherence means the performance is better and the words included in the topic are correlated with each other. Through the experiment result, as shown in Fig. 3, we can find out that the entropy based term weighting LDA such as bdc-TWLDA has better performance than standard LDA and tf-idf TWLDA in 2015 and 2016 datasets.

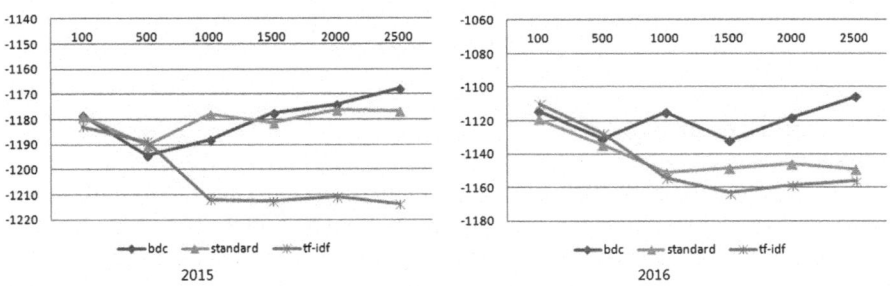

Fig. 3. Topic coherence comparison of TWLDA with different term weighting schemes.

Using TWLDA, the output of WeiboFinder is a list of topics. Each topic has a list of related words which are incident words for further study of Chinese. In addition, every word has its related posts from Weibo for reading and learning. To further demonstrate that the topics from WeiboFinder are inline with students' understanding and the words are useful for learning, we use survey to ask 20 students whether the word list about different topics is interpretable and related to the input Chinese word "Shanghai Stock Exchange Composite Index". We use Precision@n (or p@n) to check whether the words related to different topics are interpretable and could be useful for extending the Chinese word study. It is commonly used as a metric for information retrieval (Mukherjee et al. 2012 [18]). Top words are selected for comparison, here the n is set to 10. First of all, students will be asked to read the word list of each topic and find out correct topics in which half of the top 10 words are related to each other. Then they are required to label each word based on their understanding of the correct topic. If the word consists of the topic and useful for further learning about the input word, it will be labeled as correct, otherwise incorrect. The experiment result is shown in Fig. 4, our method has the best performance in all three datasets. Our proposed method using bdc has more correct words than other methods. The Precision@10 on average is around 60% using our method. The reason why we test the framework in datasets from different years is that Chinese learning from social media is time sensitive and the Chinese words related to the input word in different period could be different.

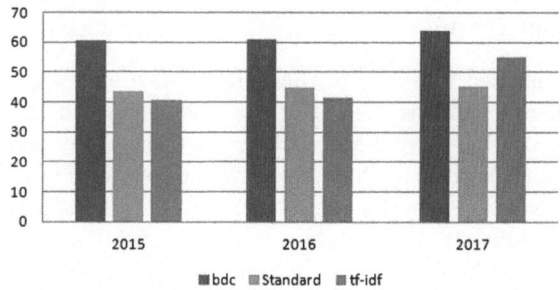

Fig. 4. Precision@10 of topics generated from 3 datasets.

5   Conclusion

The increasing popularity of social media websites has led to exponential growth of user-generated content. This user-generated content provides an useful data source for language learners. In addition, a lot of new words appear only in social media websites. In this paper, we propose an effective relevant words finding system called WeiboFinder for Chinese learning. WeiboFinder uses the data from Weibo to provide relevant topic words for Chinese learners. The experimental result demonstrates the effectiveness of our system. WeiboFinder can suggest useful words for Chinese learners and is more effective than other methods.

In the future, we will test our system in more data sets and consider learner profile generation in our system. In addition, the proposed topic generation algorithm could be used to build domain specific ontology for web-based studies.

Acknowledgments. This work is supported by the Fundamental Research Funds for the Central Universities, SCUT (NO. 2017ZD0482015ZM136), Tiptop Scientific and Technical Innovative Youth Talents of Guangdong special support program (No. 2015TQ01X633), Science and Technology Planning Project of Guangdong Province, China (No. 2016A030310423), Science and Technology Program of Guangzhou (International Science & Technology Cooperation Program No. 201704030076) and Science and Technology Planning Major Project of Guangdong Province (No. 2015A070711001).

References

1. Agichtein, E., Castillo, C., Donato, D., Gionis, A., Mishne, G.: Finding high-quality content in social media. In: Proceedings of the 2008 International Conference on Web Search and Data Mining, pp. 183–194. ACM (2008)
2. Ahmad, K., Cheng, D., Almas, Y.: Multi-lingual sentiment analysis of financial news streams. In: Proceedings of the 1st International Conference on Grid in Finance (2006)
3. Andrzejewski, D., Zhu, X., Craven, M.: Incorporating domain knowledge into topic modeling via dirichlet forest priors. In: Proceedings of the 26th Annual International Conference on Machine Learning, pp. 25–32. ACM (2009)

4. Burns, N., Bi, Y., Wang, H., Anderson, T.: Extended twofold-LDA model for two aspects in one sentence. In: Greco, S., Bouchon-Meunier, B., Coletti, G., Fedrizzi, M., Matarazzo, B., Yager, R.R. (eds.) IPMU 2012. CCIS, vol. 298, pp. 265–275. Springer, Heidelberg (2012). doi:10.1007/978-3-642-31715-6_29
5. Chen, Z., Mukherjee, A., Liu, B., Hsu, M., Castellanos, M., Ghosh, R.: Discovering coherent topics using general knowledge. In: Proceedings of the 22nd ACM International Conference on Information & Knowledge Management, pp. 209–218. ACM (2013)
6. Faizi, R., El Afia, A., Chiheb, R.: Exploring the potential benefits of using social media in education. iJEP 3(4), 50–53 (2013)
7. Faizi, R., El Afia, A., Chiheb, R.: Social media: an optimal virtual environment for learning foreign languages. iJET 9(5), 64–66 (2014)
8. Fan, R., Zhao, J., Chen, Y., Xu, K.: Anger is more influential than joy: sentiment correlation in Weibo. PLoS ONE 9(10), e110184 (2014)
9. Gao, Q., Abel, F., Houben, G.-J., Yu, Y.: A comparative study of users' microblogging behavior on Sina Weibo and Twitter. In: Masthoff, J., Mobasher, B., Desmarais, M.C., Nkambou, R. (eds.) UMAP 2012. LNCS, vol. 7379, pp. 88–101. Springer, Heidelberg (2012). doi:10.1007/978-3-642-31454-4_8
10. Hu, M., Liu, B.: Mining opinion features in customer reviews. AAAI 4, 755–760 (2004)
11. Huckin, T., Coady, J.: Incidental vocabulary acquisition in a second language. Stud. Second Lang. Acquis. 21(02), 181–193 (1999)
12. Jo, Y., Oh, A.H.: Aspect and sentiment unification model for online review analysis. In: Proceedings of the Fourth ACM International Conference on Web Search and Data Mining, pp. 815–824. ACM (2011)
13. Yang, K., Cai, Y., Chen, Z., Leung, H.F., Lau, R.Y.: Exploring topic discriminating power of words in latent dirichlet allocation. In: COLING, pp. 2238–2247 (2016)
14. Lee, M.J., McLoughlin, C.: Teaching and learning in the web 2.0 era: empowering students through learner-generated content. Int. J. Instr. Technol. Distance Learn. 4(10), 21–34 (2007)
15. Liang, H., Tsai, F.S., Kwee, A.T.: Detecting novel business blogs. In: Proceedings of the 7th International Conference on Information (2009)
16. Liu, X., Ye, S., Li, X., Luo, Y., Rao, Y.: ZhihuRank: a topic-sensitive expert finding algorithm in community question answering websites. In: Li, F.W.B., Klamma, R., Laanpere, M., Zhang, J., Manjón, B.F., Lau, R.W.H. (eds.) ICWL 2015. LNCS, vol. 9412, pp. 165–173. Springer, Cham (2015). doi:10.1007/978-3-319-25515-6_15
17. Mimno, D., Wallach, H.M., Talley, E., Leenders, M., McCallum, A.: Optimizing semantic coherence in topic models. In: Proceedings of the Conference on Empirical Methods in Natural Language Processing, pp. 262–272. Association for Computational Linguistics (2011)
18. Mukherjee, A., Liu, B.: Aspect extraction through semi-supervised modeling. In: Proceedings of the 50th Annual Meeting of the Association for Computational Linguistics: Long Papers, vol. 1, pp. 339–348. Association for Computational Linguistics (2012)
19. Peng, F., Feng, F., McCallum, A.: Chinese segmentation and new word detection using conditional random fields. In: Proceedings of the 20th International Conference on Computational Linguistics, p. 562. Association for Computational Linguistics (2004)
20. Wang, T., Cai, Y., Leung, H.f., Cai, Z., Min, H.: Entropy-based term weighting schemes for text categorization in VSM. In: 2015 IEEE 27th International Conference on Tools with Artificial Intelligence (ICTAI), pp. 325–332. IEEE (2015)

21. Wilson, A.T., Chew, P.A.: Term weighting schemes for latent dirichlet allocation. In: Human Language Technologies: The 2010 Annual Conference of the North American Chapter of the Association for Computational Linguistics, pp. 465–473. Association for Computational Linguistics (2010)
22. Xie, H., Zou, D., Lau, R.Y., Wang, F.L., Wong, T.L.: Generating incidental word-learning tasks via topic-based and load-based profiles. IEEE Multimed. **23**(1), 60–70 (2016)
23. Yang, F., Liu, Y., Yu, X., Yang, M.: Automatic detection of rumor on Sina Weibo. In: Proceedings of the ACM SIGKDD Workshop on Mining Data Semantics, p. 13. ACM (2012)
24. Zou, D., Xie, H., Wong, T.-L., Rao, Y., Wang, F.L., Wu, Q.: Predicting pre-knowledge on vocabulary from e-Learning assignments for language learners. In: Gong, Z., Chiu, D.K.W., Zou, D. (eds.) ICWL 2015. LNCS, vol. 9584, pp. 111–117. Springer, Cham (2016). doi:10.1007/978-3-319-32865-2_12
25. Zourou, K.: On the attractiveness of social media for language learning: a look at the state of the art. Alsic. Apprentissage des Langues et Systèmes d'Information et de Communication **15**(1) (2012)

Gamification of Web-Based Learning Services

Ralf Klamma[✉] and Muhammad Abduh Arifin

Advanced Community Information Systems Group (ACIS),
RWTH Aachen University, Lehrstuhl Informatik 5, Ahornstr. 55,
52074 Aachen, Germany
{klamma,arifin}@dbis.rwth-aachen.de

Abstract. Gamification is the use of game elements in non-game contexts like office work or learning. Due to its deep implications on human behavior, there are many critical voices but in principle the gamification of learning management systems is possible and different solutions are on the market. The situation is very different when users are mashing-up their personal learning environments from different Web-based learning services. This paper discusses the theoretical and technical gamification challenges of personal learning systems. It comes up with a framework that allows learning communities and individual learners even without programming experience to configure game elements and game rules in an intuitive, fine-granular and flexible way for existing Web-based learning services. To avoid changing existing code it uses aspect-oriented programming techniques. The evaluation showed that users were able to understand the concepts and could gamify Web-based learning services more easily. The gamification framework is available as open source software and will lead to more, easier and dynamic gamification of existing Web-based learning services.

Keywords: Web-based learning · Gamification · Personal learning environments · Web services

1 Introduction

The learning needs of professional Communities of Practice (CoP) in domains like engineering, healthcare, and cultural heritage are ever increasing with the digital transformation of professional practices. More and more CoP use digital media for accomplishing their goals. This has lead to the use of social software with a focus on life-long learning in professional communities [10]. To this end, personal learning environments (PLE) have become popular as collection of social software supporting the personal learning process [15]. However, their use in professional communities often lead to unproductive mixing of open source software, freemium commercial tools and emerging beta services. In the communities this can lead to major disturbances and lower the agency of the community. Also the support of CoP by PLE is not well understood on the theoretical level, e.g. pre-populated PLE can lead to lacking acceptance, distrust and uncertainty in the community, since the environment is not personal.

© Springer International Publishing AG 2017
H. Xie et al. (Eds.): ICWL 2017, LNCS 10473, pp. 43–48, 2017.
DOI: 10.1007/978-3-319-66733-1_5

Gamification of PLE uses game elements in non-game contexts to motivate players doing tasks, mostly to maintain the motivation of learners [4,16]. Gamification can be utilized in community learning environments to increase the motivation and appropriation of learning tools. By doing this, best practices and knowledge of the CoP are always developed and also shared among the members. However, existing gamification frameworks - while service oriented - are using complete or heavy integration approaches. Not all PLE are suitable to be gamified and gamification can be demotivating without proper usage, in particular in a community context. Concerning this, communities and their members should be able to design and to realize gamification strategies by themselves in a flexible enough way, i.e. the resulting PLE should work with our without gamification and this decision can be changed at any point.

In this paper, we present a gamification framework that is suitable to be used in CoP. The gamification framework is implemented as a set of Web microservices [6], so members of a CoP have the flexibility when gamifying their PLE and also the freedom to follow the needs of the CoP that changes overtime. Technically, this is realized by a light-weight integration approach using aspect-oriented programming (AOP) concepts adapted for Web engineering. Since not every member has sufficient knowledge of programming and all members of a CoP should be able to contribute [9], we developed our gamification framework based on a model-driven approach for learning service development with Web interfaces allowing CoP members to be included in the overall process of developing and mashing-up learning services. The integration of a learning service and gamification features is done without modifying the source code of the learning service. We used AOP to inject gamification features into the source code.

The rest of the paper is organized as follows. The methodological approach is presented in the next section. The paper closes with a conclusion and an outlook on further work.

2   Methodological Approach

Stanculescu et al. [13] developed a gamification framework and studied the effect of game mechanics to learning and social interaction in an enterprise environment. They focused on the use of leaderboards, badges, and the combination of both of them. The study showed the positive results in using different game mechanics in a Q&A Web application. Another study developed a strategy to motivate users based on Self-Determination Theory (SD) in social adaptive e-learning contexts [12]. They evaluated students in university courses and found high motivation of students. Other research yielded positive results for gamification in communities. Herzig et al. [8] showed that gamification improves enjoyment, ease of use, and flow experience. [14] discussed about DevHub, a website builder that implements gamification in its system. DevHub gives rewards to its users for adding more features. It also makes it more social by enabling collaborative features in building a site. Farzan et al. [5] used gamification in a company social network called Beehive. After the deployment with gamification features, the user participation has increased.

Despite the mentioned benefits, gamification also has its downsides. Andrade et al. [2] argued that the use of gamification is good as long as it is monitored and controlled. Some drawbacks, such as off-task behavior, undesired competition, and addiction might appear if the gamification is not designed carefully enough. According to them, he use of gamification in a system strongly depends on gamification designers. Gamification designers have a role to monitor and control game elements and game rules in gamification. According to Nicholson [11], a fun feeling is created using some constraints that can be achieved by a set of rules. In the gamification framework, rules are constructed by configuring some constraints in the game elements. The game elements can be seen as a stack of blocks as shown in Fig. 1a. The upper blocks depend on the blocks below. There are two main goals in the gamification framework: completing quests and increasing levels. To create a gamification, the configuration of the game elements needs to be defined in bottom-up manner, since the components above depend on the components below. Figure 1 shows the steps to configure the game elements by defining some quests and levels. To enrich the gamification process, **quests** in the gamification framework can have three states: *hidden, revealed,* and *completed.* By showing the revealed quests with their progress, players know the state of their tasks. Differentiation can be achieved by providing difficult but still feasible tasks. Our gamification framework also supports **hidden quests** that can be revealed by constraints. The process is iterated to obtain a more complex gamification as shown in Fig. 1b.

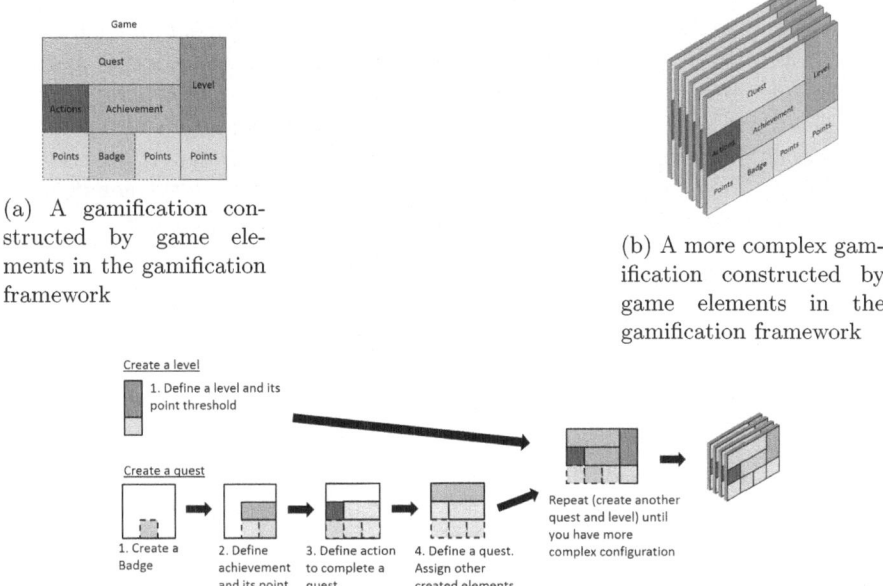

(a) A gamification constructed by game elements in the gamification framework

(b) A more complex gamification constructed by game elements in the gamification framework

Fig. 1. Steps to configure game elements in the gamification framework

Actions determine how a gamification behaves. They can be defined as the verbs of the gamification [1]. They are the possible instructions that can be performed by a learner. In the gamification framework, a member of a CoP is the learner. The gamifier bridges the learner inputs to the core mechanics. The core mechanics contain the game elements configuration and rules that are configured in the gamification manager to calculate learner's status. The gamification visualization shows the feedback from the core mechanics to the learner. Therefore, an action in the gamification framework changes states of members' game elements in the core mechanics.

Game rules are a set of constraints of game elements that construct the gamification. Member elements are the game elements that members of a CoP obtain during the game, such as their badges, their points, achievements, completed quests, and levels. The game rules in the gamification framework are about how the game elements are calculated, such as how some points are given to the members, how a quest can be completed or revealed, and how an achievement is obtained. Once an action is triggered, the game rules process all information based on the game elements configuration and the triggered action. Members of the CoP are able to configure the game elements configuration and the game rules as well as trigger an action to the game rules.

The achievement contains some rewards. It can be a badge or some points or both of them. Members configure when a quest is revealed based on how much points they have and which quest have they completed. A quest is completed after an action or a combination of some actions is performed. Members of the CoP also have a specific level depending on how much points they have.

Member points update **leaderboards** and **global leaderboards**. Points can be obtained by doing an action or getting an achievement (completing a quest). Every gamification in the gamification framework has a leaderboard to compare members in the same CoP. To be able to compare members in different CoPs (cross-community comparison), each gamification of a CoP should be comparable. Therefore, each gamification has a community type that needs to be defined by members of the CoP when they create a game in the gamification manager. Members' points in CoPs with the same community type are then compared and shown in the same global leaderboard. Each global leaderboard represents each community type.

For the sake of brevity, we cannot go in all details of the realization. The gamification framework front-ends are implemented as Web widgets developed with the ROLE framework [7], an open source SDK for developing personal learning environments. All front-end components in the gamification framework communicate with the gamification services. Each component is placed in its own ROLE space, a Web-based PLE. The gamification manager has its own space and consists of several game element widgets. The gamification framework uses AOP to inject gamification features to the PLE front-end. The injection of gamification features to a learning service source code is performed without coding so it helps members of a CoP that has no programming knowledge to gamify their learning service. The gamification features that are injected to a learning service are trigger action functions. In the gamification framework, the gamifier widget has a role to determine the place to trigger actions of a gamification in the learning service source code. Using AOP, the trigger action function can be called after a method of an HTML element event is executed.

3   Conclusions and Future Work

This paper presents our gamification framework to gamify Web services of PLE. The framework is developed based on the widely adopted Communities of Practice (CoPs) theory and emphasizes the integration of learning services mashed-up through existing Web services and gamification that needs to be less invasive than existing gamification frameworks. By doing this, all members of a CoP should be able to gamify a learning service.

The gamification framework is implemented as a set of Web services and available as open source software on Github. It uses AOP to inject gamification features. A preliminary evaluation identified possible drawbacks and benefits of using AOP in the integration process following the design process. We used the Octalysis framework [3] to assess the game elements and game rules of our gamification framework. Yet, the use of game elements was not comprehensively evaluated, We did user evaluations of psychological impacts of each selected game element and the according game rules. But, in follow-up research we will link the gamification elements to existing success awareness factors defined in community success awareness models. We expect more results when evaluating intra- and inter-community leaderboards. A larger scale evaluation is also needed, then. The evaluation of the gamification framework uses a simple to-learn-list service. A more realistic learning service like a collaborative learning service would reveal more success factors as well.

Acknowledgements. The research leading to these results has received funding from the European Research Council under the European Union's Horizon 2020 Programme through the project "WEKIT" (grant no. 687669).

References

1. Adams, E., Rollings, A.: Fundamentals of Game Design, Voices That Matter, 2nd edn. New Riders, Berkeley (2010)
2. Andrade, F.R.H., Mizoguchi, R., Isotani, S.: The bright and dark sides of gamification. In: Micarelli, A., Stamper, J., Panourgia, K. (eds.) ITS 2016. LNCS, vol. 9684, pp. 176–186. Springer, Cham (2016). doi:10.1007/978-3-319-39583-8_17
3. Chou, Y.K.: Actionable Gamification: Beyond Points, Badges, and Leaderboards. Octalysis Group, United States (2015). Revised edition
4. Deterding, S., Khaled, R., Nacke, L., Dixon, D.: Gamification: toward a definition. In: CHI 2011 Extended Abstracts on Human Factors in Computing Systems (2011). http://portal.acm.org/citation.cfm?id=1979742&picked=prox&cfid=30563557&cftoken=85856015

5. Farzan, R., DiMicco, J.M., Brownholtz, B.: ACM: spreading the honey: a system for maintaining an online community. In: Proceedings of the ACM GROUP 2009, pp. 31–40 (2009)
6. Villamor, F., Ignacio, J., Fernandez, I., Angel, C., Garijo Ayestaran, M.: Microservices: lightweight service descriptions for REST architectural style. In: 2nd International Conference on Agents and Artificial Intelligence (ICAART 2010) (2010)
7. Govaerts, S., et al.: Towards responsive open learning environments: the ROLE interoperability framework. In: Kloos, C.D., Gillet, D., Crespo García, R.M., Wild, F., Wolpers, M. (eds.) EC-TEL 2011. LNCS, vol. 6964, pp. 125–138. Springer, Heidelberg (2011). doi:10.1007/978-3-642-23985-4_11
8. Herzig, P., Strahringer, S., Amerling, M.: Gamification of ERP systems - exploring gamification effects on user acceptance constructs. In: Multikonferenz Wirtschaftinformatik, pp. 793–804 (2012)
9. Kerno, S.J.: Limitations of communities of practice: a consideration of unresolved issues and difficulties in the approach. J. Leadersh. Organ. Stud. **15**, 69–78 (2008)
10. Klamma, R., Chatti, M.A., Duval, E., Fiedler, S., Hummel, H.J., Hvannberg, E.T., Kravčík, M., Law, E.L.C., Naeve, A., Scott, P.: Social software for life-long learning. J. Educ. Technol. Soc. **10**(3), 72–83 (2007)
11. Nicholson, S.: A RECIPE for meaningful gamification. In: Reiners, T., Wood, L.C. (eds.) Gamification in Education and Business, pp. 1–20. Springer, Cham (2015). doi:10.1007/978-3-319-10208-5_1
12. Shi, L., Cristea, A.I.: Motivational gamification strategies rooted in self-determination theory for social adaptive E-learning. In: Micarelli, A., Stamper, J., Panourgia, K. (eds.) ITS 2016. LNCS, vol. 9684, pp. 294–300. Springer, Cham (2016). doi:10.1007/978-3-319-39583-8_32
13. Stanculescu, L.C., Bozzon, A., Sips, R.J., Houben, G.J.: Work and play: an experiment in enterprise gamification. In: Gergle, D., Morris, M.R., Bjørn, P., Konstan, J. (eds.) CSCW 2016, pp. 345–357 (2016)
14. Takahashi, D.: Website builder DevHub gets users hooked by "gamifying" its service (2010). http://venturebeat.com/2010/08/25/devhub-scores-engagement-increase-by-gamifying-its-web-site
15. van Harmelen, M.: Personal learning environments. In: Kinshuk, Koper, R., Kommers, P., Kirschner, P.A., Sampson, D.G., Didderen, W. (eds.) Proceedings of the 6th IEEE International Conference on Advanced Learning Technologies (ICALT 2006), pp. 815–816. IEEE Computer Society, Washington, DC (2006)
16. Zichermann, G., Cunningham, C.: Gamification by Design: Implementing Game Mechanics in Web and Mobile Apps. O'Reilly, Sebastopol (2011)

Learning Analytics

Integrating Learning Analytics into a Game Authoring Tool

Ivan J. Perez-Colado, Victor M. Perez-Colado, Manuel Freire-Moran,
Ivan Martinez-Ortiz, and Baltasar Fernandez-Manjon$^{(\boxtimes)}$

Department of Software Engineering and Artificial Intelligence, Facultad de
Informática, Universidad Complutense de Madrid, Madrid, Spain
{ivanjper, victormp}@ucm.es,
{manuel.freire, imartinez, balta}@fdi.ucm.es

Abstract. Educational games can greatly benefit from integrating support for learning analytics. Game authoring tools that make this integration as easy as possible are therefore an important step towards improving adoption of educational games. We describe the process of integrating full support for game learning analytics into uAdventure, a serious game authoring tool. We argue that such integrations greatly systematize, simplify and reduce both the cost and the knowledge required to apply analytics to serious games. In uAdventure, we have used an analytics model for serious games and its supporting implementation as a xAPI application. We describe how player interactions are automatically traced, and provide an interaction-model-trace table with the general game traces that are generated by the editor. Also, we describe the custom editors that simplify the task of authoring game-dependant analytics. Thanks to these integrated analytics, games developed with uAdventure provide detailed tracking information that can be sent to a cloud analytics server, to be analyzed and visualized with dashboards that provide game developers and educators with insights into how games are being played.

Keywords: Game learning analytics · Analytics · Serious games · Games authoring · xAPI

1 Introduction

Game analytics (GA, also called telemetry) is the process of collecting and analyzing videogame user interactions to generate a better insight of the game experience for game designers and developers to take decisions in the next project iterations [1]. For example, such an analysis can reveal which levels are too hard for the average user, or provide insights on how to increase monetization. Similarly, learning analytics (LA) is the analysis of user's interactions with educational purposes [2], for instance providing information that allows educators to better understand how the learners are applying domain knowledge in an e-learning system, and improve the educational experience in some way (e.g. evaluate student progress). Game learning analytics (GLA) is the combination of both GA and LA to allow both game designers and educators to analyze player/learner interactions to improve the use of the games in education [3].

© Springer International Publishing AG 2017
H. Xie et al. (Eds.): ICWL 2017, LNCS 10473, pp. 51–61, 2017.
DOI: 10.1007/978-3-319-66733-1_6

Although there are many platforms that provide both LA and GA, however GLA is still a complex process and there is no generally-accepted approach to apply it to serious games. For example, games must typically provide data to each analytics system (e.g. GA, LA) separately, and frequently in different formats. In addition, once the games are deployed, the GLA results are only available through each specific analytics system's proprietary analysis, reports and dashboards. As of this writing, GLA is a complex ad-hoc process specific for each game and each analytics system. However, we believe that GLA should play a critical role in the lifecycle of serious games (see Fig. 1), as it is key to allow both game and learning designers to validate their designs; and can also be used to provide formative and summative evaluation.

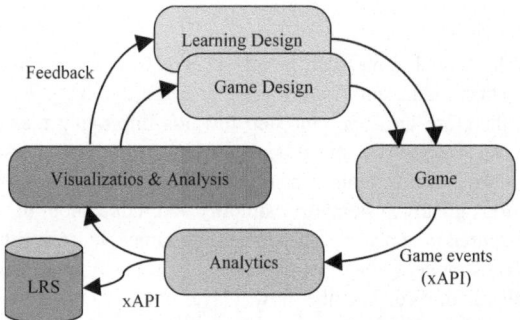

Fig. 1. Use of Game Learning Analytics in a serious game lifecycle. Use of xAPI provides a standards-based format for analysis and archival.

The process of applying GLA to educational games would be greatly simplified by having in-built support within the authoring tools, so that the resulting games can communicate with analytics services using well-known standards. This integration would systematize and simplify the usage of analytics by automatically linking the game model with the analytics model, reducing both the cost and the know-how barriers that have hampered GLA adoption in small deployments. In the following sections, we first briefly introduce uAdventure, a game authoring tool into which we have integrated GLA support. We then describe the analytics model and the user-interfaces that determine and configure how user gameplay is mapped into analytics traces. Finally, we present a discussion and conclusions that summarize the main results of this work, together with future directions for improvement.

2 An Analytics Model for UAdventure

uAdventure (uA) is a serious game authoring tool built on top of the Unity game authoring platform that supports the full development lifecycle for adventure "point and click" games [4]. It is a reimplementation of eAdventure (eA) [5], which was built using Java. The use of the Unity platform allows uA games to support a much larger range of devices and platforms. The goal of uA is to allow non-expert developers to create "point and click" educational games, including features such as scenarios, characters, dialogs, and assessment. While in eA the assessment system was based on e-learning models (e.g. SCORM), uA now extends it with support for GLA.

uA GLA support is based on a general game analytics model that is implemented according to the emergent specification promoted by ADL and called xAPI (eXperience API). A game analytics model describes how in-game interactions are reported to an analytics server, typically as a stream of events, but also sometimes as fully serialized game-states. The serious games xAPI profile [6] (SG-xAPI for short) is a general event-based analytics model that builds on the xAPI activity stream standard [7], and is therefore event-based. The main event categories found in SG-xAPI, strongly inspired by [8], are

- Completables, which describe progress along a particular level or task with a start and an end. Completables can be nested. Examples could be game, game session, level, quest, or race.
- Alternatives, which reflect in-game choices made by the player. Menus, questions, paths and dialogue choices are examples of alternatives.
- Meaningful variables, which directly echo in-game state changes such as score or character health. Note that these variables are a very small subset of the total game-state.
- Custom interactions, intended as extension points for actions not covered in the above categories.

xAPI traces are composed of a subject, a verb, an object, and optional context; for example, an xAPI trace describing that "player Alice used a key" in a given game would include Alices' identity as subject, "Used" as xAPI verb, the specific in-game key identifier as an object, and the specific door as context. This output is then passed on into existing GLA services, such as the open-source RAGE Analytics[1] system which is used in the H2020 RAGE and BEACONING projects.

Integrating GLA into a game requires both the analytics model and the definition of the server-side analyses that process this data into a format suitable for visualization within dashboards [3]. However, since uA relies on the SG-xAPI default analyses and visualizations performed in RAGE Analytics and described in [9], this work focuses exclusively on the mapping between in-game actions and the SG-xAPI traces that are sent to the server.

Point and click games are typically composed of multiple scenes woven together via a supporting narrative, where players interact on scene items or characters via mouse clicks to advance the plot. The following subsections explore the areas in which events have been analyzed and traced, starting from the lowest to the highest level of abstraction. The following subsections describe (i) session management events; (ii) user interactions with game elements inside the scenes; (iii) scene changes; (iv) meaningful variable changes; and finally, (v) completables, which are high-level tasks related to in-game progress.

---

[1] https://github.com/e-ucm/rage-analytics.

2.1 Session Events

In order to process traces sent from games into sessions, the analytics servers need to identify players. Three options are available: fully logged-in players, pseudonymous players, and fully anonymous players. When players are fully logged in, the analytics system can be integrated with an LMS to provide detailed evaluation that is tied to the player's true identity [10]. This, however, presents certain privacy and confidentiality concerns, and may not be feasible in an analytics-as-a-service setting. With pseudonymous login, players are assigned a random pseudonym when they first connect, which they will continue to use in later sessions. This allows evaluation to be carried out, without the possibility of tracing the actual identities of the players. Finally, in a fully anonymous setting, all sessions are independent of each other, and no evaluation is possible. This option is still interesting during initial pilots to gather feedback to improve learning and game design (as shown in Fig. 2).

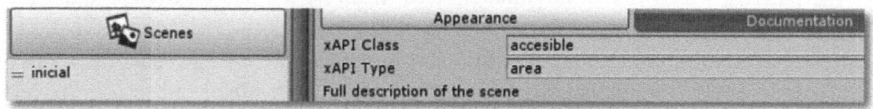

Fig. 2. Editor shows scene documentation where game designer can change scene specification, default values are, as shown: class Accessible with type Area

While necessary for analytics, authentication and authorization are not part of the analytics model itself, as they are expected to be handled by the GLA servers before any actual gameplay data is sent. uAdventure supports login (for non-anonymous use) by displaying a small login form on game startup, and transparently handles session startup with the GLA servers specified during game development.

2.2 User Interaction Events

Raw input events such as mouse movements, clicks, and keyboard inputs constitute the lowest level of abstraction in analytics. These events provide little information on their own, even when grouped to create higher-level abstractions such as dragging or double-clicking. For GLA purposes, interactions that are directly linked to game content and/or game progress, such as interactions with scene elements, are much more valuable. Elements inside scenes include items, characters or areas; and players can typically interact with them with in-game actions such as "examine" or "use".

uAdventure automatically sends "Interacted" SG-xAPI traces whenever a player interacts with an in-game element such as an item or character. The trace will identify both the object of the interaction and, if applicable, the type of interaction (such as "examine" or "eat"). Therefore, tracing such low-level interactions requires zero effort on the part of the game developer, and provides a free stream of information to perform GA (e.g. interaction heat maps). On the other hand, these events are of little help to better understand the in-game learning process; using Completables (see Sect. 2.6), which do require a certain configuration, yields much better results.

2.3   Scene and Cutscene Changes

Scenes in uAdventure are modeled after their theater counterparts: they provide backdrops within which the player moves and interacts with items and other characters. Certain mini-games are also modeled as scenes. Cutscenes are special scenes that usually imply the visualization of non-interactive content, such as slides or videos. Tracking scene changes and whether cutscenes are skipped or not provides valuable context to understand other events that are being reported by a game. Additionally, the game always knows which scene is currently open, so that information regarding both is readily available.

uAdventure uses the SG-xAPI "Accessed" verb to track scene changes, and also allows developers to further describe the scene for analytics purposes (choices include Screen, Zone, Area and Cutscene). Skipping cutscenes, such as videos, might reduce the learning value, as the player has only been exposed to a part of the potentially informative content. uAdventure uses "Skipped" verbs to signal this fact.

While access events are valuable for GA, they are not (with the exception of Skipped) so useful for LA: game developers can freely connect scenes, and there is no game-independent way to determine the game progress from these changes [11]. To infer progress, game developers can specify that scenes should be treated, in addition to Accessibles, as Alternatives (see Sect. 2.5), where by entering or leaving the scene the player is making a choice, or as a Completable (see Sect. 2.6) task such as a minigame, where entering or exiting the scene should be interpreted as actual progress.

2.4   Meaningful Variables

Game state in uA is represented mainly by variables and flags. uA condition system uses their values to control content display and behavior execution. Therefore, changes in variables are usually good candidates for analytics.

However, a game-specific analysis is required to identify the relevance of a variable (or a set of variables) for the learning process. Even if not all variables are relevant to LA, to reduce game authoring complexity, all changes in variables and flags are automatically reported. Once the data is collected, it can be mined to distinguish the variables with a larger impact on the learning process.

When a player interaction triggers several in-game consequences, so, to preserve the change context (which would allow for a more precise analysis), it is better to associate all of them together as the result of an interaction event. This is possible as, instead of sending an event per variable change, all the variable changes are stacked waiting for the next non-variable event. When the next interaction occurs, the trace generated will carry all the extensions inside.

2.5   Alternatives

Alternative selections represent a higher level of abstraction, and provide a direct measure of the student's knowledge. An alternative can be represented in many ways (e.g. text response selection, image selection, path selection); but in general, constitutes a choice where some options can be considered correct and others less so. Therefore, alternative selection is very valuable for LA and assessment, as well as to test and verify game design.

The most common types of alternatives in point-and-click games are dialogue responses for use with non-player characters [11]. uA provides a graph-based dialogue editor where questions can be identified with a unique id and, using a checkbox, marked as correct or incorrect (see Fig. 3). In uA questions without a question-id are considered not relevant for analytics purposes.

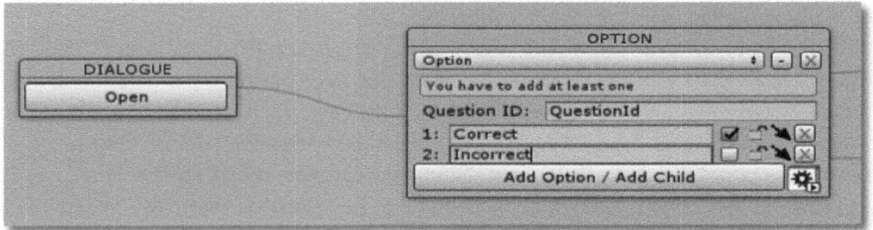

Fig. 3. Dialog Question editor allowing a game designer to specify a question id and which of the answers of that question should be considered correct or incorrect (Checkbox)

To track these events, the SG-xAPI "Selected" verb is used, where question types include menu, path or question. A result field describes the selected option identifier as response and the whether it was correct or not.

In addition to dialog responses, as mentioned in Subsect. 2.3, it is also possible to interpret scene selection as type of Alternative. In this case, as depicted in Fig. 4, each available scene exit is considered a response using the arriving scene name as response identifier. If the player passes through the exit successfully, the answer was correct, but otherwise, it was a wrong answer.

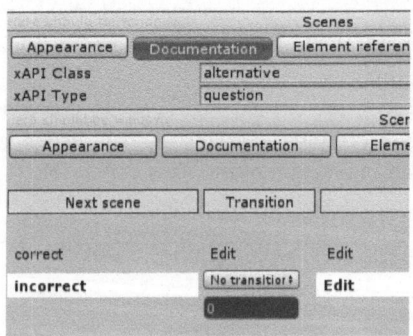

Fig. 4. Left: An Alternative scene type Question with correct and incorrect exits. Right: runtime Alternative Type Question scene from the SG First Aid Game.

2.6   Completables

Completables provide the highest level of abstraction and describe player progress along the abstract tasks that the user has to complete throughout the game. Tasks are not limited to representing game progress: they can be used to represent learning process itself, for instance by establishing a correspondence between progress and score in a given task (game design) and learning the concepts that it exercises (learning design). Completables are available in the uA editor's Analytics tab. To track completables, SG-xAPI includes the verbs "Started", "Progressed" and "Finished".

Inside of a game there could be multiple completables and they may be active at any time, even in parallel. A game with correctly configured completables is much easier to analyze than one where the underlying triggers have to be decoded from the underlying game traces (in a server-side game-specific analysis). In order to track them, the completable system lets the developer freely configure starting milestone and ending milestones. These milestones can be determined by five different triggers: (i) access to specific scene, (ii) interaction with specific item, (iii) interaction with specific character, (iv) accomplishment of another completable and (v) a boolean condition as determined by a combination of in-game variables.

Completables can be composed of several milestones; the accomplishment of each milestone defines the progress. To define them, the uA editor provides a progress editor that lets the user specify all milestones that compose the completable. Progress can either be calculated as the ratio of completed-to-total milestones, or configured for each specific completable using sliders as illustrated in Fig. 5. Finally, to associate the score, the user can select the variable that will hold its value.

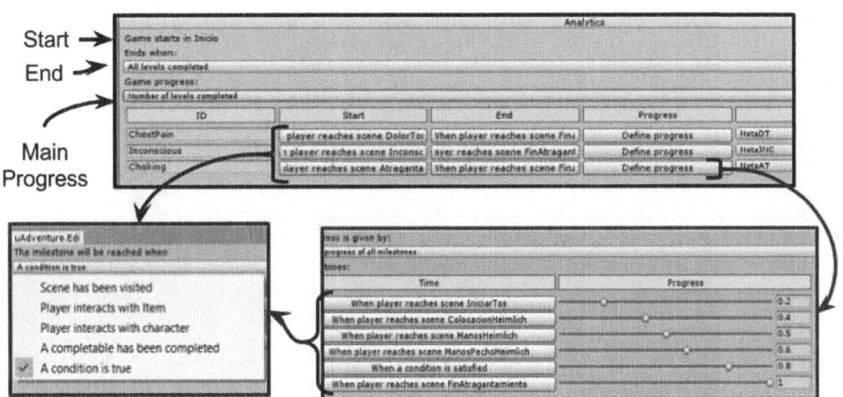

Fig. 5. uA Progress editor. (i) Top shows main completable editor, defining three cases of the serious game FirstAidGame. Progress is defined by the number of cases completed. (ii) Right shows individual completable editors, with a list of milestones to be satisfied. Progress is determined by the max of the milestones reached. (iii) Left shows milestone editor options, letting game designer to choose between a list of options to define what reach this milestone

In addition to the level-specific completables, there is a global game completable, identified using the "Game" type. When the game starts, it generates a "Started" event; whenever a completable is completed a "Progressed" trace is launched tracking the game general progress; finally, the condition associated with game end will generate the "Completed" event with the average score of all completables.

3 Mapping Game Events to SG-xAPI

Table 1 contains a summary of the mapping from game events to xAPI traces presented in the previous subsections, in increasing order of abstraction; and therefore, utility from a LA point of view: events closer to the interaction with game elements are less meaningful than the ones that are connected to game progression, such as alternatives and completables.

Table 1. Summary of game events traced inside the uAadventure authoring tool

Event	Cause	xAPI Type xAPI Verb	Target	Result R: response, S: success, Ext: extensions
NPC Interaction	Player opens NPC actions menu	Character Interacted	NPC name	Ext: Action name
Item Interaction	Player opens item actions menu	Item Interacted	Item name	Ext: Action name
Scene access	Player enters a scene	Accessible Accessed	Scene id	
Cutscene start	Player starts a cutscene	Cutscene Accessed	Cutscene id	
Cutscene skip	Player presses skip	Cutscene Skipped	Cutscene id	Ext: Percent watched
Exit selection in alternative type scenes	Player selects an exit in current scene, for menus or visual choices	(Alternative, Question Menu or Path) Selected	Exit Id	R: Arriving scene S: Based on exit conditions
Dialog choice	Player selects one dialog option	Alternative Selected	Question Id	R: Response S: Correctness
Task start	Player reaches a milestone	Completable Started	Completable Id	
Task progress	Player reaches one of the milestones	Completable Progressed	Completable Id	Ext: Milestone progress value

(*continued*)

Table 1. (*continued*)

Event	Cause	xAPI Type xAPI Verb	Target	Result R: response, S: success, Ext: extensions
Task finish	Player reaches a milestone or completes all the steps	Completable Completed	Completable Id	R: Score from variable S: Based on conditions Ext: Time
Game start	Player visits title	Game Started	Game name	
Game progress	Accomplishment of any of the levels	Game Progressed	Game name	Ext: Progress as percent of levels (tasks) completed
Game end	Milestone or all levels completed	Game Completed	Game name	R: Avg. score of all levels S: Based on conditions Ext: Time

4   Discussion and Conclusions

Serious games have frequently been evaluated by relying exclusively on (paper-based) learning assessment. In traditional e-learning, different methods have been used to connect the serious game outcome (e.g. score) to different learning systems allowing the use of serious games as any other assessment tool such as online tests; but this integration focuses on simple outcomes and provide few or no insights into the process. However, if a game fails to work for a particular set of players, knowing the exact steps they have followed inside the game is crucial to determine the reasons. Tackling this lack of flexibility requires a transformation from the traditional assessment model to the new evidence-driven model; and mapping in-game actions to events that can be used to analyze and gain insight not only on the results, but also on the process.

The uAdventure analytics model describes how player interactions are automatically captured and transformed into events that the LA system can collect and analyze. The events generated cover a wide range of situations such as scene access, element interaction and options selection. We also describe how higher-level events can be authored from within uA. Other tools that wish to integrate GLA into their games should find this analysis useful when developing their own analytics models and user interfaces.

The integration of uAdventure with GLA presents multiple benefits to game developers. First, all games developed with the tool automatically integrate free support for LA requiring minimum developer effort. This greatly reduce the GLA cost. In addition, thanks to the use of standardized events, developers do not need handle event encoding, and can automatically take advantage of several generic analyses and visualizations in xAPI-aware GLA platforms such as the (open-source and freely available) RAGE Analytics. For no added effort, uAdventure developers and users can enjoy basic analytics and assessment information, which can then be enriched by generating game-dependent events that provide richer information that links to the relevant learning situations identified in the game learning design.

During the integration, we have also identified multiple areas that can benefit from further work. For example, changes to game variables are only sent to the server as a part of future non-variable updates, instead of when they actually occur. This is part of the standard, but may confuse analyses that expect traces to be sent in the order they were generated. The uAdventure editor can also benefit from numerous usability enhancements, such as displaying information about completables directly inside of the element editors that are used as triggers in the completables' definition; or integrating game mechanics such as quests or missions that are directly tied to completables and provide explicit in-game feedback to allow users to track their own progress.

We believe that the integration between game authoring tools and game learning analytics, as described in the present work, is an is an important step towards wider usage of GLA in serious games.

Acknowledgement. This work has been partially funded by Regional Government of Madrid (eMadrid S2013/ICE-2715), by the Ministry of Education (TIN2013-46149-C2-1-R) and by the European Commission (RAGE H2020-ICT-2014-1-644187, BEACONING H2020-ICT-2015-687676).

References

1. Seif El-Nasr, M., Drachen, A., Canossa, A.: Game Analytics. Springer, London (2013)
2. Elias, T.: Learning analytics: definitions, processes and potential. Learning **23**, 134–148 (2011)
3. Freire, M., Serrano-Laguna, Á., Iglesias, B.M., Martínez-Ortiz, I., Moreno-Ger, P., Fernández-Manjón, B., Analytics, G.L.: Learning analytics for serious games. İn: Spector, M.J. et al. (eds.) Learning, Design, and Technology, pp. 1–29. Springer, Cham (2016)
4. Perez Colado, I., Perez Colado, V., Martínez-Ortiz, I., Freire, M., Fernandez-Manjon, B.: uAdventure: the eAdventure reboot - combining the experience of commercial gaming tools and tailored educational tools. In: IEEE Global Engineering Education Conference, pp. 1754–1761, April 2017
5. Torrente, J., del Blanco, A., Marchiori, E.J., Moreno-Ger, P., Fernandez-Manjon, B.: <e-Adventure>: introducing educational games in the learning process. In: IEEE EDUCON 2010 Conference, pp. 1121–1126 (2010)
6. Serrano-Laguna, A., Martinez-Ortiz, I., Haag, J., Regan, D., Johnson, A., Fernandez-Manjon, B.: Applying standards to systematize learning analytics in serious games. Comput. Stand. Interfaces **50**, 116–123 (2016)
7. xAPI - ADL Net @ www.adlnet.gov
8. Serrano-laguna, Á., Torrente, J., Moreno-ger, P., Fernández-manjón, B.: Tracing a little for big improvements: application of learning analytics and videogames for student assessment. Procedia Comput. Sci. **15**, 203–209 (2012)

9. Alonso-Fernandez, C., Calvo, A., Freire, M., Martinez-Ortiz, I., Fernandez-Manjon, B.: Systematizing game learning analytics for serious games. In: 2017 IEEE Global Engineering Education Conference, pp. 1106–1113, April 2017

10. Bienkowski, M., Feng, M., Means, B.: Enhancing teaching and learning through educational data mining and learning analytics: an issue brief. Washington, DC SRI International, pp. 1–57 (2012)

11. Mehm, F., Göbel, S., Steinmetz, R.: An authoring tool for educational adventure games. Int. J. Game-Based Learn. 3(1), 63–79 (2013)

Generating Alerts for Drops in Student Activity Levels in a Social Learning Environment

Paul Ştefan Popescu$^{(\boxtimes)}$, Cristian Mihăescu, Elvira Popescu,
and Mihai Mocanu

Computers and Information Technology Department,
University of Craiova, Craiova, Romania
{spopescu,mihaescu,epopescu,mocanu}@software.ucv.ro

Abstract. Monitoring students' activity in a social learning environment is an important issue both for students and teachers. Providing learners with notifications whenever their activity level drops has the potential to increase their motivation and engagement. This paper tackles the issue of accurately pointing when a student has a drop or an increase in activity in the context of a social learning environment. We designed and implemented a data analysis framework which generates statistical dashboards based on aggregated student activity on three social media tools (blog, wiki and microblogging tool); alerts are subsequently issued in case of a significant decrease in activity. Experimental results obtained on student data collected over the course of five years reveal a pattern regarding the average number of generated alerts. Therefore our system can be successfully used by the instructor to easily configure the number of alerts issued to the students.

Keywords: Learning analytics · Social media · Learner tracking · Activity trend

1 Introduction

Monitoring and analyzing students' activity in e-learning environments is an increasingly popular research direction [7, 15]. Predicting student grades, providing personalized recommendations, detecting undesirable students' behaviours, are some of the most tackled objectives [14]. In this context, an effective detection of activity drops allows learners to be informed about their current activity status and offers the possibility to increase their engagement in learning. It also offers instructors valuable information about students at-risk, in order to prevent potential student dropout.

Building customized learner notification systems has been addressed in [16], by automatically firing occasional alerts that direct students to particularly noteworthy comments from their colleagues, alert them when their activity is isolating them from the group, or when textual analysis of their contribution suggests high levels of agreement with the individuals with whom they interact.

© Springer International Publishing AG 2017
H. Xie et al. (Eds.): ICWL 2017, LNCS 10473, pp. 62–71, 2017.
DOI: 10.1007/978-3-319-66733-1_7

In this paper, we focus on monitoring and analyzing students' activity in a social learning environment, supported by social media tools. Indeed, these tools have the potential for enhancing communication, sharing, and cooperation, as well as building knowledge. Furthermore, social media can foster positive interactions between learners and increase learner engagement and motivation [5]. Researchers also argued that social learning represents a way to catalyse learning and innovation. Currently, since social media tools are being widely adopted as highly effective means of interaction, they are also integrated and used as facilitators of education, in a context in which learners interact with provided information by pulling it as needed [8].

Logging and analyzing activities performed in social environments can be a valuable asset for technology enhanced learning. Typically, students participating in a course that makes substantial use of social media tools as educational environment can more easily keep up their level of engagement; this prevents them from failing the course or even dropping school by being correctly and timely notified about their activity level. Under these circumstances, the difficulty lays in designing an efficient data analytics pipeline that solves the proposed task of correctly notifying learners about their social activity status, as detailed in the next section.

Therefore, the objective of our research is to design and implement such a data analysis framework which investigates when a student has a drop or an increase in activity. More specifically, the framework was built to work in conjunction with our eMUSE social learning environment [12], in which students use social media tools (blog, wiki and Twitter) to communicate and collaborate. The data analysis framework generates statistical dashboards based on aggregated student activity on the three social media tools; the aim is to subsequently issue alerts in case of a significant decrease in activity.

The rest of the paper is structured as follows: Sect. 2 provides an overview of related work and current challenges. Section 3 introduces the data analysis framework and the mechanism for alert generation. The experimental results, based on data collected over five years, are reported in Sect. 4. The paper ends with some conclusions and future research directions.

2 Related Work

An important challenge in learner tracking comes from discriminating between active learning and simply socializing when using social media tools. A set of principles were proposed in [4], which allow determining the intentions of a user (e.g., discriminating learning from browsing), grounding the learning process (by problem/task definition and experimentation) and measuring engagement in learning conversations (by usage of specific concepts that increase their understanding). Furthermore, key aspects that need to be taken into consideration when shifting from "everyday social media" to "social media tuned for learning" are presented in [3, 6]; among the dimensions of the social learning design space there may be found aspects like "reflection encouraged by UI" or "recommendations based on learning profiles and activities".

Several studies [10, 13] showed that a higher level of social presence is a good indicator of better learning results. Investigations performed for various types of course activities (e.g., Q and A, group projects) demonstrated a strong correlation between social presence and perceived learning by students.

In this context, various solutions have been proposed for building early warning systems for low activity levels of students. For instance, Macfadyen and Dawson [11] proposed a predictive model by logistic regression on tracked activity-based variables (such as number of online sessions, number of messages read/sent, etc.) which measured the student engagement and likelihood of success. While the instructional scenario did not involve the use of social media tools, many of the monitored variables had a social dimension, such as total number of discussion messages posted and total number of mail messages sent (in addition to the educational ones, such as total number of assessments completed).

Another recent example of early warning system is presented in [9]. Learning performance was characterized by using complete learning activities defined by time dependent variables. Social activity was represented by counts of participation rates in forum, while specific educational activity was represented by counts of logins, course material views and assignments. From a data mining perspective, the study used classification and regression tree (CART), supplemented by AdaBoost.

A shortcoming of existing approaches is that data models are usually obtained on datasets containing student activity for the whole period of the course. As such, usage of these models on new students at various checkpoints may need scaling for obtaining interpretable results.

Therefore, in this paper we propose a data analytics framework for identifying learner activity trends which is based on computing t-test and p-values from social activities performed in previous years and uses fitted values for determining social activity drops or increases. More specifically, the proposed approach detects when the learner has no or little activity and in this case is able to trigger an alert.

t-test [17] is generally used when there is a need to investigate the difference between two population means and its significance (provided by p-value). This statistical approach has been used extensively as general social research method [1] and also in engineering education [2]. However, to the best of our knowledge, it has not yet been applied in order to determine activity drops or increases in educational contexts, on activities performed by students while using social media tools.

3   Data Analysis Framework

3.1   Context of Study

As mentioned in the introduction, our data analysis framework was built around eMUSE social learning environment [12]. eMUSE is an educational platform which integrates several social media tools and provides various value-added services for the student and the instructor. A detailed description of the platform can be found in [12]. In particular, the functionality of interest for the current study is learner tracking: eMUSE retrieves all student actions performed on the social media tools (by means of APIs) and stores them in a local database for further processing. Starting from this data, our analysis framework can investigate students' level of activity and generate alerts if necessary, according to the procedure described in the following subsections.

There is a considerable amount of available data, since eMUSE has been used at the University of Craiova, Romania, for the past several years. More specifically, it has been applied in a course on Web Applications Design, taught to undergraduate students in Computer Science. A project-based learning scenario was implemented with the help of eMUSE. Students worked in teams of around 4 peers in order to develop a relatively complex web application of their choice. They communicated and collaborated by means of three social media tools integrated in eMUSE: (i) Blogger (used for reporting the progress of the project, for publishing ideas and resources, for providing feedback and solutions to peer problems); (ii) MediaWiki (used for collaborative writing tasks among the team members, for gathering and organizing their knowledge and resources, and for clearly documenting the project); (iii) Twitter (used for staying connected with peers and posting short news, announcements, questions, and status updates regarding the project) [12].

For the current study, data was collected from five instalments of this course, from 2011/2012 to 2015/2016, in which a total of 298 students were involved.

3.2 Data Analysis Pipeline

We have developed a data analysis framework which retrieves data from the eMUSE database, processes it and generates the corresponding alerts for the students. The whole data analysis pipeline is depicted in Fig. 1.

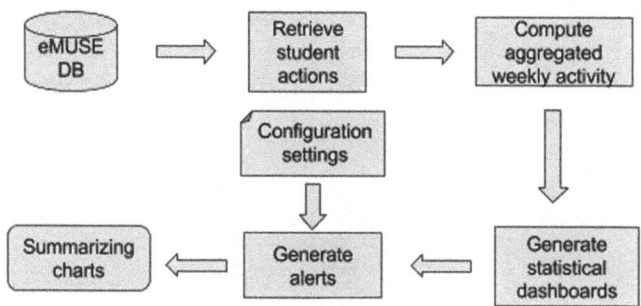

Fig. 1. Data analysis pipeline

Currently, five types of actions were monitored and recorded by eMUSE platform:

1. *blog_post-entry* (students' blog posts)
2. *blog_post-comment* (students' blog comments)
3. *twitter_post-tweet* (students' tweets)
4. *wiki_revise-page* (students' wiki revisions)
5. *wiki_upload-file* (students' file uploads on the wiki)

Our tool retrieves these actions from the eMUSE database and computes an *aggregated weekly activity count* for each student (by summing up all student actions per week, regardless of their type). These aggregated action counts are further used for computing *t*-tests and *p*-values.

Statistical dashboards are subsequently generated for each input dataset. These are further processed taking into account the configuration settings (i.e., window size, p-value and overlap) in order to generate alerts, according to the procedure described in the next subsection. The fine-tuning of the analysis process - such that a certain number of alerts are issued - is performed by setting up the parameters. By running this procedure with all possible configuration settings on all available datasets we obtain the summarizing charts presented in Sect. 4.

3.3   Alert Generation

For identifying the context when an alert is generated, we have defined a set of four states in which a student may be found at a certain moment in time: DROP, INCREASE, STEADY, NO_DATA. These states are self-evident and have the purpose to capture a reasonable number of situations we want to determine for a student. We consider that alerts need to be generated only in case of DROP or NO_DATA states, in order to boost student's engagement.

Setting students into one of the defined states is based on applying t-test for two windows of activity of the same size (i.e., same number of weeks). The first window represents the past activity interval (denoted as *Recent past* in Fig. 2), consisting of a predefined number of weeks. The second window represents the current activity interval (denoted as *Now* in Fig. 2), consisting of the same number of weeks. The sign of the t-test value discriminates between DROP (positive value) and INCREASE (negative value). However, this value does not give an indication of the importance of variance, hence we use p-value to assess the meaning of the difference in activity. Therefore, by choosing a certain threshold for p-value, we set the state of the student and thereafter his trend.

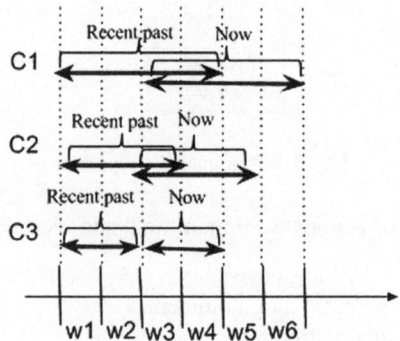

Fig. 2. Sample configurations in terms of window size and overlap

Thus, depending on the threshold that we choose for p, the number of students being identified as DROP and INCREASE may be larger or smaller, which consequently influences the number of issued alerts. For small values of p, the number of students in DROP or INCREASE states is small, including only those students who had a large variance in activity level, while most students will be identified as STEADY; therefore, a small number of alerts will be issued. As the value of p is increased, more students in DROP or INCREASE states will be identified and therefore many alerts will be issued. In an extreme case scenario where p-value is set to almost 1, any slight variation in activity level will be identified as DROP or INCREASE and thus a very large number of alerts will be issued. On the contrary, if a very small (close to 0) p-value is chosen, then only students with very large variation in activity level will be identified as DROP or INCREASE and thus a very small number of alerts will be issued. This approach needs thresholds for p-values such that the number of prospected alerts may be adjusted as needed by the instructor.

Based on the above considerations, we have designed a procedure (*computeTrend*) for deciding the state of a student depending on activity levels and threshold value:

```
procedure computeTrend (pValueThreshold,  tValue, pValue): trend {
    if (tValue == NaN || pValue == NaN)
        trend = NO_DATA;
    else
        if (pValue <= pValueThreshold && tValue < 0)
            trend = INCREASE;
        else
            if(pValue <= pValueThreshold && tValue > 0)
                trend = DROP;
            else
                trend = STEADY;
}
```

The *pValueThreshold* is a variable that sets the threshold of p-value, while *tValue* and *pValue* are the values obtained from t-test computation. The sign of computed t-tests discriminates between DROP and INCREASE states in the situation when p-value is small enough such that it signals that an alert needs to be issued.

This **computeTrend** algorithm addresses four different cases:

- We have no value for at least one of the two components t-test or p-value, which means that the status is set to NO_DATA.
- We have a *pValue* less than *pValueThreshold* and a negative *tValue*, which means that we have a rising trend activity and the status is set to INCREASE.
- We have a *pValue* less than *pValueThreshold* and a positive *tValue*, which means that we have a falling trend activity and the status is set to DROP.
- We have a *pValue* larger than *pValueThreshold*, which means we have a relatively constant trend, regardless of the *tValue*, and the status is set to STEADY.

The last step in our analysis consists in determining the prospected number of alerts depending on configuration settings. The configurable parameters are: p-value, window size (number of weeks) and overlap (number of weeks common to both *Recent past* and *Now* windows).

Figure 2 presents three sample configurations (C1, C2 and C3) for a seven week period of student activity, and is meant to offer a better intuition over the window size and overlap. Configuration C1 represents a window of four weeks with an overlap of two weeks, configuration C2 uses a window of three weeks and an overlap of one week, and the last configuration C3 has a window size of two weeks and no overlap.

Subsequently, for all available configurations, we compute the average number of alerts that are issued within the period that students take the course. In this way, we obtain a representation of the impact of p-value, window size and overlap parameters on the average number of issued alerts for a given dataset. Starting from this, the instructor can select the appropriate configuration settings, based on the desired number of alerts.

4   Experimental Results

We applied the analysis method presented in the previous section on data collected by eMUSE over 5 years (2011/2012 - 2015/2016), so we had 5 available datasets. The aggregated activity counts were computed by taking into consideration only those students who performed at least one action on one of the available social media tools.

Table 1 presents a snippet from the aggregated activity counts of 5 students from year 2015/2016. The first column represents the student's ID and the next eight columns include the activity performed in weeks 4–12.

Table 1. Sample activity dataset

Student ID	W4	W5	W6	W7	W8	W9	W10	W11	W12
5	1	2	9	0	0	3	1	0	0
6	1	2	27	66	3	2	1	2	0
7	24	4	2	2	4	1	3	1	0
8	46	3	65	18	3	34	7	19	33
9	17	0	27	17	0	3	14	2	0

For example, if we take into consideration student with ID 6, for a window of four weeks and no overlap (e.g., first window composed of weeks 4, 5, 6, 7 and second window composed of weeks 8, 9, 10, 11) we have a descending activity trend; if we have the same window size but with an overlap of two (e.g., first window composed of weeks 4, 5, 6, 7 and second window composed of weeks 6, 7, 8, 9) we may not be able to say for sure what type of trend we have. In this case, applying t-test can help identify students' activity trends and corresponding states.

In order to investigate the number of prospective alerts that would be issued, we ran the analysis with different values for the configuration parameters (window size, overlap and p-value). More specifically, we used three values for p (0.25, 0.5 and 0.75), three values for window size (2, 3, 4) and four values for overlap (0, 1, 2 and 3). We can thus explore the impact of all configurations on the prospected number of alerts, as depicted in Fig. 3.

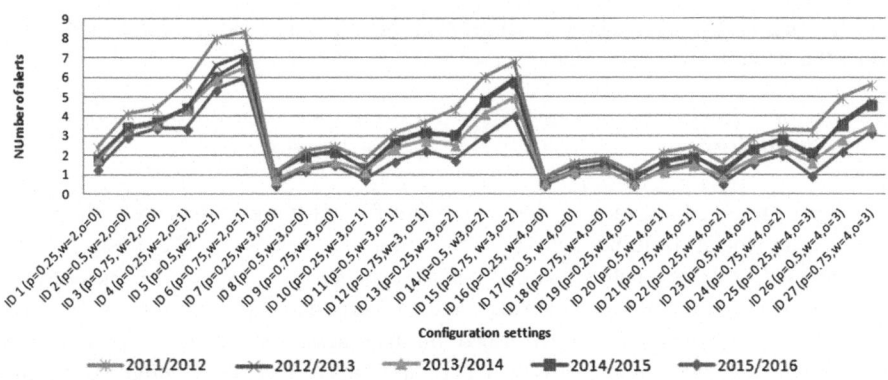

Fig. 3. Average number of alerts per student, for all available configuration settings (w = window size, o = window overlap)

By analysing the chart, we observe a pattern in prospected average number of alerts as a function of available configurations. This leads to the conclusion that we may confidently choose a certain configuration of parameters for subsequent academic years and estimate the average number of alerts that will be issued. It may also be noted that the same number of alerts can be prospected for two or more distinct configurations, therefore the instructor may choose the one that better fits the particular course settings.

For example, if the instructor wants to have an average number of three alerts per student in the next academic year, she may choose among several available configurations, as presented in Table 2. If a higher number of alerts is desired (i.e., over 6), then a smaller number of configurations are available.

Table 2. Available configurations for an average number of three alerts per student

Config. ID	p-value	Window size	Window overlap	Avg. no. of alerts
2	0.5	2	0	3.44
11	0.5	3	1	2.51
12	0.75	3	1	3.01
13	0.25	3	2	2.92
24	0.75	4	2	2.66
26	0.5	4	3	3.45

In what follows we discuss the impact of various specific configurations on the number of issued alerts. As a general rule, we can see that as the value of p increases the number of alerts also increases. Conversely, as the window size increases, the number of alerts decreases. For example, if we take two configurations with the same window size and overlap, e.g., ID 13 ($p = 0.25$, $w = 3$, $o = 2$, avg. no. of alerts = 2.92) and ID 15 ($p = 0.75$, $w = 3$, $o = 2$, avg. no. of alerts = 5.48), then we can see that the number of issued alerts almost doubles when p-value increases from 0.25 to 0.75. Similarly, if we take two configurations with the same p-value and overlap, e.g. ID 24 ($p = 0.75$, $w = 4$, $o = 2$, avg. no. of alerts = 2.66) and ID 15 ($p = 0.75$, $w = 3$, $o = 2$, *avg. no. of alerts = 5.48*) then we can see that the number of alerts more than doubles when the window size decreases from 4 to 3.

5 Conclusion

The paper presented a data analytics framework for notifying students regarding their decrease in social learning activity throughout the semester. The designed and implemented analysis pipeline takes as input the student actions on three social media tools and builds a chart with prospected issued alerts based on various configuration settings. Experimental results performed on five academic years reveal a pattern regarding the average number of issued alerts in terms of available configurations; this yields to the conclusion that our approach may be successfully used for issuing alerts in a controlled way.

One limitation of the current approach is that all monitored student actions have the same weight, which means we just add (or count) all actions; a parameterized version would assign different weights to different activities, based on their importance. As future work, we can also explore alternative settings: a finer granularity for the time-frame of logged data (currently it is weekly and may be set to daily) or a larger number of states that are defined for each student (currently it is four). Furthermore, we could also consider different window sizes for each student, depending on their learning activity patterns; a personalized approach could thus be conceived.

Acknowledgements. This work was supported by a grant of the Romanian National Authority for Scientific Research and Innovation, CNCS – UEFISCDI, project number PN-II-RU-TE-2014-4-2604.

References

1. Adeyemi, T.O.: Inferential statistics for social and behavioural research. Res. J. Math. Stat. **1**(2), 47–54 (2009)
2. Borrego, M., Douglas, E.P., Amelink, C.T.: Quantitative, qualitative, and mixed research methods in engineering education. J. Eng. Educ. **98**(1), 53–66 (2009)
3. Buckingham Shum, S., Ferguson, R.: Social learning analytics. Educ. Technol. Soc. **15**(3), 3–26 (2012)
4. Conole, G.: New schemas for mapping pedagogies and technologies. Ariadne issue 56 (2008). http://www.ariadne.ac.uk/issue56/conole
5. Dron, J., Anderson, T.: Teaching Crowds. Learning and Social Media. AU Press, Athabasca University (2014)
6. Ferguson, R., Buckingham Shum, S.: Social learning analytics: five approaches. In: Proceedings of the 2nd International Conference on Learning Analytics and Knowledge, pp. 23–33. ACM (2012)
7. Ferguson, R., Brasher, A., Clow, D., Cooper, A., Hillaire, G., Mittelmeier, J., et al.: Research evidence on the use of learning analytics - Implications for education policy. Joint Research Centre Science for Policy Report (2016). doi:10.2791/955210
8. Hagel, J., Brown, J.S., Davison, L.: The Power of Pull. Basic Books, New York (2010)

9. Hu, Y.H., Lo, C.L., Shih, S.P.: Developing early warning systems to predict students' online learning performance. Comput. Hum. Behav. **36**, 469–478 (2014)
10. Kumpulainen K., Wray, D.: Classroom Interaction and Social Learning: From Theory to Practice. Psychology Press (2002)
11. Macfadyen, L.P., Dawson, S.: Mining LMS data to develop an early warning system for educators: a proof of concept. Comput. Educ. **54**(2), 588–599 (2010)
12. Popescu, E.: Providing collaborative learning support with social media in an integrated environment. World Wide Web - Internet Web Inform. Syst. **17**(2), 199–212 (2014)
13. Richardson, J., Swan, K.: Examining social presence in online courses in relation to students' perceived learning and satisfaction. JALN **7**(1), 68–88 (2003)
14. Romero, C., Ventura, S.: Educational data mining: a review of the state of the art. IEEE Trans. Syst. Man Cybern., Part C (Applications and Reviews) **40**(6), 601–618 (2010)
15. Romero, C., Ventura, S.: Data mining in education. WIREs Data Mining Knowl. Discover **3**, 12–27 (2013)
16. Veletsianos, G., Navarrete, C.: Online social networks as formal learning environments: learner experiences and activities. Int. Rev. Res. Open Distrib. Learn. **13**(1), 144–166 (2012)
17. Zimmerman, D.W.: A note on interpretation of the paired-samples t-test. J. Educ. Behav. Stat. **22**(3), 349–360 (1997)

A Text Clustering Algorithm to Detect Basic Level Categories in Texts

Jingyun Xu[1], Yi Cai[1(✉)], Shuai Wang[2], Kai Yang[1], Qing Du[1], Jun Zhang[1], Li Yao[3], and Jingjing Li[4]

[1] School of Software Engineering, South China University of Technoloy, Guangzhou, China
5823263660qq.com, {ycai,duqing}@scut.edu.cn,
y.kai02@mail.scut.edu.cn
[2] Ideological and Political Office, Sun Yat-sen University, Guangzhou, China
wangsh73@mail.sysu.edu.cn
[3] School of Software Engineering, Beijing Normal University, Beijing, China
yaoli@bnu.edu.cn
[4] School of Software Engineering, South China Normal University, Guangzhou, China
jingjing.li1124@gmail.com

Abstract. With the rapid development of Internet and explosion of texts, an appropriate way to organize the amount of texts is necessary. Text clustering is of great practical importance for web-learning, which can group similar texts (e.g. documents, textbooks and online notes) to provide users with more valuable information. However, most of existing text clustering algorithms are very sensitive to the parameters needed to be input by users and it is hard to set an appropriate parameter as computers do not know what an appropriate parameter is. Therefore, aiming at this problem, according to the studies of cognitive psychology and our observation, this paper firstly introduces basic level categories and category utility, and then propose a text clustering algorithm to detect basic level categories in texts automatically, which is an non-parametric algorithm. The experimental results show that our algorithm significantly outperforms one basic level concept detection method, k-means and single linkage clustering on different datasets.

Keywords: Text clustering · Basic level categories · Category utility · Hierarchical clustering

1 Introduction

With the rapid development of Internet and explosion of texts, as an appropriate way to organize texts resources, text clustering [1] is of great importance and is widely used for web-learning. Based on the studies of existing text clustering algorithms, we find that the shortcoming of them is that they need setting parameters and computers do not know what a true parameter is from the use's point of view. Therefore, we firstly introduce basic level categories from cognitive psychology to solve the problem of setting parameters of the current text clustering

© Springer International Publishing AG 2017
H. Xie et al. (Eds.): ICWL 2017, LNCS 10473, pp. 72–81, 2017.
DOI: 10.1007/978-3-319-66733-1_8

algorithm. In cognitive psychology, psychologists find that basic level categories is cognitively basic and the most important property of basic level categories is that their intra-category similarity is as high as possible and their inter-category similarity is as low as possible, which is consistent of the purpose of text clustering algorithms. Therefore, it is necessary to detect basic level categories in texts automatically.

According to our observation, we find that basic level categories detected by current research works are made up of some big clusters and a bit small clusters [8]. The big clusters are basic level categories and small clusters are those extracted from basic level categories for some reasons. Figure 1 shows an example of basic level categories detected in [6], "health", "sports", "entertainment" and "finance" are basic level categories, and there are a bit small clusters around basic level categories.

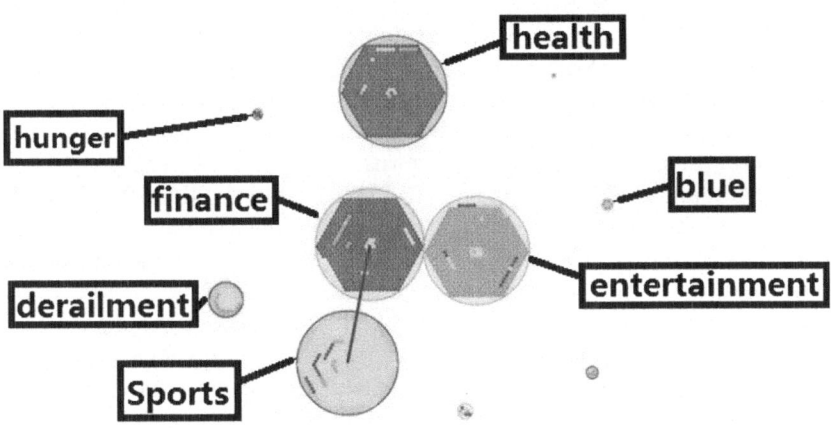

Fig. 1. An example of basic level categories detection in texts

What's more, small clusters is those clusters in which documents have common features with documents in each basic level category and at the same time, they have their own unique features. In Fig. 1, documents in the category 'diabetes' will have some features with documents in the category 'health' like 'diet' and they also have their own features like 'hunger'. we denote this kind of clusters, such as 'diabetes', as subclass of basic level categories. One possible reason for subclass is that unsupervised term weighting scheme using in text clustering just reflects the relation between a term and documents rather than the relation between a term and categories. In other words, supervised term weighting schemes do not take categories of documents into consideration. As the example we mentioned above, the term 'hunger' can distinguish documents in the category 'health' from documents in the category 'diabetes', however, it can not distinguish differences between basic level categories. As subclasses are those clusters extracted from basic level categories, classify them into basic level categories may can improve the quality of the clustering results. In this paper, we propose a text clustering algorithm to detect basic level categories in texts automatically, which is an non-parametric clustering algorithm. We conduct experiments, comparing with [6], k-means algorithm and single-linkage clustering algorithm on different datasets to verify the effectiveness of our proposed algorithm.

2   Related Work

2.1   Text Clustering Algorithms

General surveys on text clustering algorithms can be found in [1,3,4]. All in all, there are two common text clustering algorithms [14]. The one is k-means algorithm [11] and its variants [7], and the other one is hierarchical clustering algorithms [13].

As a partitional clustering algorithm, k-means and its variants detect the categories of documents by partitioning all documents into a pre-defined number of clusters [11]. They are efficient and can be implemented easily. However, the disadvantages of them is that they can be applied to text clustering in many situations only when the number of clusters is defined (Fig. 2).

In general, hierarchical clustering algorithms fall into two types: agglomerative clustering and divisive clustering [13,21]. The former algorithm represents each document as one cluster and then merges the most similar two documents into one cluster, repeats the merge process until there is only one cluster or the process has reached the termination condition, which is a bottom-up process. The divisive clustering algorithm is exactly the opposite of the agglomerative clustering algorithm, which is a top-down process. It's obvious that the disadvantages of them is that they both need setting the termination condition. The results of hierarchical clustering algorithms are usually presented in a dendrogram [20]. Figure 3 shows an example of hierarchical clustering algorithm in texts. A, B, C, D and E represent five documents.

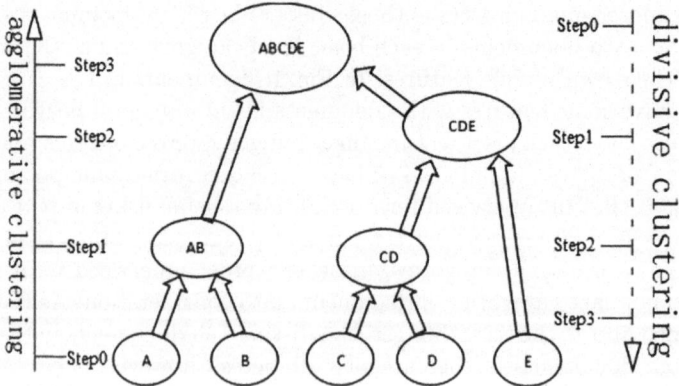

Fig. 2. An example of hierarchical based text clustering algorithm

2.2 Basic Level Categories and Category Utility

In cognitive psychology, psychologists find that basic level categories is cognitively basic [5,16]. For example, when asked "how do you get there?", you can answer "I get there by car", "I get there by transportation", or "I get there by a car with four wheels". However, most people will answer as the first one, and the first one is basic level category from cognitive psychology [18]. What's more, the most important property of basic level categories is that their intra-category similarity is as high as possible and their inter-category similarity is as low as possible, which is consistent of the purpose of text clustering algorithms [16,18]. Therefore, it is necessary to detect basic level categories in texts and the results will be more acceptable for human use than other results of common text clustering algorithms.

Category utility was given by psychologists as a metric to characterize the basic level categories [15] and they demonstrate that when category utility is the highest, categories detected in texts is basic level categories. When it comes to detecting the basic level categories in texts, the definition of category utility is as follows:

$$cu(C, F) = \frac{1}{m} \sum_{k=1}^{m} p(c_k) [\sum_{i=1}^{n} p(f_i|c_k)^2 - \sum_{i=1}^{n} p(f_i)^2] \tag{1}$$

where C is the set of clusters and each cluster combined by the documents in the clusters, F is the feature list, f_i is a feature, $p(f_i|c_k)$ i s the probability that a document of category c_k has the feature f_i, $p(c_k)$ is the probability that an document belongs to category c_k, $p(f_i)$ is the probability that a document has feature f_i, n is the total number of features, m is the total number of categories.

3   The Proposed Algorithm

Text clustering is important for web-learning, which can divide the unlabeled texts into several categories according to their characteristics. However, some existing text clustering algorithms and their variants are sensitive to the parameters needed to be input by users. What's more, it is difficult to set an appropriate parameter as computers do not know what a true parameter is from the user's point of view. In order to overcome the drawbacks of previous text clustering algorithms, we introduce basic level categories and category utility from cognitive psychology [15,16]. In cognitive psychology, psychologists find that basic level categories is the most consistent with the level of human cognition, and they are easily accepted and understood by humans [18]. Therefore, it is necessary to detect basic level categories in texts. According to our observation, we find that there are some subclasses in the clustering results in [6] except for basic level categories. Those subclasses are those extracted from basic level categories and therefore, classifying them into basic level categories can improve the quality of the clustering results in [6]. In this paper, we propose a text clustering algorithm to detect basic level categories in texts automatically, which is an non-parametric algorithm. The details of this algorithm are given in Algorithm 1.

Algorithm 1. Basic Level Categories Detection

1: Input: D,a set of documents
2: Initialize C, C is an n dimensions vector $C = (c_1, c_2, ..., c_n)$ where its element c_i is the bottom level category. C_size is equal to the number of elements in C. Set sim[n][n] as the similarity matrix of C, sim[i][j] = $sim(c_i, c_j)$. Set rounds=1, which is the time of executing clustering. $S = (s_1, s_2, ..., s_n).S_i$ is used to record the clustering result of step i.
3: **while** $C_{size} > 1$ or sim_{max}!=0 **do**
4:     Find the most similar categories in C and define a new category include all instances of them.
5:     Delete the most similar categories from C, and add the new category into C.
6:     Update the similarity matrix.
7:     $C_{size} = C_{size}$-1
8:     Record the result step=C
9:     Compute the category utility of this step
10: **end while**
11: Find the step with the highest category utility define the record of this step C as the basic level categories.
12: **if** round>1 **then**
13:     identify whether the categories in C are basic level category or not, and then using KNN to classify those are not basic level categories into basic level categories
14: **else**
15:     apply *bdc* and *chi* to preprocess the text in C, and then goto step2
16: **end if**
17: Output C

In our algorithm, firstly, we combine category utility and hierarchical clustering algorithm to detect basic level categories in texts, which have been used in [6]. Secondly, we apply *bdc* in our algorithm, which Wang et al. declare that it outperforms state-of-the-art term weighting schemes [19]. As most supervised term weighting schemes are based on feature-selection methods with different metrics and most of them are reported to approximate to *chi* [17], so we apply *chi* in our algorithm. Thirdly, as KNN is a widely used classifier [2], we choose knn as our example classifier to classify subclasses into basic level categories. Figure 4 shows an example of the process of our algorithm. At first, There are four basic level categories, which we call them blc, and six subclasses in Fig. 4, and then after applying KNN in our algorithm, the results have been presented in Fig. 4.

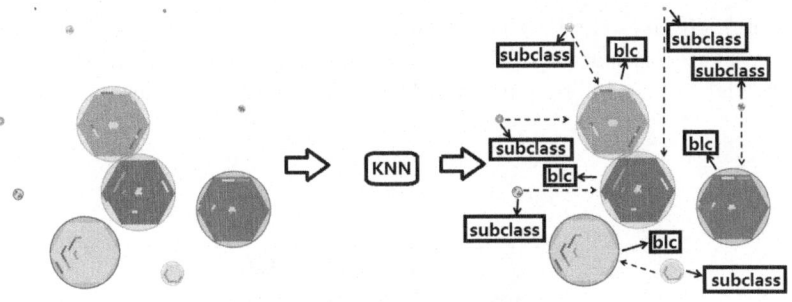

Fig. 3. The process of our algorithm

4 Experiment

4.1 Experiment Setup

In order to verify the effectiveness of our proposed algorithm, we conduct experiments on three datasets. Table 1 shows the detailed statistics of them. We use Reuters-21578 and NG20 as our datasets, which have been widely used in previous research works [12]. What's more, we crawl China news from the domestic news website and they form a Chinanews dataset, which consists of 2400 documents, and they are classified into 4 categories in advance. As Chen et al. declared their basic level categories detection method outperforms other methods [6], we choose it as one of our baselines and compare our algorithm with it on three datasets. What's more, we compare our algorithm with two parametric text clustering algorithms, k-means [11] and single-linkage clustering algorithm [9] to demonstrate that our method can solve the problem of setting parameters. For evaluation, we apply F1 score which is the aggregation of recall and precision [13].

Table 1. Statistic of the datasets

Dataset	Document	Number of categories	Category distribution
Chinanews	2400	4	600, 600, 600, 600
NG20	2500	5	500, 500, 500, 500, 500
Reuters-21578	1800	6	300, 300, 300, 300, 300, 300

4.2 Result Analysis

In this section, we first examine the impact of q by removing the words whose frequency is less than the threshold q. The value of q varies from 10 to 60. The F1 scores of the results obtained by setting different value of q are presented in Fig. 5. According to previous research works [6], We find that if we do not filter any words(q = 0), the clustering results will be the worst (0.3). Among different values of q, 40 gives the best result on F1 scores. Finally, we can conclude that basic level categories are sensitive to the value of q, which is consistent with the reasons why subclasses are extracted from basic level categories.

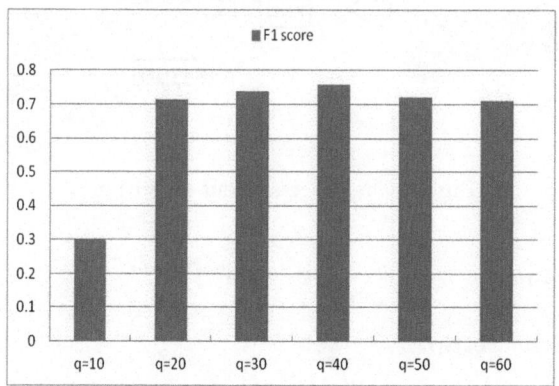

Fig. 4. The impact of threshold q

In order to improve the quality of basic level categories detected in texts, there are three main steps in our algorithm. Firstly, we apply the unsupervised term weighting scheme *tf*idf* and the unsupervised term selection method *df* [10]. Secondly, we use the supervised term weighting schemes *tf*bdc* and the supervised term selection method *chi* to classify subcategories into basic level categories. Thirdly, we use KNN to classify outliers into basic level categories. The results of different steps of our algorithm are shown in Fig. 6. According to Fig. 6, we can find that after applying *tf*bdc* and *chi*, the number of clusters becomes less than before applying. What's more, applying *tf*bdc* and *chi* can achieve better performance than not applying on F1 scores. In addition to that, applying KNN can decreases the number of clusters but F1 does not change a lot on Reuters-21578, one possible explanation is that the numbers of outliers in Reuters is only 358, which is quite small compared with that of NG20 and Chinanews.

At last, we compare the performance of our method with Chen's method [6], k-means clustering and single-linkage clustering. In Fig. 6, we show the results obtained by different methods in three datasets. On Reuters dataset, our algorithm can achieve the same effect as the k-means algorithm, but not better than it. On the Chinanews dataset, F1 scores of the result using our method and traditional k-means algorithm are both more than 0.9. As a result, we can conclude that they both achieve good performance, and k-means clustering is slightly better. On Newsgroup, it is obvious that our method is superior to the k-means algorithm. What's more, we can find that on whatever dataset, single-linkage clustering always do not achieve good performance.

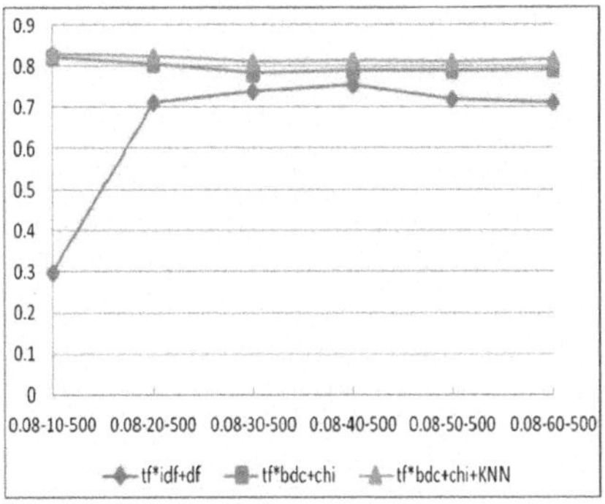

(a) Chinanews 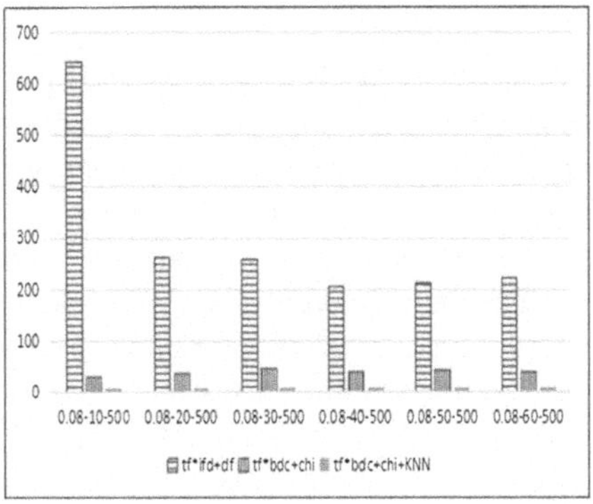   (b) Chinanews

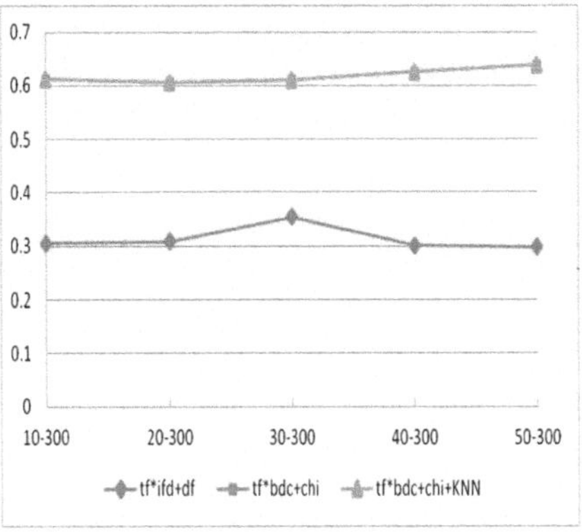

(c) Reuters-21578 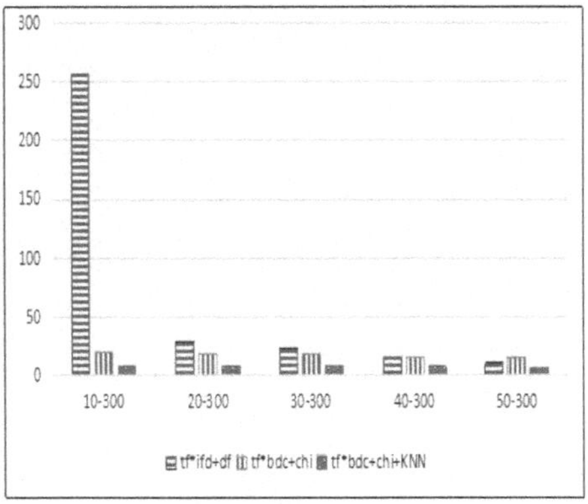   (d) Reuters-21578

Fig. 5. Comparison of different steps of our algorithm on three datasets

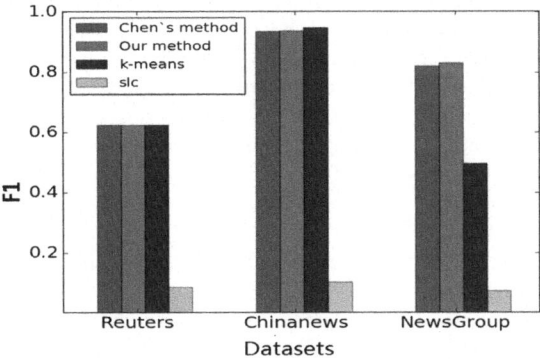

Fig. 6. Comparison of different methods on datasets

5 Conclusion

In this paper, in order to solve the problem of setting parameters in texts clustering algorithm, we introduce basic level categories and category utility from cognitive psychology, and then the purpose of text clustering is to detect basic level categories in texts. According to our obversion, we find that the categories detected by the current works are made up of big clusters and a bit small clusters. Through the analysis of the reasons, we propose a text clustering algorithm to detect basic level categories in texts, which is a non-parametric text clustering algorithm. Our experimental study shows that our algorithm can achieve better performance than other clustering methods on different datasets.

Acknowledgements. This work is supported by the Fundamental Research Funds for the Central Universities, SCUT (NO. 2017ZD0482015ZM136), Tiptop Scientific and Technical Innovative Youth Talents of Guangdong special support program (No.2015TQ01X633), Science and Technology Planning Project of Guangdong Province, China (No. 2016A030310423), Science and Technology Program of Guangzhou (International Science and Technology Cooperation Program No. 201704030076 and Science and Technology Planning Major Project of Guangdong Province (No. 2015A070711001).

References

1. Aggarwal, C.C., Zhai, C.: A survey of text clustering algorithms. In: Aggarwal, C., Zhai, C. (eds.) Mining Text Data, pp. 77–128. Springer, Boston (2012). doi:10.1007/978-1-4614-3223-4_4
2. Altman, N.M.: An introduction to kernel and nearest-neighbor nonparametric regression. Am. Stat. **46**, 175–185 (1992). Taylor & Francis
3. Anastasiu, D.C., Tagarelli, A., Karypis, G.: Document clustering: the next frontier. Technical report, University of Minnesota (2013)
4. Andrews, N.O., Fox, E.A.: Recent developments in document clustering. Technical report, Computer Science, Virginia Tech (2007)
5. Belohlavek, R., Trnecka, M.: Basic level in formal concept analysis: interesting concepts and psychological ramifications, pp. 1233–1239 (2013)
6. Cai, Y., Chen, W.-H., Leung, H.-F., Li, Q., Xie, H., Lau, R.Y.K., Min, H., Wang, F.L.: Context-aware ontologies generation with basic level concepts from collaborative tags. Neurocomputing **208**, 25–38 (2016)
7. Dhillon, S.I., Modha, D.S.: Concept decompositions for large sparse text data using clustering. Mach. Learn. **42**(1), 143–175 (2001)
8. Fisher, H.D.: Knowledge acquisition via incremental conceptual clustering. Mach. Learn. **2**(2), 139–172 (1987)
9. Gower, J.C., Ross, G.J.S.: Minimum spanning trees and single linkage cluster analysis. Appl. Stat. **18**, 54–64 (1969)
10. Jones, K.S.: A statistical interpretation of term specificity and its application in retrieval. J. Doc. **28**(1), 11–21 (1972)
11. MacQueen, J., et al.: Some methods for classification and analysis of multivariate observations. In: Proceedings of the Fifth Berkeley Symposium on Mathematical Statistics and Probability, Oakland, vol. 1, pp. 281–297 (1967)

12. Su, J., Lan, M., Tan, C.L., Lu, Y.: Supervised and traditional term weighting methods for automatic text categorization. IEEE Trans. Pattern Anal. Mach. Intell. **31**(4), 721–735 (2009)
13. Manning, C.D., Raghavan, P., Schütze, H., et al.: Introduction to Information Retrieval, vol. 1. Cambridge University Press, Cambridge (2008)
14. Manning, C.D., Schütze, H., et al.: Foundations of Statistical Natural Language Processing, vol. 999. MIT Press, Cambridge (1999)
15. Murphy, G.L.: Information, uncertainty and the utility of categories. In: Proceedings of the 7th Annual Conference of Cognitive Science Society, pp. 283–287 (1989)
16. Murphy, G.L.: The Big Book of Concepts. MIT Press, Cambridge (2004)
17. Rayson, P., Berridge, D., Francis, B.: Extending the Cochran rule for the comparison of word frequencies between corpora. In: 7th International Conference on Statistical analysis of textual data (JADT 2004), pp. 926–936 (2004)
18. Rosch, E., Mervis, C.B., Gray, W.D., Johnson, D.M., Boyes-Braem, P.: Basic objects in natural categories. Cognitive Psychol. **8**(3), 382–439 (1976)
19. Leung, H., Cai, Z., Wang, T., Cai, Y., Min, H.: Entropy-based term weighting schemes for text categorization in VSM, pp. 325–332 (2015)
20. Voorhees, E.M.: Implementing agglomerative hierarchic clustering algorithms for use in document retrieval. Inf. Process. Manag. **22**(6), 465–476 (1986)
21. Willett, P.: Recent trends in hierarchic document clustering: a critical review. Inf. Process. Manag. **24**(5), 577–597 (1988)

Community Learning Analytics Support for Audio-Visual Web-Based Learning Contents: The CIDRE Framework

Ralf Klamma[1](✉) and Marc Spaniol[2]

[1] Advanced Community Information Systems Group (ACIS),
RWTH Aachen University, Lehrstuhl Informatik 5,
Ahornstr. 55, 52074 Aachen, Germany
klamma@dbis.rwth-aachen.de
[2] Université de Caen Normandie, Caen, France
marc.spaniol@unicaen.fr

Abstract. An abundance of audio-visual (AV) learning content is available on the Web, e.g. in massive open online courses (MOOC), in Webinars and on AV streaming platforms. However, the coherence of the AV content is depending on the resources put into the production of the material. This results in a big gap between learning analytics capabilities in MOOcs and those possible in self-regulated learning communities on the Web. In this vision paper, we introduce the CIDRE (Communities of learners InterlinkeD via REssources from linked open data) framework. It aims at narrowing and ultimately bridging the gap between contextualized knowledge and learning communities by a hybrid approach: AV contents will be raised to the entity-level and interconnected withsuitable linked open data for the linked learning communities. Based on the, results, we utilize a community specific learning analytics framework. We will evaluate the approach in real learning communities using stereotypic pedagogical scenarios on the Web.

Keywords: Technology-enhanced learning · Web video · Learning analytics · Semantic annotation · Semantic enrichment · Linked open data · Entity matching

1 Introduction

Nowadays, Web-based learners have a wide range of choices, starting with massive open online courses (MOOC), going over Webinars and ending with picks from various video streaming platforms offering audio-visual (AV) educational content. The challenges are quite similar to tourism where many travelers book organized tours like cruising tours, book local tours in the lobby of their holiday resort or travel on their own from the beginning. In addition, quite similar individual travelers with similar interests organize themselves into groups to share the burden of organization and their knowledge. We see that self-regulated Web-based learners more and more organize themselves into learning communities. However, Web-based learners are facing challenges with the coherence of their AV contents, when picking it from different platforms and

© Springer International Publishing AG 2017
H. Xie et al. (Eds.): ICWL 2017, LNCS 10473, pp. 82–87, 2017.
DOI: 10.1007/978-3-319-66733-1_9

different sources. Compared with the content produced for MOOCs or even Webinars the lack of coherence make it impossible to apply already existing method for (community) learning analytics in community-regulated learning processes. First, in terms of metadata the AV content itself lacks coherence in pedagogical classification, e.g. what level of competences learners needs to have for a meaningful interaction with the content. Second, the learning communities cannot augment the AV content with their own community-specific metadata to increase the coherence within the community. If they would for example annotate the materials on the streaming platforms, we would bias the metadata by the metadata outside the community. If the annotations would be kept in an own platform, all other Web-based learners would not be able to profit from it. Third, if we like to benefit other learning communities from the automated extraction and the community-based augmentation of metadata, we need to lower the semantic distances by embedding our metadata in commonly agreed semantics. Only by solving these three challenges, we can offer automated learning community analytics comparable to what is already possible in MOOCs and Webinars nowadays. Central for this approach is MobSOS, a framework for community success aware creation of learning services [9]. We also argue that AV content produced for MOOCs and Webinars can profit from our approach by saving costs and making their contents more marketable in a wider range of learning communities. Based on the community of practice theory and our media specific theoretical extension, we propose in this conceptual position paper the CIDRE (Communities of learners InterlinkeD via REssources from linked open data) approach. The present conceptual, technical and pedagogical ideas to overcome the three challenges. For the sake of brevity, we will focus on methods for increasing the coherence of AV content and leaving out matters of cost reduction and lowering the entrance barriers. Our ideas lead to a pedagogical scenario of a more lightweight MOOC platform where Web-based learning communities are more involved in the production of learning materials than in current MOOC platforms. The platform is flexible enough also to support the creation and utilization of Webinars.

The rest of the paper is organized as follows. In the next three sections, we present our ideas for tackling the challenges mentioned above. The scenario is following these sections and a conclusion is finalizing the paper.

2   Challenge 1: Information Extraction from AV Contents

AV Web-based learning contents can be very different in terms of coherence. The CIDRE framework tackles three levels of AV content: (i) MOOCS, (ii) Webinars and (iii) AV used by self-regulated learning communities. First, we need a conceptual model for coherence in different Web mediated learning communities based on the MobSOS framework. The goals of the model are to understand the coherence requirements in the different learning communities from a pedagogical as well as from a socio-technological perspective. Furthermore, we need to operationalize the model to detect incoherence in a set of given AV content as compared to the model. Therefore, the model will utilize feature extraction methods and machine learning techniques. We will build on recent advances in deep learning to develop architectures and learning procedures adapted to our objectives. Thus, we will adapt the work of [5] to the three classes. We will also output a time-coded speech-to-text transcription of the audio channel using recent RNN-based techniques such as the one of [12]. Moreover, we will support the detection and recognition of elements such as logos, figures and texts in videos (see e.g., [8]). We will work here in two directions: first, we will develop an adapted Video Region Proposal algorithm providing spatio-temporal region considered as good candidates [13] then validated by an adapted classifier [2]. We will process text images by an OCR algorithm based on [14]. For the evaluation of our approach, we will summarize AV content in verybrief videos with two different strategies (i) keyframe selection consisting a selective the top k most informative frames and (ii) key subshot selection by grouping temporally contiguous set of frames spanning a short time interval and so producing very short video summaries. We will develop learning based algorithms [16] to apply them on supervised AV summarization. More precisely, we plan to extend our work on Part-Detection [6] to be automatically recognized the key information in videos and use them in the summarization process. CIDRE will do video captioning (see e.g., [15]) to produce models adapted to the description of AV content of our interest into meaningful textual descriptions of the content (type of material, duration, structuration) as well as a summary of the content. We will develop a sentence generator with a recurrent neural network (RNN) to model the language. A paragraph generator will be used to models the inter-sentence dependency. Both networks will be cascaded and fed with the before mentioned multimodal information.

As an output, we have text-based summarizations of AV content in different contexts like MOOCs, Webinars and self-regulated learning communities. We can define measures and key performance indicators (KPI) for coherence in our conceptual model and detect incoherence based on the KPI in arbitrary set of AV learning content.

3 Challenge 2: Metadata-Based Augmentation

Members of large-scale learning communities collaboratively enrich AV learning contents. In contrast to teacher-centered or publisher-centered approaches, the creation modes do not guarantee the coherence of metadata. In this sense, we need to support the coherence of metadata-based augmentation of learning materials by the learning environments and the according processes. While in most learning situations learners use recorded and edited AV content, in some learning situation learners use live AV streams. There is a need to capture and enrich the AV content live. To create more coherent metadata sets, we have to first develop community aware success measures and key performance indicators for the utilization of existing services within our targeted communities. In particular, we then have to deal with the distinction of pre-recorded videos, live and mobile videos. Our goal is to create augmentation services working on most common standards like HTML5, guaranteeing a wide range of application without getting trapped into technology or development lock-ins that are threatening the sustainability of our services. Thus, we study the interaction of recent Web standards for controlled creation and utilization of metadata for digital video learning materials. We will realize the services in SeViAnno (Semantic Video Annotation) [7]. Next, we will address the availability of augmentation services for digital videos and equip them with our research results. Subsequently, we focus on the adaptation of existing services from SeViAnno and SWEVA (Social Web Environment for Visual Analytics) and enhance them for live and mobile videos as well as for metadata inside the video. Moreover, we create collaborative services to link objects, persons, events und places inside videos to Linked Data on the fly collaboratively. One goal is the traceability of the augmented materials on the AV streaming platforms by using standardized hyperlinking methods in HTML5 to address AV content parts and metadata generated on the platform. Moreover, it is indispensable to trace the metadata in the learning environments and to link them back to the platforms. In return, this requires an adaption of Web standards on both sides.

4 Challenge 3: Semantics in Learning Contents

In this challenge, the aspect of creating more meaningful (semantically enriched for learning) content descriptions by raising the analytics to the entity-level. Thus, we aim at analysing the aggregated AV learning content descriptions for semantic coherence in order to reveal and (semi-)automatically modify those contents violating it. Finally, we create additional benefit to the previously aggregated and bowdlerized contents by interlinking and enriching them with content from the linked open data (LOD) cloud. We map mentions of ambiguous names onto canonical entities registered in a knowledge base such as DBpedia [1] or YAGO [4, 11]. In order to disambiguate text mentions onto canonical entities, we will pursue a disambiguation approach that is conceptually similar to the AIDA system [3]. To discover latent knowledge for learning from aggregated AV content, our research aims at developing algorithms and software for systematically aggregating, querying, mining, and analysing statistical patterns, cross-data dependencies, and temporal variabilities. At the fine-grained level, we will develop entity-level analytics tools that build on disambiguated entities in order to allow typing and examining temporal relationships among entities. At the coarse-grained level, we will investigate the semantic dependencies at large (e.g. by linking knowledge between learning communities). Further, we will apply constraint-aware reasoning in order to identify those contents that violate a semantically coherent content description based on the underlying model. To unlock this hidden potential and successfully interlink learning content with the relevant data from the LOD cloud, we contextualize these contents in the spatio-temporal processes of the learning communities. To this end, we will apply a temporal tagger, in order to identify the temporal expressions mentioned, e.g. generating a temporal scope like a sequence of learning AV content. Then, we will derive the set of location-related entity information so that we can provide geo-localized context information, as well. Further, we will also investigate the domain by computing the link-based overlap between learning contents and the LOD resources. We compute final mappings by applying a semantic scoring function deployed as entity-level analytics module.

5 A Pedagogical and Socio-Technical Scenario

We will deploy the resulting prototype in large-scale learning communities. Thus, we will do formative and summative user evaluation against the conceptual model using the assessment approach. We enable all developed services for automatic formative and summative assessment by MobSOS. Technically, this is possible through the interception of the http when using RESTful services. Conceptually, this is empowered by the operationalisation of our conceptual coherence model within the MobSOS framework. Each learning community can select and refine measures and KPIs for defining their success in reaching their learning goals based on stereotypical models for learning communities. In particular, we are interested in the correlations between coherence of the available AV content and the learning outcomes. The deployment in the learning communities will be as unobtrusive as possible by augmented existing services with the services we have developed. In the course of the scenario development in real learning communities, we will collect data from the formative assessment as well of the final summative assessment of the learning communities using the research prototype. Since the data from learning processes will flow in self-regulated learning processes, we will deploy a community learning analytics dashboard early, in order to give feedback on learning insights within the communities. We will set up also inter-community analytics to help learning community with coherences issues and give methodological support for increasing the coherence of learning contents. The CIDRE framework will provide the dashboards for a summative community learning analytics coherence assessment for researchers in community learning analytics.

6 Conclusions

The success of interlinked learning communities on the Web rests on two complementary pillars: First, on providing access to an almost abundant and continuously growing pool of Web-based learning contents (AV content), e.g. in massive open online courses (MOOC). Second, on automated community learning analytics support and tailoring of learning contents by means of community-specific and additional contextual information from the LOD cloud. For learning communities this is a great asset as the available knowledge about learner interactions, content, and multimedia semantics is a great source to handle large-scale learning processes with shrinking costs. CIDRE will operate upon available Web-based AV learning contents. These contents comprise a combination of formal and informal learning, learners in communities of practice and formal courses. As such, the contents are highly community-dependent, heterogeneous and diverse. CIDRE will offer novel and lightweight MOOC annotations covering the full spectrum from (low-level) AV content descriptions up to (high-level) semantic annotations. Thus, learners will be able to experience at the same time wider access to MOOCs and becoming more active in the selection, production and augmentation of learning content.

Acknowledgements. The research leading to these results has received funding from the European Research Council under the European Union's Horizon 2020 Programme through the project "WEKIT" (grant no. 687669).

References

1. Auer, S., Bizer, C., Kobilarov, G., Lehmann, J., Ives, Z.: DBpedia: a nucleus for a web of open data. In: Proceedings of the 6th International Semantic Web Conference, Busan, Korea, pp. 11–15 (2007)
2. Girshick, R.: Fast R-CNN. Presented at the ICCV (2015)
3. Hoffart, J., Yosef, M.A., Bordino, I., Fürstenau, H., Pinkal, M., Spaniol, M., Taneva, B., Thater, S., Weikum, G.: Robust disambiguation of named entities in text. In: Proceedings of the Conference on Empirical Methods in Natural Language Processing (EMNLP 2011), Edinburgh, Scotland, pp. 782–792 (2011)
4. Hoffart, J., Suchanek, F.M., Berberich, K., Weikum, G.: YAGO2: a spatially and temporally enhanced knowledge base from Wikipedia. Artif. Intell. **194**, 28–61 (2013)
5. Karpathy, A., Toderici, G., Shetty, S., Leung, T., Sukthankar, R., Fei-Fei, L.: Large-scale video classification with convolutional neural networks. Presented at CVPR (2015)
6. Kulkarni, P., Jurie, F., Zepeda, J., Pérez, P., Chevallier, L.: SPLeaP: soft pooling of learned parts for image classification. In: ECCV 2016 (2016)
7. Nicolaescu, P., Klamma, R.: SeViAnno 2.0: web-enabled collaborative semantic video annotation beyond the obvious. In: 12th International Workshop on Content-Based Multimedia Indexing, pp. 1–6 (2014)
8. Razakarivony, S., Jurie, F.: A novel target detection algorithm combining foreground and background manifold-based models. Int. J. Mach. Vis. Appl. **27**(3), 363–375 (2016)
9. Renzel, D.: Information Systems Success Awareness for Professional Long Tail Communities of Practice (Dissertation). RWTH Aachen University, Aachen, Germany (2016)
10. Renzel, D., Koren, I., Klamma, R., Jarke, M.: Preparing research projects for sustainable software engineering in society. In: 39th ICSE, Software in Society Track (2017)
11. Suchanek, F.M., Kasneci, G., Weikum, G.: YAGO: a core of semantic knowledge - unifying WordNet and Wikipedia. In: 16th International World Wide Web Conference (WWW 2007), pp. 697–706. ACM (2007)
12. Trigeorgis, G., Ringeval, F., Brueckner, R., Marchi, E., Nicolaou, M.A., Schuller, B., Zafeiriou, S.: Adieu features? End-to-end speech emotion recognition using a deep convolutional recurrent network. In: 2016 IEEE International Conference on Acoustics, Speech and Signal Processing (ICASSP), pp. 5200–5204. IEEE (2016)
13. Tripathi, S., Belongie, S., Hwang, Y., Nguyen, T.: Detecting temporally consistent objects in videos through object class label propagation. In: 2016 IEEE Winter Conference on Applications of Computer Vision (WACV), pp. 1–9. IEEE (2016)
14. Yang, H., Wang, C., Bartz, C., Meinel, C.: SceneTextReg: a real-time video OCR system. In: Procdings of the 2016 ACM on Multimedia Conference, pp. 698–700. ACM (2016)
15. Yu, H., Wang, J., Huang, Z., Yang, Y.: Video paragraph captioning using hierarchical recurrent neural networks. Presented at the Proceedings of the IEEE CVPR (2016)
16. Zhang, K., Chao, W.-L., Sha, F., Grauman, K.: Video summarization with long short-term memory. ECCV **9911**(4), 766–782 (2016)

Social Media and Web 2.0-Based
Learning Environments

The Role of Context for User Annotations in Searching Shared Materials

Hyeon Kyeong Hwang[1(✉)], Ivana Marenzi[2], Maria Bortoluzzi[3], and Marco Ronchetti[1]

[1] DISI, University of Trento, Trento, Italy
hyeonkyeong.hwang@unitn.it
[2] L3S Research Center, Hannover, Germany
[3] University of Udine, Udine, Italy

Abstract. One of the greatest challenges of Web 2.0 is to find the most relevant information to users' needs with minimum effort and time. Though search engines have improved greatly in the recent years, search results heavily depend on the textual search query, which does not fully reflect users' search context. In particular, teachers find it difficult to retrieve suitable materials to be used in their specific learning/teaching scenario. Tags, namely free-form user annotations, are found to be beneficial for improving search and retrieval but there has been no in-depth understanding as to which type of tags are useful and should be encouraged when designing a resource-sharing system for teachers. In this paper, we present an empirical study on the types of contextual meta-data that play an important role when teachers search for new learning/teaching materials. Based on results we collected, we propose a prototypical interface that facilitates the searching of shared resources among a community of teachers.

Keywords: Context-based search and retrieval · Social tagging · Informal learning · Language teachers · Interface design · Web 2.0

1 Introduction

A great wealth of information has been made available on the Web. However, as the amount of the information increases, the more difficult it becomes to find relevant information for a specific objective. Various Web resources can be useful for learning and teaching but it is challenging for teachers to find the most suitable resources for their specific educational scenarios; and, to our best knowledge, there are no user-friendly tools that can facilitate searching of shared resources among a community of teachers. The current work builds upon a previous study, about the use of Open Educational Resources (OERs) by teachers of different school levels [3]. The aim of the LearnWeb-OER[1] project was to investigate teachers' practices: how teachers approach Web searches, select, use and re-use OER in their teaching and learning context and develop an interface that can help non-technical users in searching efficiently materials for learning/teaching. Though the benefits of sharing learning/teaching resources with

---

[1] https://www.l3s.de/projects/internal/LearnWeb.

© Springer International Publishing AG 2017
H. Xie et al. (Eds.): ICWL 2017, LNCS 10473, pp. 91–100, 2017.
DOI: 10.1007/978-3-319-66733-1_10

other teachers in the same community were obvious, current search mechanism based on the textual string query seemed inefficient. Users were given the function to "tag" their resources but most users did not make use of the function, either due to the lack of understanding why tags were needed or due to the difficulty in choosing the "best" keywords to represent their resources. Free-form user annotations, commonly known as "tags", can enhance search and retrieval of information in collaborative settings [1, 15] and contribute to building collective vocabulary. However, the unlimited "freedom" of tagging has been shown to cause difficulties in organizing and retrieving information [15, 18]; therefore, a close examination of how particular community of teachers search and retrieve information, coupled with a bottom-up design of the system to elicit the relevant types of tag from the teachers, can not only relieve them of the cognitive burden of choosing the "right" tags but also facilitate the searching of shared resources by others in the same community. The results of semi-structured interviews with experienced language teachers [3] offered interesting insights into the factors the teachers considered relevant when choosing the learning/teaching materials. Contextual metadata such as the age of target audience, language level, trustworthiness of the source, the type of learning/teaching activity were some of the key players in the decision-making. These types of metadata cannot be automatically extracted by the system but can be elicited from the community members by appropriate and positive reinforcement and training through user-friendly interface and system design.

This paper is organized as follows: first, we provide an overview of literature on the use of tags in search and retrieval, followed by our motivation and research questions in Sect. 3. Then we discuss the methodology and results of our study in Sect. 4. In Sect. 5, we describe a model interface that facilitates the searching of shared resources, based on the study results of Sect. 4. Our provisional conclusion and discussion of the future developments are provided in Sect. 6.

2 Use of Tags for Search and Retrieval in Collaborative Environments

Since the advent of Web 2.0, social tagging systems have gained wild popularity as seen on various bookmarking systems (i.e. Bibsonomy, del.icio.us, Pinterest), media-sharing sites (i.e. YouTube, Flickr), social blogs and even commercial sites. These systems allow users not only to share online resources with others but also to annotate the resources freely with any terms users find meaningful and relevant. There are a number of distinct benefits of such tagging systems. Tagging allows multiple categorizations of a single resource, as opposed to the folder-based systems [15], which were found to demand less cognitive efforts [10]. In a collaborative setting, such freedom to choose the keywords by multiple users could be used to "harness the wisdom of the crowds" [15]. User-defined tagging helps to build a collective vocabulary called "folksonomy", which offers advantages over controlled vocabularies. Some researchers have discovered that users have various motivations for tagging [14, 17], which typically are expressed by different types of tags, as evidenced by several studies [2, 9, 14].

As social tagging systems gained popularity, many researchers looked into the possibility of using tags to improve information search [7, 19]. Tags provide several benefits because they serve as "document descriptors for other users' search queries" in users' own language [6]. However, not all types of tag are found to be useful for search [2, 7, 17]. Typically, the subject-related (content-based) tags are considered more important than the non-subjective (context-based) ones, since better search is strongly associated with building semantic taxonomy or ontology from the tags [5, 17]. However, several researchers have shown that tags' semantic relevance to the content of the resource is not the only qualifier for its usefulness for search; but rather it depends on various factors: the type of resource, users' search scope and users' perception of the purpose of the tagging systems. Bishoff et al. [2] conducted an extensive study on the potential of different types of tag for improving search. The study results showed that types of tag useful for searching shared resources were not the same as the ones useful for searching personal resources, indicating usefulness depended on the search scope. Similarly, Sen et al. [16] study showed that subjective tags such as opinions/qualities played a key role in decision-making of selecting a movie among search results, which emphasizes the role of non-content related tags in effective search of shared resources. The type of resource and the user's search scope are not the only factor that influences tagging behavior of the users. According to Heckner et al. [6], the tagging systems themselves seem to influence the choice of the types of tag. For instance, if the system was to support organization of personal resources, users tended to use tags such as self-reference, opinions/qualities and use context, which would not be so useful for others in the community.

3   Motivation and Research Questions

So far research has shown that the usefulness of types of tags hinge on various factors such as type of resource, users' search scope and the perceived purpose of the tagging systems. Nevertheless, any types of tag would be of little use if the social tagging system itself were not designed to meet the specific needs of the community it serves. In free-for-all tagging systems, users face difficulty in selecting the "right" types of tag, especially on those that support both shared and unshared resources: most users are still confused with the purpose of tags, not sure which tags are most useful for themselves or for the community. According to the recent study carried out by Kim and Rieh [8], Web users were unaware of the potential values of tags with many believing tags were for the system rather than for the users themselves. Tag recommendation systems can help users by providing tag options but the types of tags to be recommended or encouraged for better search would depend on the search context and the level of motivation for participation of the community. The community of teachers, in particular, is an example where the motivation is high because the knowledge and competence of others in the same profession are highly appreciated and beneficial [11]; however, they face difficulty in searching for new learning/teaching materials for their specific teaching scenarios because current systems do not yet support contextual search adapted for teachers.

The LearnWeb platform[2] allows users to share and collaboratively work on resources either generated by users or collected from the Web [12, 13]. Due to the growing amount of materials collected and shared by LearnWeb users, teachers noticed that it is more and more difficult to search or re-search resources on the platform. During professional courses for teachers, participants pointed out the need for a more professionally related tagging system to facilitate the search [11].

To meet this need, we investigated what type of metadata is most important and relevant for finding suitable learning/teaching materials; in order to do so we directly involved teachers in our case studies. Our research thus aims to answer the following questions:

(1) What kind of meta-data do teachers use when they search for teaching and learning materials? Are there important underlying meta-data, not overly expressed in their textual search queries? If there are any, are they content-related or contextual?

(2) Based on the results of (1), how can we best redesign existing interfaces to encourage users to provide metadata (tags) useful for community search needs? How can we visualize such metadata in search results to facilitate decision-making of selecting suitable materials?

4 Meta-data Useful for Searching Shared Teaching Materials

In this section, we revisit the qualitative summary of the results we collected during our previous research studies [3, 4, 11]. While the previous study focused on the general Web search patterns of teachers, this paper shifts the focus to identify the type(s) of metadata important for teachers when selecting materials for their context of use.

4.1 Teachers' Search Pattern and Decision-Making Strategy

In 2014, we interviewed six experienced language teachers from different Italian schools of various levels in order to investigate their Web search patterns and strategies when looking for new teaching materials [3]. The study results showed that teachers began their search with a general topic in their mind and a typical search session involved several iterations, by which key terms changed from *general to specific*. Even though teachers had other contextual requirements such as target audience, type of media and teaching activity for their searches, those were hardly included in their textual query. Instead, they used these requirements as criteria for selecting the "right" resource. The decision-making strategy of all participants showed similar patterns, especially on how teachers narrowed down search results to select particular resources suitable for their teaching scenario. Figure 1 depicts the typical decision process of participants.

---

[2] http://learnweb.l3s.uni-hannover.de.

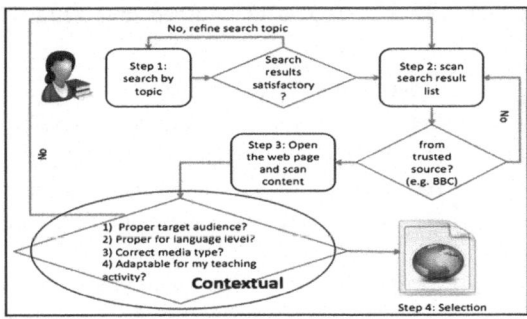

Fig. 1. The search & decision process of selecting teaching material

Resource attributes and teaching context were critical conditions for selecting the teaching materials even though they were not overtly expressed in the search queries. All participants spent a significant amount of time clicking on several "possible" search results to read the content and decide if it was appropriate for their teaching scenario. Another important factor was the "trustworthiness" of the resource. Teachers considered resources trustworthy when found in well-known portals such as BBC or Cambridge University, or shared by other trusted teachers. They often relied on the opinion of their colleagues to decide on the appropriateness of resources they found on the Web. These findings show that there is a gap between the metadata that teachers use for search and the metadata search engines use to render results. In other words, contextual types of metadata should be made available to facilitate searching but such metadata cannot be automatically extracted or inferred from the textual query. Moreover, the system itself does not have the teacher's expertise to decide which material is suitable for which type of teaching scenarios either. However, each member of teachers' communities can collaboratively provide such metadata for the resources they share, which can benefit not only themselves but also their colleagues.

4.2 Teachers' Perspective: Categorization of Resources to Facilitate Search

The results of the second phase of the study, done through search log analysis, observation fora analysis and questionnaire [3], provided insights into how teachers envision their resources to be organized for better search and retrieval through tagging resources collaboratively. According to the YELL/TELL community users, resources should be categorized as shown in Table 1, which matches the results of the first study discussed in previous section. This demonstrates there are a number of metadata that should be supported in order to facilitate the search and decision process of selection of shared materials among teachers.

Table 1. Categorization of resources suggested by teachers from YELL/TELL Community on LearnWeb

Category	Explanation and suggested dataset
Authors of the resource	The person(s) who has written or provided the resource
Type of resource	The text-type of the resource: video, song, game, text
Language	The language of the resource (English, Italian, etc.)
Language level	The level of language complexity of the resource: C2, C1, B2, B1, A2, A1
Target audience	The intended users of the resource: teachers, university students, secondary school students, primary school children, pre-school children, others
Type of learning/teaching activity	The intended learning/teaching activity of the resource: ready-to-use activities, lesson plans, teacher education materials, learning strategies, language skills, etc.
Topic	Main and high-level topic of the resource: water, food, ecology, human rights
Keywords	Additional representative concepts/expressions to describe the resource: learning style, inclusive learning etc.

5   Prototype: Redesigning the Interface to Facilitate Searching Shared Resources

Our study results showed that, while semantic keywords are important, there are other types of metadata that teachers use during the search of resources, and these are not supported in the current LearnWeb system. In this section, we show the new interfaces for eliciting such metadata from the community of users and how they can be visualized to facilitate the search and retrieval of shared resources. The key aims of the new interfaces are the following:

(1) Identify and elicit the types of metadata (those found to be important for search and retrieval) which can be provided by the community of teachers;
(2) Allow users to navigate through a hierarchical category tree in order to reduce the cognitive burden of finding specific topical keywords for searching;
(3) Visualize various types of metadata for each resource so that users do not need to click and view the content for decision-making;
(4) Provide search methods for contextual metadata such as target learners, language level and purpose of use.

5.1   Adding a New Resource: Eliciting Desired Types of Metadata

Previous observations on LearnWeb logs showed that users did not make use of the tags as expected. Thus, the new interface focuses on guiding the teacher community to provide the types of metadata useful for searching shared resources, based on studies discussed in Sect. 4. The current interface asked for minimum participation from the users in forms of free tagging and comments, whereas the new interface elicits a variety of specific metadata users can provide, as demonstrated in Fig. 2.

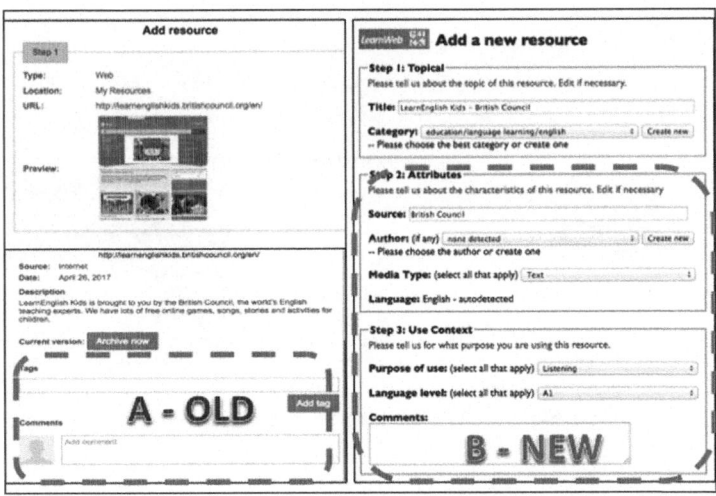

Fig. 2. Comparison of the old (L) and new interface (R) for adding a new resource (Box A-old and Box B-new show the areas of user participation in creating metadata)

Topical metadata such as title, category and keywords are automatically extracted by the system while some attributes of the resources and contextual use metadata are elicited from users. Table 2 summarizes the type of metadata, which are supported by the current LearnWeb system and by the new prototype, as well as the data provider, either automatically extracted by the system or provided by the users.

Table 2. Metadata useful for search of resources: support on old LearnWeb Interface and on the new Interface

Metadata	Semantic		Attributes		Contextual		
	Keywords	Category	Media type	Source	Audience	Level	Activity
Support? (Old interface)	Yes	No	Partial	Partial	No	No	No
Support? (New interface)	Yes	Yes	Yes	Yes	Yes	Yes	Yes
Data provider	System	System	Partial	System	User	User	User

5.2 Searching: Visualization of Contextual Metadata of Resources at a Glance

The current search interface does not provide much information about each resource other than the thumbnail and the title, making it hard for users to understand what the resource is about and whether or not it is appropriate for his or her teaching/learning needs (Fig. 3). The new search interface, on the other hand, drastically changes the amount of metadata shown to users at a glance, aiming at minimizing the efforts for selecting most relevant resources for each teaching/learning context.

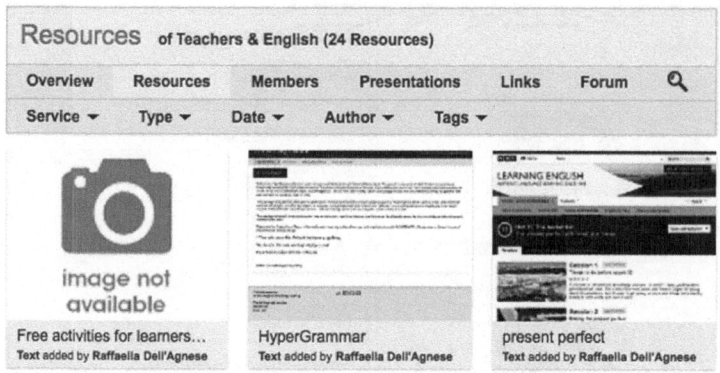

Fig. 3. Old search interface of LearnWeb

The keyword search interface (Fig. 4) focuses on allowing users to filter search results by contextual filters as well as traditional keyword search. As discussed in Sect. 4, we learned that teachers not only search by topic but also evaluate various aspects of the resources and their context of use (media type, target learners, etc.), which cannot be discerned from the resource title or description. Search results are displayed in such a way that it minimizes the need to open the link to view the content by visualizing such metadata to be reviewed instantly, reducing the time and effort need to find and choose resources. On the other hand, category navigation interface (Fig. 5) allows users to navigate topic of interest from *general to specific*, giving them a visualized hierarchical tree that eliminates the cognitive burden of knowing specific topical search terms in advance. Users are provided with the matching resources when a tree node is clicked and the results are displayed with contextual metadata as in the keyword search interface.

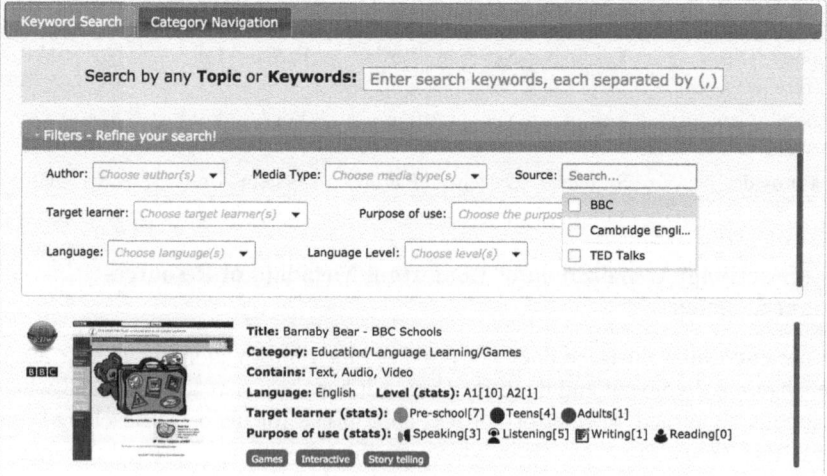

Fig. 4. New search interface by keyword with contextual filters

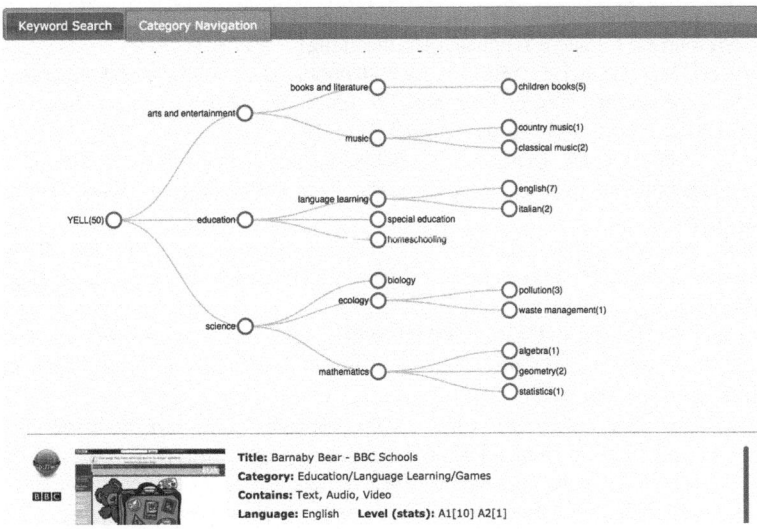

Fig. 5. New search interface by category navigation tree

6   Conclusion and Future Developments

The new interface developed for searching shared resources is the result of multiple findings: 1. analysis of user feedback, 2. logs from the LearnWeb digital environment used by language teachers for their teaching practice in schools, 3. literature on the state-of-the art of Web search, 4. previous applications developed by the researchers. The interaction between researchers and users helped us provide a tailor-made tool whose application will be tested in the next months.

The testing phase will give us insights on the validity of contextually relevant metadata filters resulting from user community/researcher interaction and will offer us the data to fine-tune or further adjust the interface. We expect to apply a similar and adapted interface for other communities of users on the bases of their own needs and filters for searching. A further development will be comparing results across different communities of users to expand on the common categories and identify the specific ones. The final outcome will be an easily adaptable and flexible interface that can be used by a variety of user-communities and eventually automatically expanding and adapting to user needs and requests.

References

1. Bergman, O., Gradovitch, N., Bar-Ilan, J., Beyth-Marom, R.: Folder versus tag preference in personal information management. J. Am. Soc. Inform. Sci. Technol. **64**(10), 1995–2012 (2013). doi:10.1002/asi.22906
2. Bischoff, K., Firan, C.S., Nejdl, W., Paiu, R.: Can all tags be used for search? In: Proceedings of the 17th ACM Conference on Information and Knowledge Management, pp. 193–202. ACM (2008)

3. Bortoluzzi, M., Marenzi, I.: Websearching for learning: How language teachers search for online resources. Lingue e Linguaggi (forthcoming)
4. Bortoluzzi, M., Marenzi, I.: YELLing for collaborative learning in teacher education: users' voices in the social platform LearnWeb2.0. Int. J. Soc. Media Interact. Learn. Environ. (IJSMILE) 2(2), 182–198 (2014)
5. Eda, T., Yoshikawa, M., Uchiyama, T., Uchiyama, T.: The effectiveness of latent semantic analysis for building up a bottom-up taxonomy from folksonomy ags. World Wide Web 12 (4), 421 (2009)
6. Heckner, M., Mühlbacher, S., Wolff, C.: Tagging tagging. Analysing user keywords in scientific bibliography management systems. J. Digit. Inform. 9(2), June 2008. ISSN 1368-7506
7. Heymann, P., Koutrika, G., Garcia-Molina, H.: Can social bookmarking improve web search? In: Proceedings of the 2008 International Conference on Web Search and Data Mining, pp. 195–206. ACM (2008)
8. Kim, Y.M., Rieh, S.Y.: User perceptions of the role and value of tags. In: Proceedings of the SIGCHI Conference on Human Factors in Computing Systems, pp. 671–674. ACM (2011)
9. Li, L., Zhang, C.: Quality evaluation of social tags according to web resource types. In: Proceedings of the 23rd International Conference on World Wide Web, pp. 1123–1128. ACM (2014)
10. Macgregor, G., McCulloch, E.: Collaborative tagging as a knowledge organisation and resource discovery tool. Libr. Rev. 55(5), 291–300 (2006)
11. Marenzi, I., Bortoluzzi, M., Kalyani, R.: YELL/TELL: online community platform for teacher professional development. In: Papadima-Sophocleous, S., Bradley, L., Thouësny, S. (eds.) CALL Communities and Culture – Short Papers from EUROCALL 2016, pp. 307–312. Research-publishing.net (2016)
12. Marenzi, I.: Interactive and collaborative supports for CLIL: towards a formal model based on digital literacy. In: Kupetz, R., Becker, C. (eds.) Content and Language Integrated Learning (CLIL) by Interaction, pp. 75–99. Peter Lang, Frankfurt am Main (2014)
13. Marenzi, I.: A multiliteracies approach for supporting language learning courses at university level. In: Jovanovic, J., Chiong, R. (eds.) Technological and Social Environments for Interactive Learning, vol. 8, pp. 249–276. Informing Science Press, Santa Rosa (2013)
14. Marlow, C., Naaman, M., Boyd, D., Davis, M.: HT06, tagging paper, taxonomy, Flickr, academic article, to read. In: Proceedings of the Seventeenth Conference on Hypertext and Hypermedia, pp. 31–40. ACM (2006)
15. Gao, Q.: An empirical study of tagging for personal information organization: performance, workload, memory, and consistency. Int. J. Hum. Comput. Interact. 27(9), 821–863 (2011)
16. Sen, S., Lam, S.K., Rashid, A.M., Cosley, D., Frankowski, D., Osterhouse, J., Riedl, J.: Tagging, communities, vocabulary, evolution. In: Proceedings of the 2006 20th Anniversary Conference on Computer Supported Cooperative Work, pp. 181–190. ACM (2006)
17. Strohmaier, M., Körner, C., Kern, R.: Why do users tag? Detecting users' motivation for tagging in social tagging systems. In: ICWSM (2010)
18. Pak, R., Pautz, S., Iden, R.: Information organization and retrieval: a comparison of taxonomical and tagging systems. Cognit. Technol. 12(1), 31–44 (2007)
19. Yanbe, Y., Jatowt, A., Nakamura, S., Tanaka, K.: Can social bookmarking enhance search in the web? In: Proceedings of the 7th ACM/IEEE-CS Joint Conference on Digital Libraries, pp. 107–116. ACM (2007)

A Preliminary Investigation
of the Appropriateness of YouTube
as an Informal Learning Platform for Pre-teens

Marié Hattingh$^{(\boxtimes)}$

Department of Informatics, University of Pretoria, Pretoria, South Africa
marie.hattingh@up.ac.za

Abstract. The introduction of Web 2.0 technologies has provided an alternative environment for informal learning to take. This paper extends previous research by investigating the appropriateness of YouTube as an informal learning platform for pre-teens. A nethnographic approach was used to analyse two YouTube videos with their associated comments from one YouTube channel – "Grant Thompson - The King of Random". The results were evaluated using parental guidelines for YouTube as proposed by Knorr [1]. The analysis has shown that learning has taken place in two instances: (1) learning-by-watching that turned into learning-by-doing when subscribers attempted to replicate the project and reported their success/failure, (2) peer-to-peer learning through discussions between different subscribers that furthered their understanding of the topic at hand. Factors that enhanced the learning experience was the self-directed interest in the topic and the fan base influence, which caused incidental learning. However, the risk associated with the informal learning environment created by YouTube that include that some projects are too dangerous for pre-teens to replicate on their own. However, the data showed that some subscribers were aware of the risk associated with these projects and admitted that they need consent from their parents. This paper contributes to literature by recommending YouTube as an informal learning platform for pre-teens under the supervision of parental vetting of the YouTube channel.

Keywords: YouTube · Informal learning · Pre-teen · Digital literacy · Web 2.0 · Digital natives

1 Introduction

The development of the Internet has revolutionized how we approach life! With the rise in uptake of Web 2.0 technologies it influenced the manner in which we communicate, how we keep up to date with current events, how we learn to name a few activities. The focus of this paper is on the latter aspect of learning.

The ubiquity of digital technologies resulted in early adoption of technologies by children. The rise of the digital natives [2] implied that children are adopting digital technologies at a much faster pace than the previous generations.

Ferguson, Faulkner, Whitelock and Sheehy [3] reported on the potential pedagogical benefits for children with the introduction of Web 2.0 technologies in schools.

© Springer International Publishing AG 2017
H. Xie et al. (Eds.): ICWL 2017, LNCS 10473, pp. 101–110, 2017.
DOI: 10.1007/978-3-319-66733-1_11

Previous research has reported on the successes of the use of Web 2.0 technologies in informal learning environments. Selwyn [4] used Facebook and Second Life project to critically review the appropriateness of the Web 2.0 technologies as alternative learning environments with the aim of integrating it into formal learning environments. Greenhow and Lewin [5] extended that discussion by proposing a model to use social media technologies in education. Due to the nature of Web 2.0 technologies and informal learning, it is relatively easy for pre-teens to self-direct the exploration of various topics that pique their interest [6].

The focus of this paper is specifically on the use of YouTube by pre-teens as a suitable platform for informal learning in an informal environment. Previous research on the use of YouTube as an informal learning platform concentrated on students between the ages of 18 to 40 [6]. Very little research has been done on the use of Web 2.0 technologies by pre-teens. The study by Ferguson et al. [3] focused on the informal learning of pre-teens using Lego Mindstorm and Scratch programming language.

Given the age of the subjects of the study, it is important to consider safe online usage of the YouTube platform. The appropriateness of YouTube as an informal learning platform will therefore have to be evaluated using parental guidelines for recommended YouTube usage.

Given this background, the objective of this research is to explore the appropriateness of YouTube as an informal learning platform for pre-teens. In meeting this objective the researcher aims to show: (1) the types of informal learning YouTube can facilitate, (2) aspects contribute to learning and (3) risk factors are involved in using YouTube as an informal learning platform for pre-teens.

A brief literature review will be provided on YouTube as an informal learning platform in Sect. 2. Section 3 will introduce YouTube guidelines for parents, which will be used to assess the results of the data that will be discussed in Sect. 5.4. Section 4 will give a brief overview of the netnographic method whereas a discussion of the results will follow in Sect. 5. The paper concludes by presenting the limitation and suggestions for future research.

2   YouTube as an Informal Learning Platform

Informal learning can be classified as learning that occurs outside a formal setting [7]. Marsick and Volpe [8] characterized informal learning as being:

- Learning is part of everyday life routine.
- Learning is prompted by an internal or external event.
- Learning takes place without conscious thought.
- Learning is incidental.
- Learning takes place through reflection and action.
- Learning takes place in connection with others.

The characteristics of informal learning provided above, is applicable to the YouTube environment. YouTube is a vast user-driven video sharing site that disseminates multimedia information. It is classified as a social networking site as it connects registered users through subscriptions that will alert subscribers of updates [9]. Consequently, users have access to a plethora of videos that covers any imaginable topic.

According to YouTube statistics, 1.3 billion users use YouTube. 300 h of video are uploaded to YouTube every minute. Approximately 5 billion videos are watched on YouTube everyday. Eighty percent of the users are 18-49 year old [10].

However, according to the Ofcom Children and Parents: Media use and Attitudes Report [11] there is a sharp increase in children age five and older watching YouTube channels, where watching these channels are becoming part of their everyday life routine. Furthermore, children usually learn through word of mouth regarding YouTube channels to visit, which prompts them to engage with the platform. They move from one video to the next without conscious thought.

3   YouTube Guidelines for Parents

Knorr [1] drafted a simple guide for parents regarding the use of YouTube to assist them in navigating the depths of the popular video sharing site. As a starting point Knorr refers parents to the tools provided by YouTube themselves to filter content which includes turning on the safety mode. She further recommends that parents should:

- Watch YouTube videos with their children
- Watch YouTube videos of their kids' favourite YouTube personality themselves
- Encourage children to subscribe to their favourite YouTube channel, as it will allow children to access the content easier.
- Investigate the creator of the YouTube channel in order to establish whether he/she will be a good role model.
- Evaluate the suggested videos that appear on the YouTube page in order to see if it is age appropriate.
- Observe if the YouTube video has an advertisement appearing before it starts.
- Read the comments in order to establish if it is appropriate for your child to read.

These guidelines will be used in Sect. 5.4 to evaluate the data collected from the YouTube videos with their respective comments as discussed in Sect. 4.

4   Research Method

The research approach employed for this study is netnography. Netnography is based on the principles of ethnography in an online environment [12]. Kozinets [12] described the method as "faster, simpler, and less expensive than traditional ethnography and more naturalistic and unobtrusive than focus groups or interviews". The approach has initially been used in online marketing research, but is now extended to other fields as well. The aim of this netnographic research was to conduct a preliminary investigation into the appropriateness of YouTube as an informal learning platform for pre-teens to early teens in an informal environment. The research followed the Kozinets [12] recommended five stages of netnography, (1) making entrée, (2) data collection and anlysis (3) providing trustworthy interpretation, (4) research ethics, and (5) member checks. These five stages are modelled on the stages involved in ethnography.

Entrée. The researcher considered two videos posted on the Grant Thompson – King of random YouTube channel: The How to make a Batarang like "The Dark Knight" (Video A) and "Soda Bottle Rope" (Video B). Video A was posted 3 years ago, whilst Video B was posted 1 month ago. The researcher was introduced to this particular YouTube channel by her pre-teen children. Upon further investigation, she noticed that the particular channel had over 7.8 M subscribers, over 2.2 B views since its joined date of 2010. The author of the YouTube channel has even published a book on his projects. The two particular videos were chosen at random. Both videos have high traffic of comments and views. At the time of the study, Video A had 9,841,898 views and 11,418 comments. Video B had 2,089,407 views and 8,197 comments.

Data Collection. The data to be collected involved watching each video and downloading all comments using a YouTube comments scraper. The data were saved in. CSV files. The data were analysed through the qualitative software, Atlas.ti.

Trustworthy interpretation. According to Kozinets [12] research is deemed to be trustworthy when the proposed procedures of netnography are followed while collecting and analyzing data. Data triangulation was used to increase the trustworthiness of this study. Triangulation was achieved by considering the large number of comments on the respective videos. Furthermore, site triangulation was achieved by considering two different videos, three years apart from the same YouTube channel (the format remains consistent), covering different topics.

Ethical procedure. The researcher followed the ethical procedure recommended by Langer and Beckman [13]. The videos and their corresponding comments posted on the YouTube channel are considered public data as it's not password protected. Therefore, the researcher did not need to obtain permission to use the data. However, the anonymity and privacy of the users were respected.

Member checks. Member checks involves the communicating the research findings to the participants in order to give them an opportunity to comment [12]. However, in accordance with Langer and Beckman [13] when data were obtained unobtrusively, it is not necessary to do member checks.

5 Discussion

An analysis of the respective videos and comments associated with the videos have provided the researcher with an overview of the type of learning, factors that can enhance learning and risk factors associated with the platform when considering the guidelines to parents for YouTube use. The study revealed that learning is multi-faceted and that the YouTube platform and environment provided by the platform lends itself to an ideal informal learning platform for pre-teens. However, given the accessibility of the platform risks have been identified which included inappropriate comments on YouTube videos and age inappropriate projects.

5.1   Types of Learning

It was observed that pre-teens are exposed to different types of learning. Firstly, by watching the videos and secondly through the comments where incidental learning takes place through discussions and pre-teens' digital abilities to engage with the platform and comment on the content.

Learning-by-watching. Reitan [14] defines learning by watching as "learning through *visual* observation". With this definition Reitan [14] proposes to extend the work of John Dewey's learning-by-doing. The nature of the YouTube channel is to show different projects or "life hacks" (how-to videos) that viewers to watch and learn how to complete a number of projects. Analysis of videos A and B showed that the presenter explained each project step-by-step, it will be relative easy for someone to replicate the project which furthers the learning process by converting the learning process into "learning-by-doing" [14]. A number of subscribers provided feedback on their own attempts through comments. The quote below illustrates the attempts of a subscriber:

"I'm in south africa and I made five batarangs thanks to this videos"

Another interesting aspect observed from the two videos is the concept of scaffolding of learning or chunking [15] which refers to presenting new information into manageable sizes for a learner's working memory. In the case of video B, the presenter referred to two previous videos that covered the projects needed to continue with making the actual rope demonstrated: firstly how to make a rope making machine and secondly how to make string from a soda bottle. This is an important concept in the learning of pre-teens as most of the projects are "new information". Furthermore, the scaffolding of learning was supported through the nature of the YouTube video where the presenter referred back to questions he got from subscribers and explained concepts they struggled with.

Peer-to-peer learning. Due to the collaborative nature of YouTube, it is possible for users to learn from one another: by telling one another of the "cool videos" or by responding to comments on posted videos. The quote below illustrates the first point:

"im from Muskegan, Michigan, your videos are awesome! i love watching these things to wow my friends and then i show them your videos and they are amazed! someone who knows how to think outside the box to create more and better things out of scrap is awesome haha"

Illustrating the second point the researcher observed a number of conversations between the various commenters. By engaging in the discussions (or just reading it) it is possible to further learning occurring spontaneously. The quote below illustrates this point:

"I have a question: Can you make the string back into the bottle?"

The above question got nine replies and 76 likes. One of the responses were:

"That's a fine question. I'd say you have to weave them like a wicker basket. and then, using temperature, melt them together as Jz said. Or use clay, but you need to dry and glaze it as well. Anyways, yes, I think this possible, but the bottle will definitely look different"

Learning from peers by reading comments can be classified as a form of incidental learning. Marsick and Watskins [8] define incidental learning as *"as a byproduct of some other activity, such as task accomplishment, interpersonal interaction..."*. The nature of the YouTube platform allows for easy incidental learning as the comments are public and anyone can partake in the discussion.

Digital Learning. Learning by watching and peer-to-peer learning occur in the context where pre-teen (the youngest indicated his age as seven years old) have developed, and are developing/improving their digital skills. Learning to be a competent computer user is also considered incidental learning as using technology is a natural response to their enquiry [8]. Although it was not possible to find "physical evidence" from data to support "digital learning skills", the researcher argues that the netnographic methodology [12] allows her to deduce from the data analysis that in the context of digital natives digital learning has occurred. Digital natives refers to the generation born into technology where "digital activity is like a mother tongue for them" [2] pre-teens navigate technology such as using the YouTube platform with ease. Their ability to do this, changes the way this generation think, changing the way they learn.

5.2   Factors that Enhance Learning

Data analysis has indicated that there were a number of factors that contributed to an enhanced learning experience. Firstly, the analysis of the comments indicated that the majority of contributors (there were inappropriate comments which will be discussed in Sect. 5.3) found the videos to be interesting. Secondly, due to the nature of the platform, the channel creator has amassed a fan base that consist of children and adults who subscribes to the channel. By subscribing to the channel they get updates regarding new projects, which creates an environment for lifelong learning [16].

Interest in the topic (product). An analysis of the comments have indicated that the subscriber found the videos considered for this study very interesting, an made reference to other projects completed by the YouTube channel creator. The following quote illustrates this:

> *"I watch all your videos when they come out. Always something interesting to be seen. I am from Montana. :)"*

The interest in the topic, allows for further learning by extending or enhancing the project presented. Gilakjani [17] stated that "If the students are not interested in the material presented, they will not learn it". Due to the nature of informal learning which is characterized by "student independent exploration" [6], the subscription and viewing of the YouTube video is voluntarily, based on intrinsic motivation to learn "cool" things.

Four areas were highlighted that underscored the interest in the topic at hand. By thinking how the products can be tested, used, improved or even suggestions for new products based on the video, allows opportunities for further learning.

Firstly, there were numerous requests to test the product.

"PLEASE!!!! Grant, please strength test the soda ropes in a unique way to see what kind of weight they can hold, or pull, with different gauges of ropes you made. lift weights, tow a car, swing from it like a vine, etc."

Secondly, there were numerous suggestions to utilize the products in everyday life.

"You should use the plastic rope you made to make something for your kids. Make like a swing tire swing or even a hammock. I think it would be really cool to see it be put to use"

Thirdly, a few suggestions were given to improve/enhance the current project. Offering improvements does not only show reflection on the part of the viewer, but also contributes to ongoing learning for those that did not know how the project could have been improved. The quote below illustrates this point:

"as an improvement you could put a double nut on the spinning end for the drill to attach it to via a socket attachment (Firmer grip, doesn't damage chuck on drill and is easier to attach)"

Finally, reflection and contextualization of the projects under consideration was also evident in the recognition of the fact that both projects recycled old materials. The following quote illustrates this:

"you should do this on the larger scale and make swings for the poor kids around you and save the earth at the same time!"

Fan base influence. It is natural for YouTube creators to be given "celebrity status", especially by young children that have a "favourite" YouTuber [1]. For this reason, Knorr [1] cautions parents to make sure that the channel creator is a good role model as children will attempt to imitate their behavior. The following quote illustrates how a child likes to "keep up" with the new content of the YouTube channel, without giving thought about the learning that takes place in the process.

"King of Random i'm your biggest fan every day after school i jump on the computer and check if you posted a video i enjoy watching them and look forward to see your future projects"

5.3   Risk Factors Associated with the YouTube Platform

The data has indicated that a number of risks are associated with using YouTube as a learning platform, especially when considering it for pre-teens. Firstly, it is difficult to protect children from inappropriate comments, which might be stated in jest; secondly, the skills required for the projects are age inappropriate as it involves the use of specialized tools.

Inappropriate comments. Due to the nature of a YouTube channel (and social media in general) it is not possible to control the comments that are posted on it. Knorr [1] cautions that comments on YouTube is notorious for being negative, and in that sense parents should educate their children about inappropriate comments. The data has indicated that there were a few inappropriate comments, mostly related to using the products produced in the videos to kill someone or commit suicide as illustrated by the quote below:

"now i can kill my family". [referring to the batarang]

Children cannot always be protected from inappropriate content and therefore should have the necessary digital literacy skills [6] to recognize and discard content as inappropriate. Although comments can be moderated by channel creators [1] and parents can activate parental control to filter out the majority of inappropriate videos, chances are that young (impressionable) will be exposed to it.

Age-skill Inappropriate projects. The safety aspect associated with the creation of the product in Video A is much more critical than that of the product in Video B. For that reason the channel creator has physically stated the risk associated with creating the product. Due to the nature of the instructional videos, children literally has a step-by-step guide to complete a project, without always considering the risks involved. However, the researcher has observed that a number of children stated that they would like to "do the project" but that they are too young to do it, or should wait for an adult to assist. The two quotes below illustrate that point.

"I am Abd-Rahman, I am 9 years old and I am from Amman, Jordan. I will let an adult do it"

"Love it but I am 12 years old. So I can't make that"

5.4   Applying YouTube Parent Guidelines

Following the analysis of the video content and comments, the researcher applied the YouTube Parent Guidelines as introduced in Sect. 3 to the data.

- *Watch YouTube videos with your child.* A number of posts indicated that a parent is watching the videos with their children. The quote below illustrates this:
- *Hey! Thanks for your videos! My kids and I really enjoy them. We'd love to see you test the strength of the different ropes. Thanks!*
- *Watch YouTube videos of their kids' favourite YouTube personality themselves.* There was no evidence that parents watched/followed the YouTube channel due to their child's interest in the channel beforehand. This is a limitation of the research methodology used.
- *Encourage children to subscribe to their favourite YouTube channel, as it will allow children to access the content easier.*
- *Investigate the creator of the YouTube channel in order to establish whether he/she will be a good role model.* The researcher was able to read under the "About" section on the YouTube channel more information on the creator of the channel. The following quote illustrates that the creator shares snippets of his personal life with the subscribers, which as a father himself, does make him a good role model, especially for pre-teens.

"You should use the plastic rope you made to make something for your kids. Make like a swing tire swing or even a hammock. I think it would be really cool to see it be put to use."

- *Evaluate the suggested videos that appear on the YouTube page in order to see if it is age appropriate.* By own admission the creator does indicate whether an adult is needed to complete a project. However, as indicated above, a number of children have stated that they were too young to complete a project without an adult.
- *Observe if the YouTube video has an advertisement appearing before it starts.* Both YouTube videos considered for this study had advertisements at the beginning of the video.
- *Read the comments in order to establish if it is appropriate for your child to read.* Even though the researcher noticed a few inappropriate comments, there was no evidence that any pre-teens reacted to it or was affected by it.

The application of the YouTube guidelines indicated that for the two videos considered, there was evidence that some parents applied recommended guidelines. However, due to the nature of the methodology, it was difficult to determine if these guidelines were followed in all instances. Using these guidelines it can be recommended that YouTube can be considered as an appropriate informal learning platform however, it needs to occur under the guidance of the parents until pre-teens have reached a level of digital literacy and maturity in order to distinguish between appropriate and inappropriate projects, comments and content (not applicable in this study).

6 Conclusion

The aim of this paper was to do a preliminary investigation into the appropriateness of YouTube as an informal learning platform for pre-teens. The paper showed that pre-teens was/would have been (it was difficult to establish the age of the commenters as they did not always state their age) exposed to different types of learning which extended beyond the expected "learning-by-watching". Rather the platform provided scaffolded learning, which were extended by peer-to-peer learning through comments and incidental learning when considering the digital skills needed to be present in order for children to partake on the platform.

This paper contributes to literature by recommending YouTube as an informal learning platform for pre-teens, previous research considered Web 2.0 technologies for pre-teens, and YouTube as an informal learning platform for students (18 years and older). This recommendation is based on the acknowledgement of parental guidance and monitoring of the pre-teen's YouTube usage as well as the need to further develop the pre-teen's digital literacy skill in order to distinguish between appropriate and inappropriate content.

The limitation of this study was introduced by the chosen research methodology that limited the analysis to the video content and comments. However, as an exploratory research project it did show that there are pre-teens using YouTube, by their own admission they learnt something from the videos. Future research is planned to address this limitation by doing interpretive research with pre-teens on their You-Tube usage to determine their perception of their extent of informal and incidental learning.

References

1. Knorr, C.: A Parent's Ultimate Guide to YouTube. Commonsensemedia.org (2014). https://www.commonsensemedia.org/blog/a-parents-ultimate-guide-to-youtube#
2. Do, H.O.W., Learn, T., To, H.O.W., Them, T.: Digital natives: how do they learn? How to teach them? September 2011
3. Ferguson, R., Faulkner, D., Whitelock, D., Sheehy, K.: Pre-teens' informal learning with ICT and Web 2.0. Technol. Pedagog. Educ., vol. 22, June 2015 (2013)
4. Selwyn, N.: Web 2.0 applications as alternative environments for informal learning - a critical review. Paper for CERI-KERIS International Expert Meeting on ICT and Educational Performance, pp. 16–17 (2007)
5. Greenhow, C., Lewin, C.: Social media and education: reconceptualizing the boundaries of formal and informal learning. Learn. Media Technol. 41(1), 6–30 (2016)
6. Tan, E.: Informal learning on YouTube: exploring digital literacy in independent online learning. Learn. Media Technol. 38(4), 463–477 (2013)
7. Rogoff, B., Callanan, M., Gutiérrez, K.D., Erickson, F.: The organization of informal learning. Rev. Res. Educ. 40(March), 356–401 (2016)
8. Marsick, V.J., Watkins, K.E.: Informal and incidental learning. New Dir. Adult Contin. Educ. 2001(89), 25 (2001)
9. Wattenhofer, M., Wattenhofer, R., Zhu, Z.: The YouTube social network. In: ICWSM (June 2012)
10. Fortunelords.com: YouTube Statistics – 2017 (2017). https://fortunelords.com/youtube-statistics/. Accessed: 10 May 2017
11. Ofcome: Children and Parents: Media Use and Attitudes Report, October 2014
12. Kozinets, R.V.: The field behind the screen: using netnography for marketing research in online communities. J. Mark. Res. 39(1), 61–72 (2002)
13. Langer, R., Beckman, S.C.: Sensitive research topics: netnography revisited. Qual. Mark. Res. Int. J. 8(2), 189–203 (2005)
14. Reitan, J.B.: Learning-by-watching as a concept and as a reason to choose professional higher education. In: International conference on Engineering and Product Design Education, September 2015
15. Baker, R.: Examples of scaffolding and chunking in online and blended learning environments (2010). https://papers.ssrn.com/sol3/papers.cfm?abstract_id=1608133. Accessed 7 Aug 2017
16. Lin, Y.-M., Lee, P.-C.: Informal learning: theory and applied. Int. J. Bus. Commer. 3(5), 127–134 (2014)
17. Gilakjani, A.P.: Visual, auditory, kinaesthetic learning styles and their impacts on english language teaching. J. Stud. Educ. 2(1), 104–113 (2011)

Mining Domain-Specific Accounts for Scientific Contents from Social Media

Jun Wang[1]([✉]), Junfu Xiang[2], Yun Zhang[2], and Kanji Uchino[1]

[1] Fujitsu Laboratories of America, Sunnyvale, CA 94085, USA
{jun.wang,kanji}@us.fujitsu.com
[2] Nanjing Fujitsu Nanda Software Tech. Co., Ltd., Najing, China
{xiangjf.fnst,zhangyun.fnst}@cn.fujitsu.com

Abstract. This paper proposes a machine learning based approach to automatically create an initial set of domain-specific accounts by matching real-world authors of the latest domain-specific publications to corresponding social media accounts. An efficient approach based on social network analysis is further applied to extend the initial set by finding more domain-specific accounts of various types and filtering out irrelevant general or non-domain-specific accounts. Our experiments on Twitter are used to verify feasibility and effectiveness of the proposed methods.

Keywords: Domain-specific scientific contents · Social network analysis · Social media

1 Introduction

Social media allow researchers and research institutes to communicate and collaborate in ways that disregard institutional boundaries, and is used for keeping up-to-date with topics, following other's work, discovering new ideas or publications, promoting current work/research and making new research contacts [1]. However, massive information overload on social media poses significant challenges to new learners and novice researchers of a specific domain, who attempt to promptly engage in scientific communication and interaction on social media and efficiently stay up-to-date with the latest domain-specific research progress. Generally, it often needs significant time and efforts to manually collect appropriate informative accounts to follow and find relevant high-quality contents to read, especially in cutting-edge technology domains.

To address the above problem, we first propose a machine learning based approach to automatically create a initial set of domain-specific accounts by matching real-world authors of the latest domain-specific publications to corresponding social media accounts. Second, an efficient approach based on social network analysis is further applied to extend the initial set by finding more domain-specific accounts of various types and filtering out irrelevant general or non-domain-specific accounts with low *domain-specificity*. These identified domain-specific accounts can be used as informative sensors to filter and aggregate valuable domain-specific scientific contents. Our experiments using Twitter are used to verify feasibility and effectiveness of the proposed methods.

H. Xie et al. (Eds.): ICWL 2017, LNCS 10473, pp. 111–118, 2017.
DOI: 10.1007/978-3-319-66733-1_12

2   Related Work

Hadgu et al. [2] presented an approach for the identification and classification of computer scientists on Twitter. They first manually complied a list of Twitter accounts of computer science conferences as seeds, and mainly extracted candidates for computer scientists from accounts following at least one of the seed accounts or followed by one of the seed accounts. Ke et al. [3] employed a list-based snowball sampling method for breadth-first search on Twitter lists[1], which started from a given initial set of scientist accounts and expanded to identify more scientists in a wide range of domains. Wang et al. [5] proposed a method based on heuristic rules to discover domain-specific accounts by matching real-world authors extracted from the latest domain-specific publications to corresponding Twitter accounts. As shown in Sect. 4, the approach in [2] have very low coverage of target accounts due to the limitation of the seed accounts. The method in [3] is inherently blind towards those scientists who are not listed, and given the threshold of 10 lists, it favors precision over recall, so there is a much larger population of scientists who were not identified in this way. Furthermore, the list-based method skews towards the elite and high profile science communicators. Our paper improves the handcrafted heuristic rules in [5] using an automated machine learning method with significantly higher performance. Both [2] and [5] were only identifying the target set from the initial set of candidates and did not further extend the target set using social network analysis presented in our paper.

3   Mining Domain-Specific Accounts

3.1   Creating an Initial Set of Domain-Specific Accounts

The latest publications reflect the state of art of a specific domain, so they are valuable sources for discovering active domain experts [4]. For better engagement and communication, researchers and scholars are highly likely to provide their real names and professional profiles on social media. If we can match real-world authors extracted from the latest publications to corresponding social media accounts, we can create an initial set of high-quality domain-specific accounts [5]. An author name often matches multiple accounts with the same name [5], and we can identify which account really matches the author using machine learning. Social media user profiles often provide informative signals for identifying correctly matched accounts. For instance, some *domain-specific terms* reflecting research interests, such as "machine learning", "deep learning", "artificial intelligence" and "natural language processing" can often be found in descriptions of many machine learning researchers' profiles, and *occupational terms* such as "professor", "researcher", "PhD student" and "scientist" can also be found in descriptions of their profiles. URLs of personal academic pages are often contained in researchers' profiles and contain useful signals as well. For example,

---

[1] https://support.twitter.com/articles/76460.

we can check if a URL contains academic domains (such as ".edu" or ".ac.uk") and "~". We can further check if its page content contains the featured *domain-specific terms* and *occupational terms*. We also noticed that, even if an account has no description or URL in its profile, sometimes we can still identify the account with high reliability by checking if the featured *domain-specific terms* and *occupational terms* appear in profile descriptions of its following accounts.

Most authors found multiple Twitter accounts with the same names, and many had more than a dozen [5]. Before we can distinguish matched accounts from non-relevant ones, we have to fetch a large of number of candidate accounts with the same names for feature extraction, and classify each candidate one by one. So creating a large initial set using the machine learning method based on matching authors is relatively computationally expensive. All identified accounts in the initial set are owned by persons, who are authors of recent publications. Sometimes a person has an informative account in a domain but does not publish papers recently, and the account will not be found and matched. Some non-personal social media accounts, such as corporate research labs, academic institutions or groups and conferences, are also informative in a domain. To address the above problems, we propose a light-weight and efficient approach, which can start from a relatively small initial set of domain-specific accounts and leverage network connections among these accounts to find more domain-specific accounts including non-personal accounts.

3.2 Extracting More Domain-Specific Accounts Based on Social Networks Analysis

The domain-specific accounts in the initial set identified in Sect. 3.1 can be put into a target set. These accounts followed by the accounts in the target set but not contained in the target set can be put into a candidate set. For each account in the candidate set, we extract its *number of total followers NTF* in the whole social network and its *number of local followers NLF*, which is the number of its followers appearing in the target set. We create a measurement *domain-specificity* defined as NTF/NLF, which can be used to effectively filter out general or non-domain-specific accounts as background noises from the candidate set. As shown in Fig. 1, for a general or non-domain-specific account, such as a celebrity or mainstream media, even its number of local followers appearing in the target set of domain-specific accounts is not small, but the number is only a tiny proportion of its huge number of total followers, so finally the *domain-specificity* is low. Instead, a domain-specific account is more likely to engage and communicate with other accounts in the same domain, so a large proportion of its total followers is also more likely to come from accounts in the target set of domain-specific accounts, and that leads to a high *domain-specificity* .

First, any account with NLF lower than a threshold TH will be removed from the candidate set. Second, we sort the accounts in the candidate set by *domain-specificity* in descending order, and finally keep only the top N accounts in the candidate set. We add the N accounts into the target set. Generally, a larger N extends the target set faster with lower confidence in precision, and a smaller N extends the target set slower with higher confidence in precision. The above process of extending the target set by finding more domain-specific accounts may be repeated with R rounds if necessary. When we get adequate domain-specific accounts in the target set, these accounts can be ranked based on various metrics. For example, we can exploit the links among these accounts and calculate PageRank, or we can leverage the bipartie links between these accounts and contents they created or shared and calculate ranking of the accounts and contents by modeling a mutually reinforcing relationship [5].

4   Experiments

We selected *machine learning* domain for experiments, because it is a rapidly changing domain, in which a lot of new publications and social media contents are generated daily. ICML and NIPS are the two most important annual academic conferences on machine learning, so they are good sources to catch up with the latest progress and find active researchers/authors in the domain. Twitter is a public information channel and suitable for disseminating and discussing academic and research contents, so we selected Twitter for our experiments. We used the Twitter user search API and returned authors finding Twitter accounts with the same names. In order to verify feasibility of finding corresponding Twitter accounts owned by authors, we extracted all authors from the proceedings of ICML2016 and NIPS2015 respectively, and manually checked if each author really owns a Twitter account. As shown in Table 1, near 30% (288/988 and 321/1078) of authors own corresponding Twitter accounts, and quantitatively verified our assumption that social media such as Twitter are widely used in community of researchers with real names. With the data of ICML2016 and NIPS2015, we further analyzed the methods for identifying scientists on Twitter proposed by Hadgu et al. [2] and Ke et al. [3]. Hadgu et al. acquired 92% candidates for identifying target scientists from accounts following conference accounts, but Table 1 showed that only a small proportion (103/288 and 106/321) of the accounts matching conference authors were actually following corresponding official conference accounts, so their method has very low coverage. The list-based method of Ke et al. also can only find a small proportion (80/288 and 86/321) of accounts matching conference authors.

XGBoost[2] has empirically proven to be a highly effective approach to predictive modeling and accumulated an impressive track record of winning a vast array of competitions, so it was selected for identifying accounts matching authors. We used 3 datasets for training/testing in Table 2. Feature extraction was conducted as described in Sect. 3.1. Table 3 showed that, even with small training datasets our machine learning based method can get performance significantly better the method based on heuristic rules used by [5].

---

[2] https://github.com/dmlc/xgboost.

Table 1. Statistics of the authors in ICML2016 and NIPS2015. (NA is the number of authors; NS is the number of authors finding Twitter accounts with the same names; NM is the number of authors having really matched Twitter accounts; $NMFC$ is the number of authors having matched Twitter accounts which followed the corresponding official conference account; $NML1$ is the number of authors having matched Twitter accounts which were contained in at least one Twitter list; $NML10$ is the number of authors having matched Twitter accounts which were contained in at least 10 Twitter lists.)

Conference	Official account	NA	NS	NM	$NMFC$	$NML1$	$NML10$
ICML2016	@icmlconf	988	718	288	103	187	80
NIPS2015	@NipsConference	1078	779	321	106	197	86

Table 2. Training/Testing datasets for identifying accounts matching authors. (The numbers of positive examples are slightly lower than the numbers of matched accounts in Table 1, because some matched accounts identified by human were protected or not accessible. The Arxiv2016 dataset was obtained from the experimental data used in [5].)

Dataset	Positive examples	Negative examples
ICML2016	274	328
NIPS2015	302	325
Arxiv2016	110	129

Table 3. Results of identifying accounts matching authors by XGBoost. (The overlapped positive/negative examples between the training dataset and the testing dataset have been removed from the testing dataset. ICML2016 and NIPS2015 have 67 and 71 overlapped positive and negative examples, respectively. ICML2016 and Arxiv have 9 and 14 overlapped positive and negative examples, respectively. NIPS and Arxiv have 10 and 8 overlapped positive and negative examples, respectively.)

Training data	Testing data	Precision	Recall	F1
ICML2016	NIPS2015	93.42%	90.64%	92.01%
NIPS2015	ICML2016	94.87%	89.81%	92.27%
Arxiv2016	ICML2016	93.83%	86.04%	89.76%
Arxiv2016	NIPS2015	91.01%	86.64%	88.77%
Heuristic Rules [5]		81.16%	77.78%	79.43%

We merged the positive examples from ICML2016, NIPS2015 and Arxiv2016 datasets and obtained 634 unique domain-specific accounts, which were used to initialize the target set. The method of social network analysis illustrated in

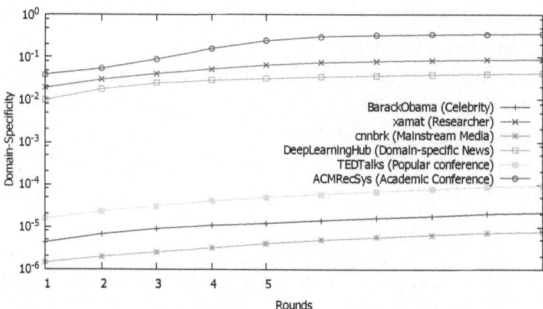

Fig. 1. Real examples of non-domain-specific and domain-specific accounts can be clearly divided by their *domain-specificity* (NLF/NTF) measurements, which are always in different orders of magnitude in each round. $(TH = 5, N = 1000, R = 10)$

Sect. 3.2 was used to find more domain-specific accounts of various types and extend the target set. Each account in the candidate set should have at least TH followers, and the top N accounts with the highest *domain-specificity* in the candidate set will be added into the target set. The process of extending the target set can be repeated for R rounds. Figure 1 showed that NLF/NTF is an effective *domain-specificity* measurement for filtering out the popular non-domain-specific accounts but keeping the domain-specific accounts.

We merged ICML2016, NIPS2015 and Arxiv2016 datasets into one training dataset and trained a new predictive model for checking if the accounts newly added into the target set in each round are relevant to the domain, and Fig. 2 showed that the relevant percentage is still stable even after multiple rounds. The results demonstrated that our method of finding new domain-specific accounts are really robust and efficient. We sorted 10634 accounts obtained in 10 rounds and listed top 15 accounts by PageRank in Table 4, and also listed some top accounts of different types in Table 5.

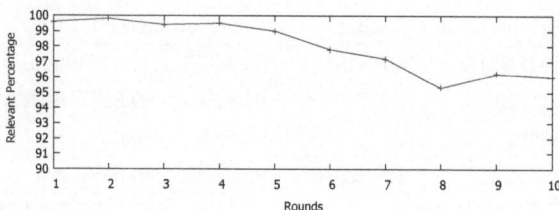

Fig. 2. Relevant Percentage of the accounts newly added into the target set in each round. $(TH = 5, N = 1000, R = 10)$

Table 4. Top 15 Accounts sorted by PageRank. ($TH = 5$, $N = 1000$, $R = 10$)

Name	Account	PageRank	NLF	NTF	NLF/NTF
Yann LeCun	@ylecun	4.72×10^{-3}	2852	46.6 K	6.13×10^{-2}
Andrew Ng	@AndrewYNg	4.15×10^{-3}	3310	124 K	2.68×10^{-2}
Andrej Karpathy	@karpathy	3.25×10^{-3}	2528	51.1 K	4.95×10^{-2}
Nando de Freitas	@NandoDF	3.20×10^{-3}	2046	23.7 K	8.64×10^{-2}
Stanford NLP Group	@stanfordnlp	2.97×10^{-3}	2369	30.8 K	7.69×10^{-2}
DeepMind	@DeepMindAI	2.81×10^{-3}	1973	65.1 K	3.03×10^{-2}
Fei-Fei Li	@drfeifei	2.79×10^{-3}	1984	53.4 K	3.71×10^{-2}
NIPS	@NipsConference	2.55×10^{-3}	1764	9682	1.82×10^{-1}
Demis Hassabis	@demishassabis	2.45×10^{-3}	1800	63 K	2.86×10^{-2}
Jure Leskovec	@jure	2.41×10^{-3}	1744	18.6 K	9.39×10^{-2}
Hugo Larochelle	@hugo_larochelle	2.34×10^{-3}	1789	21.2 K	8.46×10^{-2}
Hal Daume III	@haldaume3	2.23×10^{-3}	1763	8476	2.08×10^{-1}
Oren Etzioni	@etzioni	2.16×10^{-3}	1052	8661	1.21×10^{-1}
Alex Smola	@smolix	2.15×10^{-3}	1607	8668	1.85×10^{-1}
Fernando Pereira	@earnmyturns	2.12×10^{-3}	1404	7835	1.79×10^{-1}

Table 5. Real examples of some top accounts of different types.

Type	Examples
Corporate	@DeepMindAI, @allenai_org, @MSFTResearch, @GoogleBrain
Academic	@stanfordnlp, @MIT_CSAIL, @uwcse_ai, @NYUDataScience
Conferences	@NipsConference, @icmlconf, @kdd_news, @CVPR
News	@mxlearn, @DeepLearningHub, @TlkngMchns, @arxiv_cs_cl
Software	@tensorflow, @TorchML, @PyTorch, @scikit_learn

5 Conclusion

This paper proposes a framework for mining domain-specific accounts and relevant scientific contents from social media, and a real system has been implemented for identifying informative Twitter accounts and filtering and aggregating valuable up-to-date contents in the machine learning domain. The experiments on real data have demonstrated its feasibility and effectiveness compared with previous work.

References

1. Coleman, V.: Social media as a primary source: a coming of age. EDUCAUSE Rev. **48**(6), 60–61 (2013)
2. Hadgu, A.T., Jäschke, R.: Identifying and analyzing researchers on twitter. In: Proceedings of the 2014 ACM Conference on Web Science, WebSci 2014, pp. 23–32. ACM, New York (2014). http://doi.acm.org/10.1145/2615569.2615676
3. Ke, Q., Ahn, Y.Y., Sugimoto, C.R.: A systematic identification and analysis of scientists on twitter. PLoS ONE **12**(4), e0175368 (2017)
4. Wang, J., Xiang, J., Uchino, K.: Topic-specific recommendation for open education resources. In: Li, F.W.B., Klamma, R., Laanpere, M., Zhang, J., Manjón, B.F., Lau, R.W.H. (eds.) ICWL 2015. LNCS, vol. 9412, pp. 71–81. Springer, Cham (2015). doi:10.1007/978-3-319-25515-6_7
5. Wang, J., Xiang, J., Uchino, K.: Domain-specific recommendation by matching real authors to social media users. In: Chiu, D.K.W., Marenzi, I., Nanni, U., Spaniol, M., Temperini, M. (eds.) ICWL 2016. LNCS, vol. 10013, pp. 246–252. Springer, Cham (2016). doi:10.1007/978-3-319-47440-3_27

Constructing a Usability Guidelines List for Educational Social Networks

Gerti Pishtari[1(✉)] and Gilberto Lacerda Santos[2]

[1] Tallinn University, Tallinn, Estonia
gerti.pishtari@tlu.ee
[2] University of Brasilia, Brasilia, Brazil
glacerda@unb.br

Abstract. Social Networks are playing an important role in Education. However, many existing ones lack on ergonomics, which directly affects their potential as learning platforms. For this reason, pedagogical usability is of central importance during the development, as well as in the process of maintenance of educational social applications. As a consequence of incomplete and uneasy to use checklists for similar applications, as well as the nonexistence of usability guidelines for social networks as educational environments, this paper presents the first steps of a new usability guideline list. Feedback from the validation show that our guidelines are perceived as well constructed by experts.

Keywords: Usability guidelines · Educational social networks · Usability evaluation · MapLango

1 Introduction

With the explosion of digital technologies, we have been witnessing drastic changes in almost every aspect of our society. Education, doesn't make the exception! One particular consequence of this process is that education today extends beyond classrooms. Social networks are an example of these technologies. They represent today the typical environment that allows interactions with a large number of people and communities, encourage collaboration and discussion, meanwhile promoting direct sharing and manipulation of written, audio, and visual content [22]. With the reorganization of knowledge acquisition, these technologies are transforming basic patterns of knowledge and of communication interchange in society, as well as what knowledge means [16]. At the same time, the importance that social networks are gaining in education is underlined by many studies. Based on the 2010 data from the EDUCAUSE Center more than 90% of students that were interviewed responded that they use social services, such as Facebook, Twitter, or LinkedIn [25] Ito et al., while discussing their pedagogical value, suggest that youth's participation in this network means a new way of thinking about the role of education [15]. While reflecting over these data, it is inevitable not to consider social networks as important factors in today's learning processes. Even though there are many studies that treat the utilization of social networks in learning activities [4, 7, 21], there is no literature regarding usability criteria, about this specific context.

© Springer International Publishing AG 2017
H. Xie et al. (Eds.): ICWL 2017, LNCS 10473, pp. 119–122, 2017.
DOI: 10.1007/978-3-319-66733-1_13

When considering an evaluation, the challenge is to decide what to evaluate, who is going to do it and when it will take place [8]. Responding to the first one, a usability evaluation of an application in an educational context include two aspects, cognitive and technical. Cognitive aspects have to do with pedagogical strategies of the specific social environment, while technical ones refer to usability, or the quality of human-machine interactions, as well as design characteristics. It should be emphasized that the lack of such guidelines affects two main groups. The developers, during the overall software lifecycle process. Starting from the conception, where their ideas should fit with a targeted group, up to the creation of prototypes, maintenance and upgrade processes. The other group concerned are activity designers at the moment that they need to choose a specific environment for different pedagogical and learning activities.

Considering this context, while constructing a guideline list to evaluate the usability of a social network in an education context, existing recommendations, that are related with the topic should be classified and analyzed. Other missing characteristics should be added by analyzing social networks in general, as well as the ones designed for educational purposes. All of these, must be filtered by considering and having as a reference a chosen theoretical framework, based on specific literature and learning theories.

2   Exploratory Stage

To build up our instrument, the methodology that we selected was anasynthesis. Developed by Legendre [23], and later adapted by Silvern [17], it consists in a cycle of four basic steps: analysis, synthesis, prototype, and simulation that lead to the production of an instrument.

The first step was to analyze all the sources that were considered as relevant. Later, a systematic process of synthesis followed, until obtaining the final list of criteria. The literature that was considered was organized into three groups, learning theories, ergonomics, and social networks.

Our list is mainly developed having in mind constructivist and connectivist points of view. The second is proposed as a theory that describes better our digital age, where action is needed without personal learning and where information derives outside of our primary knowledge [2]. Several sources of guidelines [6, 9, 20, 24] and existing learning models [19] were considered. All the criteria that derived from these guidelines were classified and crosschecked. In general, criteria such as interactions, development of autonomy, problem solving situations, feedback and engagement were considered as important.

Ergonomics were especially considered related with educational software, usability and cognitive processes. Two different sources were treated: (a) international standards directly related with the topic [10–14]; (b) important authors in the field of ergonomics [1, 3, 5, 22]. The same procedure of crosschecking guideline lists was repeated, as in the case of learning theories. Regarding Ergonomics, the most important elements that were identified are: functionality, accessibility, ease of use, clear defined goals, security and content organization.

There is a lack of literature regarding the ergonomics of social networks as learning environments. Due to this fact, we analyzed several existing social networks categorized as: common, professional, academic and educational. The goal was to recognize and compare important features, from which we could enrich further our list of criteria. From the process of synthesis of all the information gathered, we were able to come up with a first prototype. All the criteria are gathered into seven groups: general considerations, design process and maintenance, pedagogical guidelines, appearance, functionality, social network elements, security.

3 Preliminary Results and Future Work

To validate the content of our guidelines we are using a quantitative approach, the modified model of Lawshe [26]. Six experts are participating in this procedure. Two experts in technology enhanced learning, two experts in development, and two in human computer interactions. For each item, every expert had to choose between the levels of importance defined by the model. From the preliminary results the overall body of the guidelines is accepted with a $CVI = 0.82 > 0.58$. The experts were also asked to answer 3 questions. Are there important aspects that were not included in the list? Do you consider the instrument useful to support the usability evaluations of Educational Social Networks? Are there guidelines that you consider that are missing?

The process will continue through several cycles based on the feedback given by the experts regarding missing guidelines and modifications that are necessary for existing ones. After the validation of content, we plan apply the evaluation of MapLango, which is a social network based on geo-localization that helps users to learn French [18]. Our guidelines can be transformed into a checklist and experts will have to go through it to identify specific problems. At the end of this procedure a semi-structured interview will give more feedback about the effectiveness and understandability of the guidelines.

4 Conclusion

This paper introduces the preliminary results about the process formulating a usability guidelines list for educational social networks. Results from the validation of content through the modified model of Lawshe show that the list is being perceived as well constructed and useful by experts. Despite positive feedback from experts, there are many issues regarding specific guidelines that are being considered through the multiple cycles of validation.

Regarding future works, the guidelines will be used to evaluate educational social networks that are still in development. This could bring more evidence of the efficiency of our list compared to other lists of criteria.

References

1. Ahlstrom, V., Longo, K., Truitt, T.: Human Factors Design Guide Update (Report Number DOT/FAA/CT-96/01): A Revision to Chap. 5–Automation Guidelines (No. DOT/FAA/CT02/XX) (2001)

2. AlDahdouh, A.A., Osório, A.J., Caires, S.: Understanding knowledge network, learning and connectivism. Int. J. Instr. Technol. Distance Learn. **12**(10), 3–21 (2015)
3. Bailey, R.W., Barnum, C., Bosley, J., Chaparro, B., Dumas, J., Ivory, M.Y., John, B., Miller-Jacobs, H., Koyani, S.J.: Research-Based Web Design & Usability Guidelines. US Department of Health and Human Services, Washington, DC (2006)
4. Beer, D., Burrows, R.: Sociology and of and in Web 2.0: Some initial considerations. Sociol. Res. Online **12**(5), 17 (2007)
5. Bevan, N., Kincla, S.: HCI Design Foundation Study Final Report (2004)
6. Calvani, A.: Rete, comunità e conoscenza: costruire e gestire dinamiche collaborative. Edizioni Erickson (2005)
7. Carlson, S.: The net generation goes to college. Chronicle High. Educ. **52**(7), A34 (2005)
8. Heller, R.S.: Evaluating software: a review of the options. Comput. Educ. **17**(4), 285–291 (1991)
9. Honebein, P.C.: Seven goals for the design of constructivist learning environments. In: Constructivist Learning Environments: Case Studies in Instructional Design, pp. 11–24 (1996)
10. ISO 13407: Human-centred design processes for interactive systems (1999)
11. ISO 14915: Software ergonomics for multimedia user interfaces (2002)
12. ISO 16982: Ergonomics of human-system interaction - Usability methods supporting human-centred design (2002)
13. ISO 19796: Information technology - Learning, education and training - Quality management, assurance and metrics (2005)
14. ISO/IEC 25040: Systems and software engineering - Systems and software Quality Requirements and Evaluation (SQuaRE) - Evaluation process (2011)
15. Ito, M., Horst, H.A., Bittanti, M., Stephenson, B.H., Lange, P.G., Pascoe, C.J., Martínez, K.Z.: Living and Learning with New Media: Summary of Findings from the Digital Youth Project. MIT Press, Cambridge (2009)
16. Lave, J., Wenger, E.: Situated Learning: Legitimate Peripheral Participation. Cambridge University Press, Cambridge (1991)
17. Legendre, R.: Dictionnaire actuel de l'éducation. Editions Guérin Eska, Montréal (2005)
18. Petit, T., Santos, G.L.: Aplicativo MapLango: design de uma rede digital educacional para a aprendizagem nômade de línguas. Lang. Learn., p. 2 (2013)
19. Pettenati, M.C., Cigognini, M.E.: Social networking theories and tools to support connectivist learning activities. Int. J. Web-Based Learn. Teach. Technol. (IJWLTT) **2**(3), 42–60 (2007)
20. Ranieri, M., Fadini, U.: Formazione e cyberspazio: divari e opportunità nel mondo della rete. ETS (2006)
21. Rosen, D., Nelson, C.: Web 2.0: a new generation of learners and education. Comput. Sch. **25**(3–4), 211–225 (2008)
22. Scapin, D.L., Bastien, J.C.: Ergonomic criteria for evaluating the ergonomic quality of interactive systems. Behav. Inform. Technol. **16**(4–5), 220–231 (1997)
23. Silvern, L.C.: Anasynthesis revisited: systems engineering in a time of educational lethargy. Educ. Technol. **20**(1), 40–46 (1980)
24. Siemens, G.: Knowing knowledge (2006). http://www.lulu.com/, ISBN 978-1-4303-0230-8
25. Smith, S.D., Caruso, J.B.: The ECAR study of undergraduate students and information technology, p. 118. Educause, Colorado (2010)
26. Tristán-López, A.: Modificación al modelo de Lawshe para el dictamen cuantitativo de la validez de contenido de un instrumento objetivo. Avances en medición **6**(1), 37–48 (2008)

Assessment and Accessibility
in Higher Education

Code Review in Computer Science Courses: Take One

Zuzana Kubincová[(⊠)] and Martin Homola

Comenius University in Bratislava, Mlynská dolina,
842 48 Bratislava, Slovakia
{kubincova,homola}@fmph.uniba.sk

Abstract. Code review is an important tool regularly employed in information systems development practice. In this preliminary study we tested employment of code reviewing in educational setting in two Computer Science university-level courses: (a) in the first course we collected code reviews using an existing Learning Management System (LMS) that we regularly use to administer peer reviews; (b) in the other one we collected them using GitLab, an industrial strength source code management system. We compare results obtained from both experiments. Compared to our existing LMS, GitLab is readily equipped with more elaborate features for reviewing, commenting, and discussing code submitted by others, and the process is similar to industrial practice. However, as we also learned, the code reviewing workflow in GitLab is too open, which may be limiting in educational practice (e.g., the comments are immediately visible to everyone, hence it may happen that very active students leave little space for the remaining reviewers). This shows interesting directions for future research: one, to develop specific code-reviewing tool tailored to educational practice; but also to come up with novel methodologies which would enable to use real industrial tools while overcoming the issues pointed out in our study.

Keywords: Code review · Peer review · Education · Tools

1 Introduction

Code review is an activity when a computer program code is reviewed by peers with the aim to find and fix its defects and thus improve the program quality. During this activity a reviewer reads the code (without compiling or executing it) and tries to understand its behavior and to detect and correct its defects by herself [2,16]. This activity is essential especially in development large software applications since it can reveal 50–70% of defects [20]. To improve the process of code reviewing as well as its results new methods are continuously developed and studied [8,16]. There is also research dealing with the influence of the personality on the person's performance on a code reviewer task [4,5]. However, as pointed out in the study of Bacchelli and Bird [1], nowadays, code reviewing is less formal and less strict than e.g. 30 years ago: "The reviews are less about defects and

H. Xie et al. (Eds.): ICWL 2017, LNCS 10473, pp. 125–135, 2017.
DOI: 10.1007/978-3-319-66733-1_14

instead provide additional benefits such as knowledge transfer, increased team awareness, and creation of alternative solutions to problems."

As already found out by researchers [11,18] code review can serve as an activity suitable for educational purposes, where it can have various benefits on the learners. The other argument for employment of code review in our teaching practice, is that since it is widely viewed as a well-established best practice in software engineering, graduates of computer science, software engineering, and related university programs should gain experience in this area, and should be equipped with basic code reviewing skills.

In this paper, we report on a preliminary qualitative study, that we conducted in order to prepare a wider application of code review in our university Applied Informatics curriculum. In the study we have focused on programming project assignments that students develop independently, and we have evaluated two systems to deliver the code reviews: our own previously developed LMS system with basic peer review capabilities [15]; and Gitlab, a widely used open-source code management platform with good code review capabilities.

The aims of our preliminary study were: (a) to test and evaluate both systems for code-reviewing associated with a real programming project assignment; (b) to better understand the requirements for delivering code reviews in educational settings, and to help us decide whether we want to continue using our own LMS system (with necessary enhancements) or it is better to switch to an established code-review platform with code-review features such as Gitlab or Github; (c) to evaluate also students' and teachers' perception and acceptance of the code reviewing activity.

Our small sample of students, and the teachers involved in our experiments, perceived the activity positively, which encourages us to employ code-reviews more widely in our educational practice. Our evaluation of the systems shows, that while many useful features are offered by Gitlab, some requirements inherent to educational setting are not so easily met. We therefore plan to improve our own LMS system in the future, extending it with selected code-reviewing features.

2   Related Work

There are many possible ways how to integrate code reviewing into educational activities. Trytten [13] has developed a new design of code review activity for her introductory programming course. This activity comprised individual as well as team code reviews. Students who were divided into small groups performed the code review activity in three phases: at first individually, then within their group and afterwards also between groups. All of them reviewed the same code and answered a set of questions prepared by teachers. The activity ended in a whole-class discussion about the answers. Code reviewing was accepted by students quite positively. They gained some experience in reading code, have seen alternative designs for their own code and have learned about the necessity of well-developed communication skills in teamwork. Hundhausen et al. adapted the formal code review process for use in computer science courses and implemented 'pedagogical code review' [9]. Students in groups of 3–4 people were assigned roles of author, reader, inspector and recorder and in several rounds (according to the number of group members) read each other's program code, evaluated it against a predefined list of best coding practices, discussed all found issues and recorded them. All these steps were performed under the supervision of an experienced moderator. An analysis of this activity confirmed its positive influence on the improvement of the students' code quality, stimulation of more sophisticated discussions about programming issues and practices and raise of the sense of community. There are also studies reporting the effort of the researchers to refine the definitions of roles and documents related to peer reviewing process with the aim to standardize the process and also the research in code review area and to simplify the communication among the researchers in this field [19].

Additionally, activities of this kind can also make a contribution to the student's final grade in the course. Wang et al. used this approach in two different programming courses for freshmen using an online assessment system EduPCR developed directly for this purpose. As they presented in their report [18], they observed significant improvements of student learning in various aspects, such as student programming skills, collaborative learning competence, compliance with coding standards, time management capability and competence of giving and accepting criticism. Li [10] also used marks assigned to students by their peers during code review process in final grading, although he did not employ any supportive tool for code review. Similarly to the previous study he concluded that this activity motivated students to learn coding standards and facilitated the communication among them.

GitLab and GitHub are web-based source code management services usually used in software development. Although they are starting to emerge as collaborative platforms for education [3,6,7,17,21], studies introducing educational use of these services are not focused on code reviewing. On the other hand, several studies can be found in the literature, presenting new tools developed to facilitate the employment of code review in educational settings [12,18,22]. Since these tools are usually not available, we used GitLab and our own LMS with basic peer review functionality in our courses.

3 Experiments

To evaluate the potential of code review in computer science university courses, we conducted two preliminary experiments. Each experiment was with a different course at a different study level, and also used a different platform to administer the code review process.

3.1 Experiment 1: Undergraduate Course

The first course was an optional undergraduate-level (Bachelor) course on NoSQL database systems. There were 10 students enrolled, who took part in a practical project assignment, which was individual. The task was to implement an application on top of a non-relational database. The actual choice of the application and the database was free. While the project assignment was compulsory to pass the course, the code-review part was not (however, students who did not participate in this part were penalized by one level of overall grading for the course). All 10 students submitted the project, but only 7 participated in reviewing.

The students used the Gitlab platform to create a git repository, and to share it with their colleagues for code-review and comments. We followed the methodology similar to those mentioned in our previous works [14,15] where after the first initial deadline the students were assigned to review each other's work (2 reviewers per project, randomly assigned). They were given 10 days for review and 7 additional days to process the feedback. Then they submitted a new version for teacher's evaluation. This makes the review process immediately useful for the students, and, in case of code reviews it also simulates the real world application of this type of reviewing to some extent.

The choice of the Gitlab platform had some influence on the review process: the reviewing was not blind in any sense – the reviewers knew the identity of the code author and vice versa. Also, the comments appeared in the system at the moment they were submitted and were immediately visible to the author but also to the other reviewers (even if they did not submit their comments yet).

The students were given predefined criteria on which to focus their reviews: (a) choice of database system for the problem, (b) suitable database model, (c) optimal usage of the database system and its API, (e) code structure, modularity, and quality, (f) code organization and comments.

Gitlab permits to add comments to every line of code (of the merge request created by the students during submission) and in addition to add an overall comment at the bottom. The students were instructed to comment the lines of code as much as possible when useful, and to write the rest to the overall comment.

3.2 Experiment 2: Master's Course

The second course was an optional Master's course on Web programming. There were 34 students enrolled. In our experiment we focused on a project assignment which was one of the activities in the course. The goal of the project was to implement a web application – an educational game. Students had to choose the game topic from a list provided by the teacher.

The project assignment was not compulsory, and did not contribute to the evaluation. It was part of a set of alternate assignments students could undertake in order to qualify to the exam. In the end, 11 submissions were delivered, 7 from 2-member teams, and 4 by individuals.

Submissions, and code reviews administration were handled by our own LMS system. Students had 3 weeks to develop and submit the project. Consequently, each submission author (a team or an individual) was randomly assigned 3 other submissions for the code review. Since this code review activity was not evaluated by the teacher, it was entirely voluntary. Students were encouraged to participate to help their colleagues to better understand the shortcomings of their projects. In the end the authors of 6 submissions took part in it.

Our LMS was designed based on our own requirements and was built from-scratch. In addition to common usage as LMS, it has been used to administer peer review based activities so far. It does not offer all functionalities usually employed for code reviewing however, it is equipped with configurable peer-review forms. The reviewers downloaded the submissions assigned for review, examined the code and afterwards they filled in the reviewing form prepared by the teacher. The form consisted of 10 questions corresponding to the same criteria, used in evaluation by the teacher. The criteria focused especially on required features and capabilities, employment of required technology, difficulty and technical quality of the implementation, and code documentation.

The students rated each criterion by 1–5 points and also by verbal justification of their rating. The reviewing process was blind – each reviewer was aware of the project author, but the authors did not know who reviewed their project.

As mentioned above, the system we used was not originally developed for code reviewing, thus it misses some functionality useful for this activity. However, it features other supportive functions that are helpful when working in teams, e.g., team formation, random assignment of projects for code reviewing, or peer reviewing of the team-mates' contribution to the join work. Also, some of them were even familiar with the system as they used it before in other courses.

4 Results

4.1 Participation in the Activity

In the first experiment, 10 students delivered the submissions, and 7 of them submitted it in time in order to get reviewers assigned. Each was assigned 2 reviewers, and received on average 16.43 comments from both reviewers combined. The students also responded to these comments averaging 6.43 replies per students (while 3 students did not respond at all).

In the second experiment the assignment was a team one. Here, 11 teams delivered the submission. Each team was assigned 3 other assignments to review. Only 6 teams participated in the reviews, 5 of them filled in all three assigned reviews and the remaining team missed out on one review. There was no way how to reply, but it was possible rate the review. Only 5 reviews were rated altogether, i.e., on average only 0.84 reviews were rated out of the 3 assigned to each submission.

We can see that a lower percentage of students participated in the feedback phase in the second experiment. Partly this could be because of the lengthy structured review form they had to complete at once, but this observation is not highly conclusive, due to large differences in the settings of the two experiments and also between the student groups.

4.2 Students' View

After the experiment, we conducted a survey focused on students perception of code review activity. Students from both courses were asked to fill in a questionnaire consisted from 15–18 questions. The core of both questionnaires was the same, however some questions were different according to the scenario used in code review process in a particular course.

The aim of the survey was to get insight into the opinions and attitudes of the students both towards the code reviewing activity and towards the different tools that we tested. The questionnaire was delivered online, and 4 students from each course responded to it.

Several questions of the questionnaire concentrated on the students' perception of the usefulness of the activity: students were asked how they profited from comments received from their peers but also from commenting the program code of the others. Students in both groups mostly appreciated that the received feedback helped them to detect shortcomings of their project they have not noticed before submitting (Fig. 1). When asked if reviewing the code submitted by others was somehow useful, they predominantly indicated the answers "It was useful to realize a variety of errors occurring in computer programs," and "It was useful to gain experience in code reviewing" (Fig. 2). They largely concluded that this skill will be useful in their future job (more so, the group that used Gitlab), as depicted in Fig. 3.

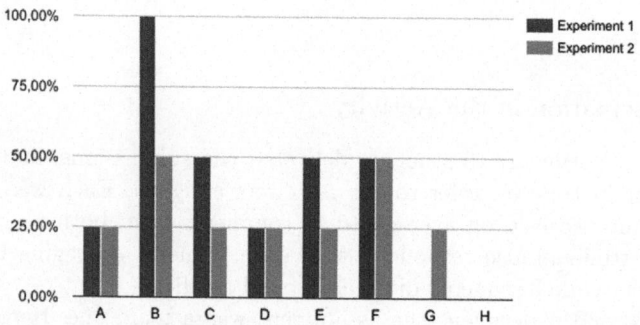

Fig. 1. What was the benefit of the comments you received from your colleagues? A – It helped me better understand the assignment of the project; B – It helped me to fix the shortcomings I did not notice before submitting; C – I learned how to review the code; D – It helped to improve my programming skills; E – I learned to accept constructive criticism; F – I learned to learn in cooperation with others; G – Nothing; H – Else.

We also tried to find out the students' opinion about what kind of feedback they received, as well as about the code review process in general. We asked if the feedback was more on the fundamental issues or minor improvements in programming and code standards. The students from Experiment 1 leaned slightly towards the latter, while those of Experiment 2 leaned more towards the former (Fig. 4).

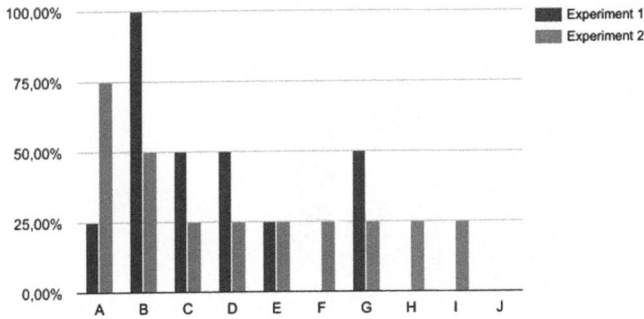

Fig. 2. What benefits you gained by commenting on colleagues' projects? A – I gained experience with code reviewing; B – I realized a variety of errors occuring in the program code; C – When looking at my colleagues' projects, I realized the shortcomings in my project; D – I improved my programming skills; E – I improved my communication skills; F – I learned to learn in cooperation with others; G – I learned to give constructive criticism; H – I earned extra points; I – I have never commented on projects; J – Else.

(a) Experiment 1.   (b) Experiment 2.

Fig. 3. Do you think that the experience you gained in assessing the work of others will be useful for you in future programming practice? A – Certainly yes; B – Rather yes; C – Rather yes; D – Certainly no.

Both groups agreed on that the received comments were mostly sufficiently specified. Regarding the form of feedback they would prefer to receive, the opinions of students differed according to the group they belong to. While the students of Experiment 1 stressed the importance of commenting particular lines of the program and giving the feedback also in the form of the corrected program code; the students of Experiment 2 indicated that it is enough to assess the project as a whole and it is sufficient to point out the defects. We observe that the preference of particular workflow matches the one which the students experienced in the experiment. This is quite natural to expect since they did not have a chance to try the other workflow. In the future it would be interesting to compare these two workflows more thoroughly.

The commenting in Experiment 1 was non-anonymous (this is inherent to Gitlab and similar tools), while the reviewing in Experiment 2 was blind. Both groups were mostly neutral to this setting, it did not bother anybody. Both group expressed their preference towards randomly selected reviewers. The students in

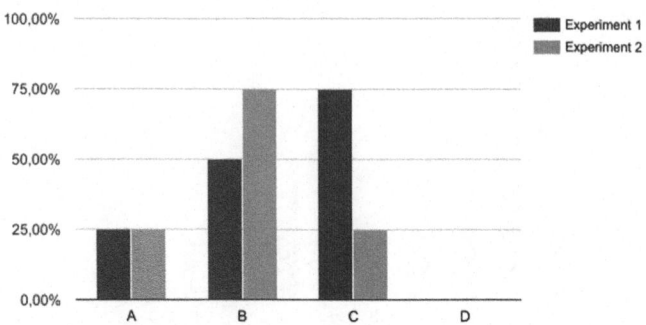

Fig. 4. What kind of feedback did you get? A – Fundamental to the proposal; B – Fundamental to the implementation; C – How to improve the code; D – I have not received any comments.

Experiment 1 were able to reply to the comments, which some found beneficial. As mentioned above, in Experiment 2 there was no such option.

When asked about their experience with the provided system that supported the activity, the Gitlab system in Experiment 1 was viewed as non-problematic, while our own LMS system in Experiment 2 was reported to have some navigation issues (difficulty to find the reviews).

As for the evaluation of the whole code review activity, the students perceived it positively, even very positively in Experiment 1. This difference may be related to the different scenarios, e.g., the possibility to improve the project according to comments available only in Experiment 1, but also perhaps to the fact that the students in Experiment 1 were more satisfied with the provided tool.

4.3   Teacher's View

We also conducted an interview with the teachers responsible for both courses. The scope of the interview was broader, however we summarize the observations related to their perception of the activity and its usefulness.

In general, the teachers were aware of the code review feedback, and they also perceived its usefulness to certain degree. Their impression was that most of the feedback was on minor coding issues, however, there were notable exceptions. One such exception was when in Experiment 1, i.e., the database course, the students we able to communicate via comments the fact that the data model details, which were not submitted with the code of the submission is in fact needed for evaluation. Some of the students were even able to agree on passing additional files via comments which improved their reviewing experience as well as their feedback on the submission. This indicates that the discussion between the submission's author and the reviewers may be very useful.

Students also reflected on the other projects they reviewed during assessment. It happened that some of them felt the other projects were better then their own, they suggested they should be graded lower.

Another observation was on the commenting workflow inherent to Gitlab (Experiment 1), where the comments are immediately accessible to everyone as soon as they are posted. This may cause problems when there were 2 or more reviewers assigned on a submission, and one of them overly active and quickly comments on most issues. The other reviewers may find that they have nothing to add. Such a problem does not appear in our own LMS, where the reviews are only visible once the deadline for reviewing expires.

5   Conclusions

In this study we tried two distinct supportive tools for implementing a code-review activity in university courses: our own LMS system with peer-review functionality, and Gitlab code management system. Regarding our aim (a) to test and evaluate both systems we conclude that, feature-wise, Gitlab and similar environments may offer a number of useful features for code review administration, and their workflow, which are not part of basic LMS system. But on the other hand these code management platforms lack other features which make their administration in the educational setting easier for the teachers: e.g., submissions overview, randomized reviewer assignment, postponed review delivery based on a deadline, anonymization, etc. Students working with Gitlab and similar systems also need some basic experience, and face some "industrial" overhead like working with git repository, creating merge requests, etc.

This experience also helped us with our aim (b) to better understand the requirements for delivering code-review activities in educational settings. While some of these requirements are met by Gitlab, some other important requirements related to anonymisation, and postponing review delivery until all students submit their comments cannot be achieved easily in such systems. This suggests the idea to extend our existing LMS system with advanced code-reviewing features such as commenting upon arbitrary line of code, etc., while keeping the new features in line with these requirements.

In regard to our aim (c) to evaluate students' and teachers' perception and acceptance of the activity, we may conclude that the activity was useful, and it was viewed predominantly positively by our small sample of surveyed students, and also by the teachers. This encourages us to extent our study in the future, to a larger, statistically significant sample.

Acknowledgments. The authors would like to thank to Roman Hrušecký, Ján Kľuka, Alexander Šimko, and Jozef Šiška – the lecturers who cooperated on this study.

References

1. Bacchelli, A., Bird, C.: Expectations, outcomes, and challenges of modern code review. In: Proceedings of the 2013 International Conference on Software Engineering, pp. 712–721. IEEE Press (2013)
2. Boehm, B.W., et al.: Software Engineering Economics, vol. 197. Prentice-Hall, Englewood Cliffs (1981)

3. Bonakdarian, E.: Pushing Git & GitHub in undergraduate computer science classes. J. Comput. Sci. Coll. **32**(3), 119–125 (2017)
4. Da Cunha, A.D., Greathead, D.: Code review and personality: is performance linked to MBTI type? Technical report CS-TR-837, University of Newcastle upon Tyne (2004)
5. Da Cunha, A.D., Greathead, D.: Does personality matter? An analysis of code-review ability. Commun. ACM **50**(5), 109–112 (2007)
6. Feliciano, J.: Towards a collaborative learning platform: the use of GitHub in computer science and software engineering courses. Ph.D. thesis, University of Victoria (2015)
7. Feliciano, J., Storey, M.A., Zagalsky, A.: Student experiences using GitHub in software engineering courses: a case study. In: Proceedings of the 38th International Conference on Software Engineering Companion, pp. 422–431. ACM (2016)
8. Höst, M., Johansson, C.: Evaluation of code review methods through interviews and experimentation. J. Syst. Softw. **52**(2), 113–120 (2000)
9. Hundhausen, C., Agrawal, A., Fairbrother, D., Trevisan, M.: Integrating pedagogical code reviews into a CS 1 course: an empirical study. ACM SIGCSE Bull. **41**(1), 291–295 (2009)
10. Li, X.: Incorporating a code review process into the assessment. In: 20th Annual Conference of the National Advisory Committee on Computing Qualifications (NACCQ), Hamilton, pp. 125–131 (2007)
11. Li, X., Prasad, C.: Effectively teaching coding standards in programming. In: Proceedings of the 6th Conference on Information Technology Education, pp. 239–244. ACM (2005)
12. Tang, M.: Caesar: a social code review tool for programming education. Ph.D. thesis, Massachusetts Institute of Technology (2011)
13. Trytten, D.A.: A design for team peer code review. ACM SIGCSE Bull. **37**(1), 455–459 (2005)
14. Homola, M., Kubincová, Z., Culík, J., Trungel, T.: Peer review support in a virtual learning environment. In: State-of-the-Art and Future Directions of Smart Learning, pp. 351–355. Springer (2016)
15. Dropcová, V., Homola, M., Kubincová, Z.: Students' acceptance of peer review. In: Vincenti, G., Bucciero, A., de Carvalho, C.V. (eds.) eLEOT 2015. LNICST, vol. 160, pp. 52–59. Springer, Cham (2015). doi:10.1007/978-3-319-28883-3
16. Uwano, H., Nakamura, M., Monden, A., Matsumoto, K.: Analyzing individual performance of source code review using reviewers' eye movement. In: Proceedings of the 2006 Symposium on Eye Tracking Research & Applications, pp. 133–140. ACM (2006)
17. Villarrubia, A., Kim, H.: Building a community system to teach collaborative software development. In: 2015 10th International Conference on Computer Science & Education (ICCSE), pp. 829–833. IEEE (2015)
18. Wang, Y., Li, H., Feng, Y., Jiang, Y., Liu, Y.: Assessment of programming language learning based on peer code review model: implementation and experience report. Comput. Educ. **59**(2), 412–422 (2012)
19. Wang, Y., Yijun, L., Collins, M., Liu, P.: Process improvement of peer code review and behavior analysis of its participants. ACM SIGCSE Bull. **40**(1), 107–111 (2008)
20. Wiegers, K.E.: Peer Reviews in Software: A Practical Guide. Addison-Wesley, Boston (2002)

21. Zagalsky, A., Feliciano, J., Storey, M.A., Zhao, Y., Wang, W.: The emergence of GitHub as a collaborative platform for education. In: Proceedings of the 18th ACM Conference on Computer Supported Cooperative Work & Social Computing, pp. 1906–1917. ACM (2015)
22. Zeller, A.: Making students read and review code. ACM SIGCSE Bull. **32**(3), 89–92 (2000)

Revisiting Assertion-Reason Question Format: Case of Information Security Course

A. Kayode Adesemowo[(✉)] [iD] and Mxolisi Mtshabe [iD]

School of ICT, Nelson Mandela University, Port Elizabeth, South Africa
kadesemowo@iee.org, s218208960@live.nmmu.ac.za

Abstract. Technology enhanced learning is shaping the face of teaching and learning in innovative way more than ever before. A number of higher education institutions, especially in sub-Sahara Africa are fast-tracking the adoption of blended learning with renewed focus on web-based learning. The pressure on lecturers/faculties to deliver keeps increasing. In the area of assessment, multiple-choice-questions have hold sway and are de-facto where psychometric and validity is of the essence. Assertion-reason questions types, the higher-order variant of multiple choice questions, have not received the same level of adoption and scrutiny. This paper by revisiting Williams (2006) contributes to discourse on assertion-reason questions types. It contributes to the body of knowledge in the domain of information security training and summative assessment. The paper affirms that assertion-reason questions are indeed challenging, and aligns to learning outcome for an information security course, as well as contribute to aspects of sustainable assessment.

Keywords: ARQ · Assertion reason · Question type · Sustainable assessment · Higher order · Information security

1 Introduction

Apart from learning analytic, another area of teaching and learning (T&L) that is receiving due attention is assessment. This section introduces assessment and provide a structure for the paper.

1.1 Sustainable Assessments

Much has been said of assessment for and assessment of learning [1–5, 9, 17]. Much of these have touched on formative and summative assessments, as well as the notion of authentic assessments. Beyond what Boud and Soler [4], regard as the "unhelpful binary division between summative and formative assessment" and the unending narrative of authentic assessment [9], is the shift towards sustainable assessment.

Boud and Soler [4], posit that sustainable assessment "shift assessment discourse away from the notion that assessment is a unilateral act done to students, to that of assessment that is mutually constructed between learners and assessors/teachers." What then is the focus of sustainable assessment is the capacity to evaluate evidence, appraise

© Springer International Publishing AG 2017
H. Xie et al. (Eds.): ICWL 2017, LNCS 10473, pp. 136–146, 2017.
DOI: 10.1007/978-3-319-66733-1_15

situations and circumstances astutely, draw sound conclusions and act in accordance with this analysis [4]. With that said, one might then want to know if there is a role for and if text-based assessment can contribute towards sustainable assessment. This paper looks at the case of assertion-reason question type (text-based) assessment in an information security course.

1.2 Structure of the Paper

The rest of the paper is structured as follows. Multiple choice question (MCQ) format is reviewed, followed by the concept of assertion-reason question type. Thereafter, the research problem domain is presented with methodology. The findings are presented and discussed. The paper then concludes with thoughts and way forward.

2 Sustainable Assessment and Assertion-Reason Questions

In this section, concepts and the higher-order challenge faced with MCQ types are reviewed. The need for assertion-reason question types is then looked into.

2.1 Multiple-Choice Question Formats

Assessments whether 'pen-and-paper' or computer assisted (e-assessment) or projects can be text-based or psychomotor or portfolio [2]. For text-based assessment, three major types have typically been multiple-choice, short answer and essay. There are others.

MCQ after being mooted during the first world war (WW1) era has become an efficacy tool, (yet most controversial), when one look at accuracy and fairness of assessment [18]. In the sense that there is little or no assessor/lecturers' subjectivity. However, is MCQ valid or reliable? This paper will carefully avoid the unending debate on validity and reliability of MCQ.

There has been questions about the depth of learning that MCQ format offers vis-à-vis learning outcome and capability for real world decision making task, post the study-era. There is even the query of lack of assessment of learning. This paper will not attempt to provide answers in this regard. Rather, this paper looks at types of MCQ formats and narrow down to a specific type, which is assertion-reason question (ARQ).

MCQ format can be simple 'true-or-false' or 'yes-or-no'. It can also be simple linear listing of direct options. A variant of this is what could be called "most correct option" MCQ format, where all or most of the answer are probable, however, only one is the most suitable. This type provides a springboard to some level of 'higher-order' thinking. Nonetheless, constructivist are of the view that higher order thinking skills are not assessed [18]. One criticism of MCQ that stands out is the lack of authenticity, or rather put the notion that real world tasks are not usually multiple-choice tasks. They (real-world tasks) are complex in nature, requiring analytical reasoning [17, 18].

2.2   The Push for Higher Order

What has happened since the late 1990's is the evolution of a type of MCQ which attempt to introduce higher order thinking into MCQ format. This being the ARQ. Although, when ARQ was first introduced is debatable, whether one is from Europe or from the Americas. What is important though is the nature and format of ARQs.

At the heart of question construct representation is the nature of the question item and the level within a T&L taxonomy that it seeks to address. Bloom's being the most referenced T&L taxonomy [10, 12]. Others include Heer's, an adaptation of Anderson and Krathwohl, whose model is actually a revision of Bloom's [8]. Worth mentioning here is the Scalise and Gifford's taxonomy (focusing on e-assessment) that was discussed in Shute et al. [14]. This paper refers the reader to the papers cited herein for details about these taxonomies.

The concept of higher order can be summarized as one that seeks to engage a learner/student as to the ability of the learner to:

- Learn the fundamental for the subject area;
- Read through (comprehend) and apply their own mind to the current context;
- Carry out an analysis; and
- Be able to synthesize some form of knowledge;
- Where need be, engage on (in-depth) evaluation exercise.

Beyond just learning the fundamentals, being able to comprehend, apply one's mind, analyze and synthesize knowledge, is considered to being able to operate at the cognitive hierarchy level. At the bedrock of constructivism in T&L, is being able to synthesize or better still 'construct' knowledge. The debate about MCQ format is centered on this. In the sense that, MCQ format types are not believed to push a learner to the domain or hierarchy level of analyzing and synthesizing. Herein comes the ARQ format type; to assess at cognitive hierarchy level especially being able to synthesize and possibly construct knowledge.

2.3   A Look at ARQ

The construct of an ARQ format in its simplest form, is providing a statement of fact and a reason to establish/sustain the statement. Let us look at an example in Table 1.

Table 1.   An author's constructed example of a simple ARQ format

Assertion		Reason
South Africa and Nigeria are members of the 55 member-states African Union (AU)	Because	They are sovereign countries within Africa
(a) [correct]	True; True (correct reason)	
(b)	True; True (incorrect reason, but the reason is true on its own)	
(c)	True; False	
(d)	False; True	
(e)	False; False	

This ARQ states that South Africa and Nigeria are members of the 55 member-states African Union (AU) because they are sovereign countries within Africa. Here, the statement of fact is that South Africa and Nigeria are members of the AU, which is true. Equally true is that the AU comprised of 55 countries (and is the successor of the previous Organization of African Unity – OAU. However, is the reason provided also true? One then need to understand the structure or constitution or the working of the AU: Being that of member states must be a country in Africa and must be sovereign. With that understanding and reasoning, one is able to say, yes, the reasoning is equally true as both are sovereign (independent) countries. We will see later in this paper that ARQ need not be this 'simplistic'. ARQs could derive from subject matter case studies, for which, the student will be put to task on higher order thinking.

To reinforce this, we look at another ARQ example: *WannaCry is a ransomware* <u>*because*</u> *it has spread to over '100' countries in May 2017, affecting over '100 000' computers.* To answer this, a student must look at the assertion – is Wannacry a ransomware. Yes, it is. This requires an awareness and understanding of information security (what is a malware and a ransomware). For the reason part, the student must carefully consider; yes it is true that Wannacry spread to over '100' countries and affecting '100 000' computers, however, does that qualifies it to be a ransomware? From an information security point-of-view, it is not so. It could as well just be any virus or worm or malware spreading. This then comes down to knowing what a ransomware is, within the discipline of information security. Hence, "B" is now the correct answer.

As Williams [18], puts it, a student is not merely selecting an option. Rather, the student is expected to determine if the assertion is true or not. This comes from an understanding of the subject. In engineering, information technology (IT), accounting, and in our case information security, the student must have the foundational knowledge and the capability to calculate or put the principles to use. The student must be able to reflect on the "reason" and determine if it provides an accurate *explanation* for the "assertion".

Unlike MCQs that usually test only one issue/concept, ARQs test two issues/concepts within a single question (this being the assertion and the reason statements), as well as the validity of the joining "because" statement [18].

In this section, it has been shown that ARQs are designed to address what might be the inherent deficiency in MCQs in their (MCQ) inability to assess higher order thinking. What then need to be studied is if ARQs are fulfilling this expectation.

3   Research Problem and Design

In this section, we discuss the rationale for the paper and the research project approach.

3.1   Research Rationale

This paper revisits Williams [18], decade old paper on the use of ARQ at an Australian business school. The circumstances as at then, are also prevalent in South Africa as at today and most of third-world countries. In the last two years, there has been rolling agitations and protests on fees, inclusion and transformation. At the heart of these, it seems it is about black equity students gaining access and having increasing throughput from the universities. This is seemly in line with provisions in section 29(1) of the South African Constitution and articles 16 and 17 of the 1990 Kampala declaration.

Two things from these are that lecturers are laden with increasing assessment peda-gogical and administrative tasks and secondly, the (fast-tracking) push for blended learning with a focus on the online learning aspect of blended learning.

Surely, online learning through the use of learning management system (LMS) covers a wide spectrum of the scholarship of teaching, learning and assessment [13]. Regarding the aspect of assessment that is being addressed in this paper, it can be said that with increasing number of students entering higher education institutions (HEI), there is increasing load on lecturers (especially) when there is no commensurate increase in the appointments of additional lecturers. Adesemowo et al. [2] on their reflection on introducing secure e-assessment, further highlighted that although e-assessment "might introduce initial extra burdens on lecturers but substantially alleviates the marking load afterward." Is this also the case of ARQ whether paper and pen or electronic.

This paper therefore *seeks to understudy the relevance of ARQ in the T&L of principle of information security courses.* More so, a search through academic databases (EBSCO hosts, Web of Science, Scopus, and Google Scholar) shows that literature is very thin in addressing ARQ in information security or cyber security. Nonetheless, the security aspects of (securing) assessments are being addressed [2, 15].

3.2   Research Design

This paper adapts the ARQ probing questionnaire in Williams [18] and that of Ogude and Bradley [11].

Over a hundred students initially registered for the information security principle course (SSO2000), taken by students in their second year and some (from other streams) in their third year. Out of the registered students, 73 took the mid-year test (Big June Test – BJT), which was conducted on the university's Moodle based LMS and secured with safe exam browser – SEB [2]. At the end of the BJT and in order to exit from the SEB enabled secure mode, the students are re-directed to an online questionnaire (ques-tionpro.com). Sixty students started the quiz with forty-six (46) completing.

4   Findings and Discussion

Before presenting and discussion the result, a moment will be taken to show the construct representation of the BJT.

4.1   BJT ARQ Structure

The BJT was made up of 25 questions as shown in Table 2. Questions one to twenty were MCQs with negative marking for incorrect answers. There were given to students at random from a pool of questions.

Table 2. Design of the mid-year big June test (BJT)

Weight	Construct representation	
20% I Q1 – Q20	MCQ I negative marking. Factual recollection	
10% I Q21 (5 sub Qs)	MCQ I understating of information security principles	
10% I Q22 (5 sub Qs)	MCQ I understanding of access controls principles	
20% I Q23 (10 sub Qs)	ARQ I Access control scenario	
20% I Q24 (10 sub Qs)	ARQ I varying information security concepts	
20% I Q25 (10 sub Qs)	ARQ I Security breaches and mitigation scenario	

In Williams [18], there were no negative marking and the students were allowed multiple attempts. The negative marking was to dissuade students from thumb sucking [15]. To allay fears and impact of negative markings, the students have been well oriented in formative pre-class pop quizzes. This trained them in the process of answering the questions. This also included introduction to and how to answer ARQs. Students also participate in the generation of ARQs.

Care was taken to avoid 'double negatives' in the questions [6]. This is important as it might affect the readability of the questions.

Questions 21, without negative marking, consisting of five sub questions, tests the students understating of information security principles of confidentiality, integrity, availability as well as threat, risk and authorization.

Question 22, also consisting of five sub questions, on the other hand tests the students understanding of access controls principles.

Questions 23 to 25, each carrying a weight of 20%, consist of 10 sub questions each. Question 23 and 25 are made up of scenario based ARQ format, whilst Q24, focusses on varying information security concepts. Question 23, partly shown in Fig. 1, has two MCQs.

4.2 Finding on Use of ARQ in Information Security Course

Patterned after Williams' [18] survey instrument, we asked students about their experience with ARQs.

The findings summarized in Fig. 2, correlates to a large extent with Williams [18] findings on ARQ being able to assess at cognitive level. This further collaborate with earlier findings from Ogude and Bradley [11]. However, there are some differences, which we will explain later on.

In Williams [18], the survey instruments used odd-numbered Likert-scale type of options. This was because in Williams's case, some of the students had had no exposure to ARQ. More so, there was no pre class test trials to expose all of the students unlike the case in this research study. The elimination of the "middle" line is to force all respondents to give a response based on their experience on ARQ. Hence, this research study focuses on 'usability' rather than 'perception'.

It was also found that some of the respondent are more concerned about the impact of the ARQ on their marks. This fear came to light from post semester test (BJT) probing engagement. Hence, rather than some of the students commenting on ARQ, they tend to commend on their experience of the "test". This post-survey probing is essential as Hassan and Wium [7], pointed out "[S]tudent evaluations can sometimes be viewed as a 'personality contest' rather than as a tool for measuring teaching performance". This can be seen in the response that will be looked into below.

4.3 Findings: Useful but not Useful

When asked if "ARQ tests are good indicator of deeper learning", their responses shows an "agree" 46.51% against to a "limited extent" of 27.91. However, when asked if "ARQ test engage me at higher-order cognitive level", the responses moved around to "limited extent" of 34.88% and an "agree" of 34.88%.

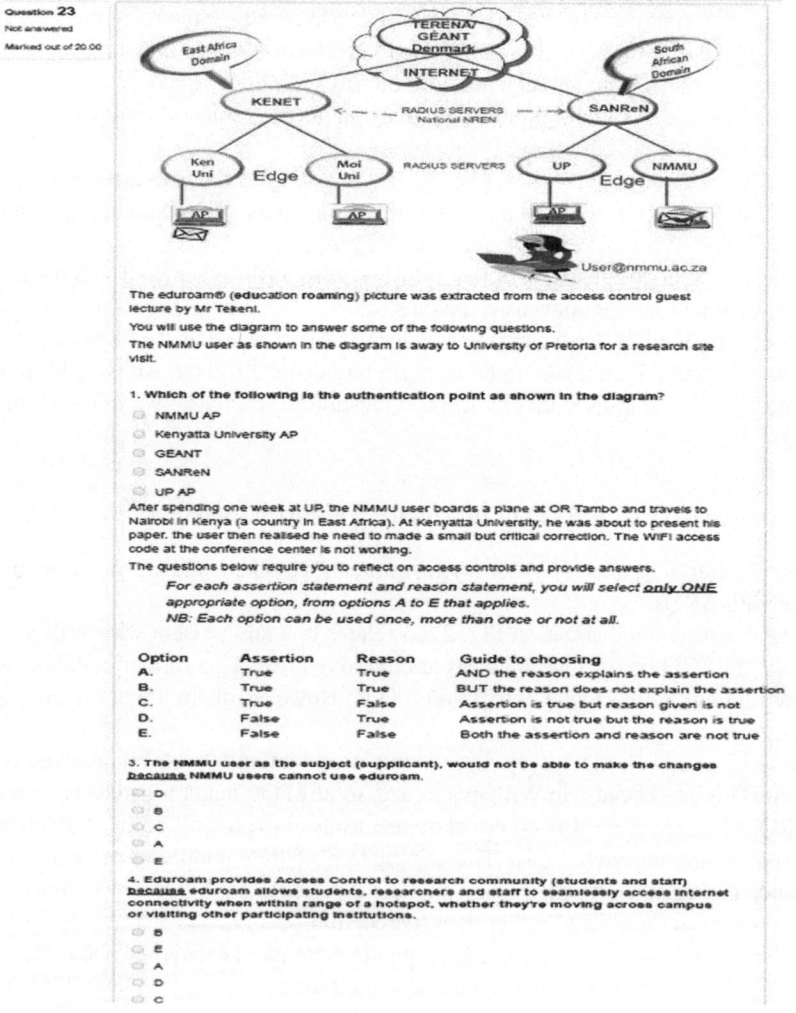

Fig. 1. Extracts of Q23: made up of an access control scenario, two MCQs and eight ARQs.

However a further probing shows more insight. The response to "ARQ test my ability to analyse situations" shifted to an "agree" of 48.84% and "limited extent" of 20.93%.

This was further entrenched in "ARQ test my ability to evaluate situations", where "agree" is 45.24% and "limited extent" is 26.19%.

What can be seen is that with careful construction of survey instrument and proper probing questions, Hassan and Wium [7], noted that nonetheless their limitations, student feedback can still provide vital evidence for assessment and improvement thereof. This is critical in validating the result from student feedbacks as is being done in this research study and many others.

With that said, and having probed the students further in post study engagement, as highlighted in the preceding paragraphs, it can then be said with relative confidence, albeit not so strongly, that "ARQ test my ability to apply my knowledge of InfoSec principles" (Agree of 34.88 and limited extent of 30.23%).

There is still a concern though as there was a close call between the view if "ARQ simply test my factual knowledge of InfoSec" where it was observed there is a combined "definitely not and limited extent" of 53.49% against a combined "agree and definitely yes" of 46.51%.

Against the backdrop of students' personality factor and the fear factor of course marks as highlighted by Hassan and Wium [7], the findings herein whilst correlating with Williams [18], must still be given careful thought. It is advised that lecturers and policy makers must tread with cautions when using ARQ for summative assessment, especially high-stake assessment. For this, the students must have gone through series of formative ARQ assessments and students' confidence level in ARQ must be high.

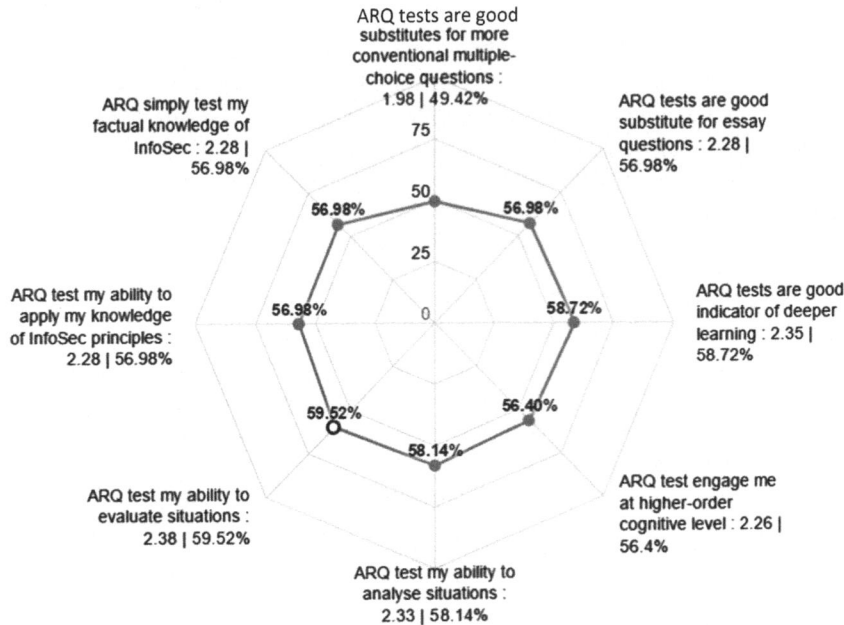

Fig. 2. The use of ARQ assessment.

4.4   Findings: Relevance of ARQ

Earlier on in the paper, it was said that at the bedrock of constructivism in T&L is the ability to comprehend and synthesize or construct knowledge. In so doing, one will be faced with challenges that stretches a person beyond just learning the fundamentals. Hence, the paper *seeks to understudy the relevance of ARQ in the T&L of principle of information security courses.*

It has been highlighted in the last section that with relative confidence, ARQ allows applying knowledge of InfoSec principles. What must be found out is whether ARQ are indeed challenging and assisting with learning information security principles. To assist in this regard, three responses will be looked at.

ARQ format as it relates to intellectual challenge

68.18% were of the view that the ARQs are very challenging, with a further 25% believing that the ARQ format is moderately challenging. This finding follows the same pattern as was found out in Williams [18], which further affirms earlier findings by Sircar and Tandon [16].

ARQ format as it relates to learning outcomes

Findings as it relates to learning outcome for information security principle is not the same as those of Williams's [18] where 64% were of the view that the learning outcomes associated with ARQ tests were superior to those associated with MCQs.

What was found in this research study is that whereas 58% (38% ARQ produced moderately superior outcomes, 20% superior outcome) were of the view that ARQ tend to produce superior outcomes, there is a 22% contrary view that ARQ produced significantly inferior outcomes.

Due to the fact that the questionnaire was anonymous, there was no way to correlate the findings with the marks of the student. However, there are some of the students who expressed opinion of understanding the outcomes to be their assessment mark!

Once again, when using ARQ for summative assessments, great care must be taken as students tend to believe that although the ARQ to an extent is useful and help them to learn, their preference would still be for traditional MCQ. This is because they (the students) believe MCQ allow them to perform better (achieve higher grade!).

A beep into the ARQ marks

To conclude on the findings and discussion, the performance in the ARQ will be looked at. Q23 with the access control case study, partly shown in Fig. 1, has the lowest average of 8.03 (n = 73), followed by Q25 with the security breach scenario having 8.11 (n = 73). Q24 is a standard ARQ format with the highest average of 8.27 (n = 73).

What was observed is that the highest score of 18/20 (n = 1) was in Q23, yet having the lowest mean. The highest score in Q24 is 16/20 (n = 3). Q24 has the most score of 14 s. All of Q23, Q24 and Q25 have two scores of 12 each. Invariably, Q23 presented the toughest challenge and at the same time the highest mark!

A bit of learning analytics on the marks point out that had negative marking been introduced for the ARQs, the mean marks would have been lower than what they are (as presented above). This will clearly affirm the students' viewpoint of finding the ARQ more challenging as well as expressing the view that they (the student) performed better with traditional MCQ.

5 Conclusion

This paper does not want to be seen as equating ARQ as the same as authentic, although it can attempt to in some ways. Also, this paper does not equate ARQ to sustainable assessments even though it can be used as a platform for sustainable assessments. In two ways ARQ can though. The nature of scenario based ARQ are mimic of post study real-life decision making. Also, ARQ can follow the path of 'questionfunding', where students either participate in the generation of ARQ (as was partly done in this research study) or contribute questions as was the case in Sircar and Tandon [16].

This paper has shown that indeed ARQs are found to be more challenging than MCQs and that they could align learning better to information security learning outcome. A unique contribution of this paper is the use of scenario based ARQ in information security courses. What remains to be seen is how ARQ stack up with carefully constructed scenario-based Cloze questions [1]. This paper also examined the use of ARQ in summative assessment and points out the 'tread carefully path'.

It is important to restate here that care must be taken to scaffold students into answering ARQs, otherwise, students will remain fixated on the grammar of the ARQ and their assessment marks, instead of achieving on learning outcome the ARQ enhances.

As web based learning get further entrenched, and both virtual learning environment and personal learning environment increasingly comes to the fore, concepts such as ARQ will take more prominent place in assessment for e-learning and technology for learning.

All of these open the door for critical realism approach to interrogating the ontology and epistemology of ARQ as a *reality*. Thereby, the concept, content, and context of ARQ can then be interrogated.

What would also be of interest is a longitudinal study over a three to five year period as well as comparative study of ARQ in undergraduate and postgraduate information security courses.

References

1. Adesemowo, A.K., et al.: Text-based sustainable assessment: a case of first-year information and communication technology networking students. Stud. Educ. Eval. **55**, 1–8 (2017)
2. Adesemowo, A.K., et al.: The experience of introducing secure e-assessment in a South African university first-year foundational ICT networking course. Africa Educ. Rev. **13**(1), 67–86 (2016)
3. Beller, M.: Technologies in large-scale assessments: new directions, challenges, and opportunities. In: von Davier, M., et al. (eds.) The Role of International Large-Scale Assessments: Perspectives from Technology, Economy, and Educational Research, pp. 25–45. Springer, Netherlands, Dordrecht (2013)
4. Boud, D., Soler, R.: Sustainable assessment revisited. Assess. Eval. High. Educ. **41**(3), 400–413 (2016)

5. Clarke-Midura, J., Dede, C.: Assessment, technology, and change. J. Res. Technol. Educ. **42**(3), 309–328 (2010)
6. Dermo, J.: e-Assessment and the student learning experience: a survey of student perceptions of e-assessment. Br. J. Educ. Technol. **40**(2), 203–214 (2009)
7. Hassan, S., Wium, W.: Quality lies in the eyes of the beholder: A mismatch between student evaluation and peer observation of teaching. Africa Educ. Rev. **11**(4), 491–511 (2014)
8. Heer, R.: A Model of Learning Objectives. http://www.celt.iastate.edu/teaching-resources/effective-practice/revised-blooms-taxonomy/
9. Newhouse, C.P.: Using digital technologies to improve the authenticity of performance assessment for high-stakes purposes. Technol. Pedagog. Educ. **24**(1), 17–33 (2013)
10. Van Niekerk, J., von Solms, R.: Using Bloom's taxonomy for information security education. In: Dodge, R.C., Futcher, L. (eds.) Information Assurance and Security Education and Training, pp. 280–287. Springer, Heidelberg (2013)
11. Ogude, A.N., Bradley, J.D.: Ionic conduction and electrical neutrality in operating electrochemical cells: pre-college and college student interpretations. J. Chem. Educ. **71**(1), 29 (1994)
12. Paul, R.W.: Bloom's taxonomy and critical thinking instruction: recall is not knowledge. In: Wilsen, J., Binker, A.J. (eds.) Critical Thinking: What Every Person Needs To Survive in a Rapidly Changing World, pp. 519–526. Foundation for Critical Thinking, California (2012)
13. Rust, C.: The unscholarly use of numbers in our assessment practices: what will make us change? Int. J. Scholarsh. Teach. Learn. **5**(1), 1–6 (2011)
14. Shute, V.J., et al.: Advances in the science of assessment. Educ. Assess. **21**(1), 34–59 (2016)
15. Sim, G.: Evidence based design of heuristics: usability and computer assisted assessment. University of Central Lancashire (2009)
16. Sircar, S.S., Tandon, O.P.: Involving students in question writing: a unique feedback with fringe benefits. Am. J. Physiol. **277**(6 Pt 2), S84–S91 (1999)
17. Wiggins, G.P.: Assessing Student Performance: Exploring the Purpose and Limits of Testing. Wiley, New York (1993)
18. Williams, J.B.: Assertion-reason multiple-choice testing as a tool for deep learning: a qualitative analysis. Assess. Eval. High. Educ. **31**(3), 287–301 (2006)

Web Accessibility for the Visually Impaired: A Case of Higher Education Institutions' Websites in Ghana

Millicent Akotam Agangiba[1(✉)], Emmanuel Boahen Nketiah[2], and William Akotam Agangiba[2]

[1] Department of Information Systems, University of Cape Town, Cape Town, South Africa
agnmil001@myuct.ac.za
[2] Computer Science and Engineering Department,
University of Mines and Technology, Tarkwa, Ghana
emmaboahen6@gmail.com, waakotam@umat.edu.gh

Abstract. Globally, the use of web-based resources has increased tremendously among Higher Education Institutions (HEIs). This move has made access to information more convenient and easy for most students. However, while providing this benefit, some students may be excluded because they cannot use standard modes of access. Students with disabilities are most at risk of being excluded from access, particularly those who are visually impaired and use assistive technologies such as screen magnifiers and screen readers. Websites of education institutions serve as virtual gateway to access immediate information for students and should therefore be accessible. Yet, web accessibility is under-explored in Ghana. In this study, we evaluate based on the Web Content Accessibility Guidelines (WCAG 2.0); the accessibility of some HEIs' websites in Ghana using diagnostic automatic tool. The findings show that most HEIs websites failed to comply with perceivable and operable principles of WCAG 2.0. The study also shows that despite a growing awareness of web accessibility issues worldwide, visually impaired students in Ghana are likely to be experiencing barriers in accessing web content from these institutions. The study recommends increasing awareness, training web developers and users, and developing contextualized web accessibility guidelines as some needed steps to ensure the integration of visually impaired students into the digital society.

Keywords: Web accessibility · Higher education institutions · Students with disabilities

1 Introduction

The web is a major source of information. Many activities which used to require a lot of time to be accomplished can now be done by just a click of a button. This has made access to information more convenient and easy for most people. However, while providing this benefit, there are dangers that some people will be excluded because they require other supporting technologies for access. In the context of Higher Education Institutions (HEIs), students with disabilities (SWDs) are most at risk of being excluded from access, and in particular the visually impaired who use assistive technologies such

© Springer International Publishing AG 2017
H. Xie et al. (Eds.): ICWL 2017, LNCS 10473, pp. 147–153, 2017.
DOI: 10.1007/978-3-319-66733-1_16

as screen magnifiers and screen readers. Although there are other forms of disabilities; mobility, speech, cognitive among others, visual impairment is considered the most restrictive type of disability [1, 2].

Worldwide over one billion people live with disabilities; 80% of them reside in developing countries and 285 million visually impaired [3]. It is estimated that 10% of Africa's population is disabled [3, 4]. Education among PWDs particularly in developing countries is generally low. This is because PWDs are often marginalized and so do not get equal access to education [5].

Information technology, particularly the World Wide Web is increasingly playing a pivotal role in higher education in the provision of administrative, academic and student services. Websites of HEIs are very crucial as they serve as a virtual gateway; providing timely and vital information to students and therefore should be accessible. For a website to be accessible; it should be interactive, easy to navigate and use regardless of device [6]. With the advent of the Internet, it is perceived that PWDs would have equal opportunity to education through diverse channels such as E-learning and Distance learning. Today, the use of the web is a required as part of student life since most of the information needed for day-to-day activities on campus can be found on the institutions' websites. With most physical classrooms now transforming into virtual with the help of the web; access to the web becomes even more crucial. However, web accessibility in HEIs remains a challenge for SWDs particularly the visually impaired [7–9].

This study is motivated by the fact that demand on web accessibility is continually increasing [9, 10]; however, most studies conducted on web accessibility have focused on developed countries and developing countries have been given minimal attention [10]. There is dearth of such study in Ghana and Africa as a continent. This study investigates web accessibility in HEIs and raises awareness on importance of accessibility particularly in a web-based learning environment.

The rest of the paper is structured as follows: Sect. 2 summarizes previous studies on web accessibility in HEIs. Section 3 discusses methodology adopted for data sampling and evaluation process. Results and discussions are covered in Sect. 4 and finally Sect. 5 concludes the paper with final remarks.

2 Literature Review

2.1 Related Works

Research on web accessibility has been on the increase, since the emergence of the web. For students to take full advantage of information and services provided by HEIs, their websites have to be technically accessible. This is particularly important for the visually impaired who employ assistive technologies (e.g. JAWS, NVDA, ZoomText) to efficiently access the web [2].

Many research studies examining accessibility of HEIs websites in developed countries conclude that there are several accessibility barriers. For instance, a study in [8] reported that 98% of Australian university websites fail to meet minimum criteria required for accessibility according to WCAG 1.0. Similar findings were reported in several other studies in [11–13]. On the African continent, few studies on web accessibility have been conducted. These studies have focused on E-government or E-commerce websites. For example, in [1] web accessibility conducted on South African business websites showed that most of them were not accessible. Other studies conducted in [2, 10, 14] report similar findings on E-government websites.

This study focuses on one African country; Ghana. Ghana is located in West Africa with an estimated 10% of its population living with disabilities [15]. Presently in Ghana, many HEIs are moving most of their resources online with distance education becoming more popular by the day [6]. Moreover, distance education is presently seen as means of expanding college and university level education especially in Africa where there is limited infrastructure and the student to teacher ratio is high [16, 17]. Accessible web is therefore crucial for equal access as well as effective learning in HEIs.

2.2 Web Content Accessibility Guidelines

In 1999, Web Accessibility Initiative (WAI) developed the Web Content Accessibility Guidelines (WCAG) to guide designers of websites. These guidelines are to enhance web accessibility for PWDs [18]. WCAG provides information on how to make a web page or web application more accessible to PWDs. It is made up of 14 guidelines and 65 checkpoints to ensure the accessibility of websites for a wide range of disabilities. Three priorities of web accessibility are defined by WAI based on the checkpoints: Priority 1 (16 checkpoints), Priority 2 (30 checkpoints) and Priority 3 (19 checkpoints). These priorities conform to three levels of criteria of accessibility: Level A, Level AA and Level AAA. Website conformance to Level A means all problems relating to Priority 1 must be fixed. For a website to attain Level AA, accessibility issues in Priorities 1 and 2 should be fixed. Website conformance to Level AAA means Priorities 1, 2 and 3 must be passed. According WCAG, a website must conform to Level AA criteria to provide accessibility to PWDs. Many developed countries have since established their own web guidelines using WCAG as the basis [2]. WCAG has two versions; WCAG 1.0 and WCAG 2.0 established in 1999 and 2008 respectively. The next section discusses the methodology used for this study.

3 Methodology

3.1 Selection of Evaluation Tool

According to WCAG 2.0, for a website to be accessible it should meet four requirements: be perceivable, be operable, be understandable and robust [19]. These requirements can be assessed using web evaluation tools. A web evaluation tool is a software that helps to analyze web pages by comparing the written codes on the webpage to WCAG guidelines [18]. They are used as effective and quick means of detecting accessibility errors since human judgement is laborious, bias and time consuming [20, 21]. In this study, aDesigner developed by IBM was selected to analyze the accessibility of the websites. aDesigner is a disability simulator specifically designed to check accessibility flaws in websites for the visually impaired (from low vision to total blindness) [22, 23]. In addition, aDesigner is open source which makes it easily accessible. It has two types of extensible visualization engines which includes blind usability simulation engine for simulating the case of blind usage of the website under evaluation and low-vision simulation engine for simulating the case of low-vision usage of the website under evaluation.

3.2 Evaluation Process

The study selected twelve websites of public HEIs in Ghana with additional, three websites belonging to government agencies responsible for tertiary education. aDesigner was then used to determine their compliance to WCAG 2.0. Evaluation of websites were conducted only on homepages; as it has been well established that errors on homepages mostly run through the rest of the websites [11]. Again, students are likely to visit homepage first before linking up to other pages. The evaluation was carried out in within a period of two weeks. URLs of each website were entered into aDesigner. Test evaluation was conducted in two stimulation modes low vision (L) and blindness (B) for each website. Reports were generated based on WCAG principles for each website. Results on critical accessibility errors were recorded in each case. aDesigner also indicates rating of each website's performance in terms of accessibility. Ratings range from 0–3 where 0 is the poorest performance while 3 indicates the highest performance in terms of accessibility. For the sake of anonymity, each website was coded with a number. Findings from evaluation are discussed in the following section.

4   Findings and Discussions

4.1   Findings

After evaluating each website with aDesigner, two reports were generated (summary and detailed). Summary report comprises of the rating given to the webpage after the evaluation with the total number of accessibility errors found and results obtained for the four WCAG principles of accessibility (Perceivable, Operable, Understandable, Robust). The detailed report indicates the guidelines violated. The results for adherence to WCAG principles are shown in Table 1.

The analysis shows that most websites have large number of problems relating to perceivable principle. This is followed by the violation of operable principle. Websites are quite robust and the understandable principle was the least violated. The low scores in principles "Perceivable and Operable" mean that these websites will be less usable for the visually impaired students since they will have difficulty operating the interface to retrieve content. Additionally, websites may not be compatible with some web browsers [24]. Critical accessibility errors were identified in all websites for both low vision and blind simulation. Example website No. 1 had as many as 215 and 46 accessibility errors for low vision users and blind users respectively. Based on the ratings, only one website (see column 6 No. 9) was found to be accessible for users with low vision.

Detailed report generated pointed out various derelictions which resulted in critical errors. Notable among them were: lack of alternative text for images; missing table

Table 1. Results on WCAG principles

Website	Perceivable (%)	Operable (%)	Understandable (%)	Robust (%)	Rating	Critical Errors
No. 1	0	31	95	85	0(L), 0(B)	215(L),46(B)
No. 2	19	16	90	80	0(L), 0(B)	79(L),28(B)
No. 3	0	78	93	91	0(L), 0(B)	51(L), 37(B)
No. 4	72	47	93	93	0(L), 0(B)	24(L),5(B)
No. 5	0	10	86	73	0(L), 0(B)	57(L),33(B)
No. 6	58	82	100	100	0(L),1(B)	91(L),8(B)
No. 7	0	79	89	83	0(L), 0(B)	57(L),20(B)
No. 8	36	71	95	100	0(L), 0(B)	65(L),7(B)
No. 9	0	84	95	100	2(L), 0(B)	22(L),30(B)
No.10	42	0	86	88	0(L), 0(B)	160(L),25(B)
No.11	22	11	81	78	0(L), 0(B)	112(L),34(B)
No.12	7	18	84	87	0(L), 1(B)	143(L),36(B)
No.13	0	73	90	88	0(L), 0(B)	132(L),33(B)
No.14	0	55	100	85	1(L),1(B)	110(L),33(B)
No.15	52	61	83	95	0(L),0(B)	76(L),2(B)
Average	**20.5**	**47.7**	**90.7**	**88.4**		

Key: L = Result for Low Vision test; B = Result for Blind test.
Ratings: 0 = Very Poor; 1 = Poor; 2 = Good; 3 = Very Good.

headers and tags; lack of intra-page linking, missing tab indices to help navigate keyboard; missing titles on frames; fixed font size, poor contrast of image and text color.

4.2 Discussions

The findings indicate that most websites are not accessible to the visually impaired. Several of the websites use images and graphics which most screen readers are unable to read. Appropriate alternative text should therefore be used to describe images for users with screen readers. Empty string (" ") can also be used as an alternative text in instances where that images may not really matter to the blind user. Many tables also lacked tags. Tables without tags are difficult for bind user to visualize. Tables need to be well structured and tagged to make them accessible. Websites also lacked intra-page links to facilitate navigation and linking from one page to the other. Options to change fonts were missing from most websites. The use of absolute-size keywords (e.g. "large"), relative-size keywords (e.g. example, "larger") will enable low vision users enlarge fonts. Many forms lacked titles; shielding blind users from knowing which input details are required which makes the webpage less perceivable. Poor foreground and background color contrast were identified on many of the websites. The use of sharp contrasting colors for the foreground and background is recommended to help improve accessibility. The results confirm findings of similar studies conducted in [1, 2, 14, 21] on E-government and E-commerce websites on the African continent.

5   Conclusions and Recommendation

Web accessibility is an important requirement for the visually impaired to have easy access to online web content. In this study, website evaluation of fifteen higher education institutions in Ghana revealed that the visually impaired students will encountered several challenges accessing these websites. This lack of accessibility will exclude potential visually impaired students who rely on web-information to effectively study or those who might be interested in some information from these institutions' websites. Findings further show that, none of the websites is accessible to the visually impaired. We therefore advocate the need to create more awareness by incorporating accessibility into curriculum of educational institutions to help sensitize society. Accessibility policy which helps to enforce compliance [21, 24] is still lacking in most developing countries and Ghana is no exception. There is need to implement web policies, train web developers on accessibility requirements for persons with disabilities who employ assistive technologies. Disability oriented organizations should help to champion the creation of awareness on web accessibility in the digital society. The findings of this study are significant in several ways. The study is the first of its kind examining web accessibility in Ghanaian universities thereby raising contextual awareness. The findings also provide insights into how to develop and improve HEIs websites to be more accessible by all students, and particularly students with visual impairment.

Acknowledgment. The first author is grateful Schlumberger Foundation, Faculty of the Future Fellowship and L'Oréal-UNESCO for Women in Science Sub-Saharan Africa for funding support.

References

1. Venter, S., Lotriet, H.: Accessibility of South African Web sites to visually disabled users. SA J. Inf. Manag. **72**(2), 1–14 (2005)
2. Boussarhan, I., Daoudi, N.: The accessibility of moroccan public websites: evaluation of three e-government websites. Electron. J. e-Government **12**(1), 67–81 (2014)
3. UNESCO: Disability Data and Statistics, Monitoring and Evaluation: The Way Forward - a Disability-Inclusive Agenda Towards 2015 and Beyond (2014)
4. WHO: World report on disability 2011. Am. J. Phys. Med. Rehabil. Assoc. Acad. Physiatr. **91**, 1–350 (2011)
5. Mitra, S., Posarac, A., Vick, B.: Disability and poverty in developing countries: a snapshot from the world health survey (2011)
6. Boateng, J.K.: Accessibility considerations for e-learning in Ghana (2015). http://transform2015.net/live/Resources/Papers/Accessibilityconsiderations.pdf. Accessed 10 Apr 2016
7. Pino, M., Mortari, L.: The inclusion of students with dyslexia in higher education: a systematic review using narrative synthesis. Dyslexia **20**(4), 346–369 (2014)
8. Harper, K.A., DeWaters, J.: A quest for website accessibility in higher education institutions. The internet and higher education. Internet High. Educ. **11**(3), 160–164 (2008)
9. da Silva, P., Alturas, B.: Web accessibility: study of maturity level of Portuguese institutions of higher education. In: Information Systems and Technologies (CISTI), pp. 1–7 (2015)

10. Adepoju, S.A., Shehu, I.S.: Accessibility evaluation and performance analysis of e-government websites in Nigeria. J. Adv. Inf. Technol. **7**(1), 49–53 (2016)
11. Kurt, S.: The accessibility of university web sites: the case of Turkish universities. Univ. Access Inf. Soc. **10**(1), 101–110 (2011)
12. Michailidou, E., Mavrou, K., Zaphiris, P.: eInclusion@ cyprus universities: provision and web accessibility. In: CHI 2012 Extended Abstracts on Human Factors in Computing Systems, pp. 1637–1642 (2012)
13. van Rooij, S.W., Zirkle, K.: Balancing pedagogy, student readiness and accessibility: A case study in collaborative online course development. Internet High. Educ. **28**, 1–7 (2016)
14. Asiimwe, E.N., Lim, N.: Usability of government websites in Uganda. Electron. J. e-Government **8**(1), 1–12 (2010)
15. Commonwealth Human Rights Initiative (CHRI): Access to Information for Persons with Disabilities (2011). http://www.humanrightsinitiative.org/publications/ghana/CHRIDISABOOKLET.pdf. Accessed 15 May 2016
16. Asunka, S.: Online learning in higher education in sub-saharan Africa: Ghanaian University students' experiences and perceptions. The International Review of Research in Open and Distance Learning (2008). http://www.irrodl.org/index.php/irrodl/article/view/586. Accessed 27 Oct 2016
17. Brady, K.P., Holcomb, L.B., Smith, B.V.: The use of alternative social networking sites in higher educational settings: a case study of the e-learning benefits of Ning in education. J. Interact. Online Learn. **9**(2), 151–170 (2010)
18. Brewer, J.: Web accessibility highlights and trends. In: Proceedings of the 2004 International Cross-Disciplinary Workshop on Web Accessibility (W4A), pp. 51–55 (2004)
19. W. W. W. C. (W3C): Web content accessibility guidelines (WCAG) 2.0 (2008). http://www.w3.org/TR/WCAG20/. Accessed 15 Apr 2016
20. Bradbard, D., Peters, C.: Web accessibility theory and practice: an introduction for university faculty. J. Educ. Online **7**(1), 1–46 (2010)
21. Yaokumah, W., Brown, S., Amponsah, R.: Accessibility, quality and performance of government portals and ministry web sites: a view using diagnostic tools. In: 2015 Annual Global Online Conference on Information and Computer Technology (GOCICT), pp. 46–50 (2015)
22. Michalska, A.M., You, C.X., Nicolini, A.M., Ippolito, V.J., Fink, W.: Accessible web page design for the visually impaired: a case study. Int. J. Hum. Comput. Interact. **30**(12), 995–1002 (2014)
23. Takagi, H., Asakawa, C., Fukuda, K., Maeda, J.: Accessibility designer: visualizing usability for the blind. In: ACM SIGACCESS Accessibility and Computing, pp. 177–184 (2004)
24. Abu-doush, I., Bany-mohammed, A., Ali, E., Al-betar, M.A.: Towards a more accessible e-government in Jordan: an evaluation study of visually impaired users and Web developers. Behav. Inf. Technol. **32**(3), 273–293 (2013)

Open Educational Resources and Recommender Systems

Reciprocal Recommender System for Learners in Massive Open Online Courses (MOOCs)

Sankalp Prabhakar[1]([⊠]), Gerasimos Spanakis[2], and Osmar Zaiane[1]

[1] University of Alberta, Edmonton, AB T6G 2R3, Canada
{sankalp,zaiane}@ualberta.ca
[2] Maastricht University, 6200 MD Maastricht, Netherlands
jerry.spanakis@maastrichtuniversity.nl

Abstract. Massive open online courses (MOOC) describe platforms where users with completely different backgrounds subscribe to various courses on offer. MOOC forums and discussion boards offer learners a medium to communicate with each other and maximize their learning outcomes. However, oftentimes learners are hesitant to approach each other for different reasons (being shy, don't know the right match, etc.). In this paper, we propose a reciprocal recommender system which matches learners who are mutually interested in, and likely to communicate with each other based on their profile attributes like age, location, gender, qualification, interests, etc. We test our algorithm on data sampled using the publicly available MITx-Harvardx dataset and demonstrate that both attribute importance and reciprocity play an important role in forming the final recommendation list of learners. Our approach provides promising results for such a system to be implemented within an actual MOOC.

Keywords: Reciprocal recommender systems · MOOC · Information retrieval

1 Introduction

Higher education is an area that has thus far embraced, but arguably has not been fundamentally altered by the growth of the Internet. This has been rapidly changing over the last few years with the rise of Massive Open Online Courses (MOOCs) as a way of learning that lets students participate on their own terms and conditions via Internet. Number of students that signed up for at least one course in year 2015 has crossed 35 million - up from an estimated 16–18 million the previous year[1].

MOOC courses integrate the connectivity of social networks, the facilitation of an acknowledged expert in a field of study and a collection of freely accessible online resources. MOOC learners are diverse, originating from many

---

[1] Data collected by https://www.class-central.com.

© Springer International Publishing AG 2017
H. Xie et al. (Eds.): ICWL 2017, LNCS 10473, pp. 157–167, 2017.
DOI: 10.1007/978-3-319-66733-1_17

cultures across the globe in all ages and backgrounds [6]. Despite this diversity, three main attributes unite them: A desire to learn, a desire to connect to a global community and a desire to experience and consume content online. Our work focuses on exploring the possibilities of assisting MOOC learners in the process of self-organization (e.g. forming study groups, finding partners, encourage peer learning, etc.) by developing a reciprocal recommender system that will recommend learners to each other based on a predefined set of preferences (e.g. interests, age range, location, qualification, gender, etc.). Moreover, lack of effective student engagement is one of main reasons for a very high MOOC dropout rate [11]. Although many thousands of participants enroll in various MOOC courses, the completion rate for most courses is below 13%. Further studies [5,15] have been made to show how collaboration or active learning promotes student engagement. Therefore, we believe that recommending learners to each other will foster better student collaboration and would help mitigate the dropout rates to some extent.

The remainder of the paper is organized as follows. Section 2 presents some related work on the criteria of recommendations in MOOCs. In Sect. 3, we talk about the data and the proposed model for generating and ranking recommendations. Soon after, in Sect. 4, experimental results and evaluation are presented. Lastly, Sect. 5 concludes the paper and presents future work.

2   Related Work

Recommender systems for MOOCs have been developed, but their main focus has been on recommending courses to learners [2,3]. i-Help peer recommendation [4] was an early effort towards this area but the matchmaking process is not clear and there is no evaluation of the results. People-to-people recommender systems have been studied in the general context [8] involving techniques such as collaborative filtering, semantic-based methods, data mining, and context-aware methods as well as testing performance and effect of recommender systems. However, they have not found much application in the context of education.

Some of the most significant work in reciprocal recommendation has been done in the domain of online dating. The subject is more relevant here because a successful match only occurs when both recommended people like each other or reciprocate. In their work [1], authors built a Content-Collaborative Reciprocal (CCR) system. The content-based part uses selected user profile features and similarity measure to generate a set of similar users. The collaborative filtering part uses the interactions of the similar users, including the people they like/dislike and are liked/disliked by, to produce reciprocal recommendations. Other approaches include RECON [12], a reciprocal recommender system for online dating which utilizes user preferences to calculate compatibility scores for each other.

Our research draws inspiration from some of the works mentioned above. More specifically, our system takes into account one of the MOOC particularities: there is no extended history for learners' preferences, thus traditional collaborative filtering systems are not directly applicable. Moreover, the idea of reciprocity and peer recommendation is relatively new not only to the area of MOOC but also to the recommendation systems and gains more ground with many such applications.

3 Proposed Method

In the next few subsections, we talk about our data model along with the design and description of our recommendation algorithm.

3.1 Data

The data used in our research comes from the de-identified release from the first year (Academic Year 2013: Fall 2012, Spring 2013, and Summer 2013) of MITx and HarvardX courses on the edX platform [10]. For our analysis and without loss of generality, we selected records with attributes about age, location, qualification and gender. Moreover, we enhance this information with synthesized data about learners' interests. This information is not available via the mentioned dataset but is potentially useful for recommending learners to other learners.

A brief overview of the dataset attributes can be found in Table 1. The *user_id* is a numerical unique identifier for different learners, *age* of the learner is calculated using the year of birth obtained from the original dataset, *gender* is another binary attribute followed by *location*, which has information about the resident city of the learner. Furthermore, the *qualification* attribute has been divided into 5 levels: less than secondary, secondary, bachelors, masters and doctorate. The *interest* attribute contains one or more values about learners' interest. A sample of our dataset can be seen in Table 2.

Table 1. Dataset attribute description

Attribute	Short	Type	Comment
user_id	id	Numeric	Unique identifier
Age	age	Numeric	Calculated using year of birth
Gender	gen	Binary	M(ale)/F(emale)
Location	loc	Categorical	City of the learner
Qualification	qua	Ordinal	5 levels
Interests	int	Hierarchical, Categorical, Multi-Value	Info about learners' interests

Table 2. Dataset sample

id	age	gen	loc	qua	int	crs
1	32	M	Frankfurt	Doctorate	ML	Machine learning, java, python
2	28	M	Los Angeles	Bachelors	AI	Java, python
3	27	F	Edmonton	Bachelors	Science	Python, sociology
4	22	F	Las Vegas	Secondary	Soccer, AI	History, general studies

3.2   Preference and Importance Modeling

When users sign up on a MOOC platform, they provide preferences for the above mentioned attributes, which would be used to recommend similar learners to them. These preferences are based on value ranges for attributes in Table 1, and can include none, one or more (even all) of these attributes. A description of the value ranges of preferences for each of the attributes is mentioned below:

- **Age:** the age preference attribute is divided into these 5 levels: less than 20, 20–25, 25–30, 30–35, 35 and above.
- **Gender:** male or female gender options.
- **Location:** *same city* (if learners prefer meeting in person), *same country or timezone* (to facilitate communication).
- **Qualification:** one or more qualifications out of the five levels available.
- **Interests:** users can define their own interest preference which might or might not be similar to their own interest.

A sample of user preferences can be seen in Table 3. It must be noted that not all five preference attributes are required to be defined by a user. One or more (but not all) of these attributes can be left empty, at which point the algorithm simply ignores these in the recommendation process as it considers them irrelevant. In Table 3, 'x' denotes no preference for the given attribute by the user.

Moreover, users can further define whether they have some preferences that are more important to them i.e. if they have a priority for their preferences (highlighted in bold in the preference Table 3). For instance, looking at preference p_4 in Table 3, we can tell that this user prioritizes *location* and *qualification* over other attribute preferences.

Table 3. Sample of user preferences

pref	age	gen	loc	qua	int
p_1	**30–35**	**M**	Same city	>=Masters	x
p_2	x	x	x	Bachelors	Football
p_3	**25–30**	F	x	x	x
p_4	<=25	x	**Same timezone**	**<=Bachelors**	x

3.3   Recommendation Algorithm Description

In the next subsections, we will discuss our recommendation algorithm in detail. In short, we first build a similarity matrix which has the compatibility scores (based on user preferences) between the users. The compatibility scores helps us to generate ranked recommendations. Next, we re-rank the users based on their preference priority.

Building Similarity Matrix. Given the preferences of a user, we compute the 'distance' of this user, with every other user based on their attribute values. It is to be noted that, 'the lower the distance score, the greater the similarity'. For instance, using the data sample in Table 2, distance of a user (with $id = 1$) to other users could be computed as follows:

- **Ordinal Variables** (age, qualification): Preferences for *age* and *qualification* attributes are divided into levels in such a way that adjacent levels have a distance of 1, as shown in the data (Sect. 3.1). Once the distance between users for these attributes are calculated, it is then normalized in the range [0–1] by dividing it by the maximum distance possible.
- **Nominal Variables** (gender, location): Preferences for *gender* and *location* attributes are mapped to a binary distance metric. For instance, if the *gender* of two users are same, then the distance 'd'_{gen} is 0, otherwise 1. Similarly, the same computation is applied to the *location* or any other nominal variable.
- **Hierarchical Variables** (interests): For preference attributes that come from a hierarchy there is a similarity measure based on the hierarchy tree. This measure, based on the edge counting between nodes by the shortest way, presents a method to evaluate the semantic similarity in a hierarchical tree structure. The hierarchy we used for *interests* of users is based on WordNet [9] and the similarity measure used is based on the Wu and Palmer method [14] *score* which considers the depths of the two synsets in the WordNet taxonomies, along with the depth of the LCS (Least Common Subsumer). Score for this similarity is between 0 and 1, since we are implementing our system in a distance measure (and not similarity) the final value of distance between the interests is $[1 - score]$.

Finally, the 'distance score' of a user x with any other user y is the mean of the attribute distances:

$$distance\_score(x, y) = \frac{\sum_{i=1}^{N} d_i(x, y)}{N} \tag{1}$$

where d_i is the distance for attribute i between users x and y and N represents the total number of attributes (in our case $N = 5$). For instance, the 'distance score' of user 3 ($id = 3$) with the other users can be computed as follows:

$distance\_score(userid : 3, userid : 1) = \frac{1/4+1}{5} = 0.25$, (as *age* range difference is 1 and *gen* difference is 1)

$distance\_score(userid : 3, userid : 2) = \frac{0+1}{5} = 0.2$, (as *age* range is same, but *gen* is different)

$distance\_score(userid:3, userid:4) = \frac{1/4+0}{5} = 0.05$, (as age range difference is 1 and gen is same)

Table 4 below shows the 'Similarity Matrix' with distance scores between all users in the sample dataset (Table 2)

Table 4. Similarity matrix

user_id	1	2	3	4
1	x	0.3	0.5	0.6
2	0.2	x	0	0.15
3	0.25	0.2	x	0.05
4	0.45	0.1	0.3	x

Ranking Recommendations by Importance. After the user preferences and the distance scores are computed, the list of recommended users generated for user x are as follows: Every user y will receive a distance score that reflects how many preferences of user x match with the attributes of user y and vice-versa. We call this measure 'reciprocal score'. The reciprocal score between users x and y is the harmonic mean of the distance scores between them. It is to be noted that distance scores of zero are replaced by a small value like 0.001 in order for the harmonic mean to be computed. A ranking is generated using the reciprocal scores (harmonic mean), it is then verified if the preference priority for attributes as denoted by the user is satisfied or not.

For instance, the reciprocal score for user $id:3$ is shown in Table 5. Note that the reciprocal score is symmetric as the name suggests, i.e. y's score in the recommendation list for x is the same as x's score in the list for y. However, as the lists contains only the top-N recommendations, user y may be in the top-N recommendations for user x but the opposite may not be true.

Table 5. Reciprocal score for user $id:3$

y	p(3, y)	p(y, 3)	harmonic_mean
1	0.25	0.5	0.333
2	0.2	0.001	**0.002**
4	0.05	0.3	0.086

Given the reciprocal scores in Table 5, the list of top-3 recommendations for user $id:3$ will be: [2, 4 and 1]. Furthermore, user $id:3$ has noted preference priority for age attribute (see bold values in Table 3). Since user $id:2$ satisfies this criterion, it will remain at the first position and users $id:4$ and $id:1$ will follow. If this was not the case, then a re-ranking of recommended users is done based on the preference priority of the user for the given attributes.

4   Experiments and Results

4.1   Evaluation Metrics

The goal of the current work was to primarily explore the role of reciprocity in the formulation of the recommendations for MOOC. It should be noted here that an actual evaluation of a (reciprocal) recommender system requires on-line deployment of the algorithm to one of the existing MOOC platforms. Since this was not possible in our case, we had to build measures based on the data available.

For a reciprocal system (like the one in our case) we need to define 'what is a successful recommendation?'. We say that, "learner y is a successful (reciprocal) recommendation (out of the K-total) for learner x, if and only if x is also in the top-K recommendations of learner y". This condition factors the reciprocity element which is essential to measure the performance of a reciprocal system like ours. Using this logic, we modify the definitions of precision and recall [13] for each learner as follows: "In order to compute the precision for learner x, we divide the number of successful recommendations by the total number of rec-ommendations (i.e. K) generated for leaner x". "Similarly, in order to compute the recall for learner x, we divide the number of successful recommendations by the total number of learners that have x in their top-K recommendation list". These definitions can be formalized in the following equations:

$$P_x = \frac{N_x}{K}, R_x = \frac{N_x}{N*_x} \tag{2}$$

where P_x is the precision for learner x, R_x is the recall for learner x, N_x is the number of successful recommendations for learner x (as defined before), K is the total number of recommendations generated and $N*_x$ is the number of learners that have x in their recommendation list.

The total precision and recall of the dataset based on the recommendation algorithm is defined as follows:

$$P = \sum_{i=1}^{M} \frac{P_i}{M}, R = \sum_{i=1}^{M} \frac{R_i}{M} \tag{3}$$

where P_i and R_i are the precision and recall respectively for learner i (as declared previously) and M is the total number of learners.

Moreover, in order to evaluate the rankings of the algorithm, we utilize a modified definition of the Discounted Cumulative Gain (DCG) [7], a popular measure of ranking quality. DCG originates from information retrieval where ranking positions are discounted logarithmically. Since for our system, we only care about the rank alignments and not the relevance of ranking positions, hence we do not require the logarithm discounting. When applied to our case, 'DCG' is the measure of 'reciprocity' or 'rank alignment'. In other words, a perfect rank alignment is when - "for all learners i, present at a position j in the list of top-N recommendations of learner u, if u is also present at the same position j in the list of top-N recommendations of i".

Assuming each learner u has a "gain", g_{ui} from being recommended to another learner i, then the average Discounted Cumulative Gain (DCG) for the recommendation list of K learners is defined as follows:

$$DCG = \frac{1}{M} \sum_{u=1}^{M} \frac{\sum_{j=1}^{K} g_{ui_j}}{S} \tag{4}$$

where M is total number of learners, S is the number of successful recommendations, j denotes the position in the ranking list and g_{ui_j} is the gain of learner i (in position j) for learner u.

Division by the number of successful recommendations guarantees that maximum DCG will be 1, provided that a user has successful recommendations, otherwise the value is 0.

The gain g_{ui}, is 0 if learner u is not in the top-K recommendation list for learner i (no gain for the reciprocal recommendation system here) and if is present, then the gain is defined as follows:

$$g_{ui} = \frac{1}{1 + |diff_{ui}|} \tag{5}$$

where $diff_{ui}$ is the difference in positions between the ranking of user i in the recommendation list of user u and the ranking of user u in the recommendation list of user i. This equation provides a value of 1 if the reciprocal rankings between learners i and u agree, otherwise it discounts this gain.

Finally, DCG can be divided by the ideal DCG for the recommender system which would lead to the normalized discounted cumulative gain (NDCG). Ideal DCG is 1 provided that all users have at least one successful recommendation (each user can have a maximum DCG of 1, so divided by the number of users that gives 1), otherwise it is a reduced value.

$$NDCG = \frac{DCG}{DCG*} \tag{6}$$

Consider the following Table 6 of six learners: [1, 2, 3, 4, 5, 6] with successful recommendations highlighted in circles.

Overall precision for this system is 0.44, recall is 0.40 and the NDCG is 0.73 (DCG is 0.61 and DCG* is 0.83).

We conducted our experiments with 5 different samples of 1000 user records from the dataset. From each of these samples, we ranked users by comparing their reciprocal scores and recommended the top-N [5, 10, 15, 20] users in the list. The results were averaged across the samples for each of these top-N recommendations. Our precision, recall and 'DCG' scores are compared against the 'baseline', wherein the reciprocity factor was not accounted for. The 'baseline' model builds the list of top-N recommendations without looking at reciprocity, very similar to a traditional recommender system.

Table 6. Ranked recommendations, $K = 3$

Rank/learner	1	2	3	4	5	6
1	2	③	①	6	1	3
2	③	4	②	⑤	④	2
3	4	5	④	③	6	1
4	5	1	5	1	2	4
5	6	6	6	2	3	5
Precision	0.33	0.33	1.00	0.67	0.33	0.00
Recall	0.33	0.33	0.75	0.50	0.50	0.00
DCG	0.50	0.50	0.67	1.00	1.00	0.00

The precision and recall graphs are shown in Fig. 1. As expected, precision and recall increase with 'N', which means that in the case of precision, if a learner y is present in the top-N recommendation list for learner x, then the chances that x is also present in the recommendation list of y increases with increasing value of 'N'. The same holds true for recall as well.

We also calculate the 'Normalized DCG' or 'NDCG' as shown in Fig. 2. The value of 'NDCG' decreases if the 'top-N' recommendations increase. This makes sense because with higher number of recommendations, the difference in ranks for two positions in the recommendation list will increase, thereby resulting in an overall decrease in 'gain'.

In summary, the precision and recall scores for 'reciprocal' model far exceeds the scores for 'baseline' model whereas the 'NDCG' values for 'reciprocal' is slightly better than the baseline model across all values of top-N recommendations.

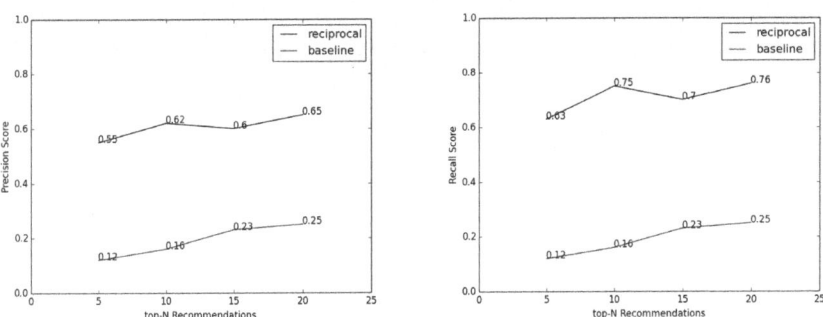

Fig. 1. Precision and recall graph

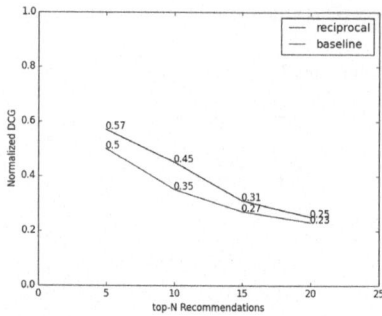

Fig. 2. NDCG graph

5   Conclusions and Future Work

In this paper we proposed an algorithm that allows learners to reach out and communicate with other similar learners and it thereby facilitates meaningful discussions and encourages peer learning. Results show that our system performs better than the baseline system on the measures of precision, recall and discounted cumulative gain. As future work, we plan to incorporate some more learner attributes like 'communication frequency', 'leadership ability' etc., based on the historical interaction of users on various MOOC forums. This will certainly help to improve the list of recommendations. Moreover, we plan to conduct tests on an actual MOOC platform to measure the quality of recommendations. Such an experimentation will evaluate how reciprocal recommendation can improve learners' experience but it should be noted that it requires longer times and greater difficulties in implementation. Case studies reveal that with the number of participating users in MOOCs increasing exponentially every year, it is quite challenging to establish the same kind of communication that exists within a classroom. However, with this proposed model, we believe we can bridge that gap to some extent.

References

1. Akehurst, J., Koprinska, I., Yacef, K., Pizzato, S., Kay, J., Rej, T.: CCR-a content-collaborative reciprocal recommender for online dating. In: IJCAI, pp. 2199–2204 (2011)
2. Apaza, R.G., Cervantes, E.V., Quispe, L.C., Luna, J.O.: Online courses recommendation based on LDA. In: SIMBig, pp. 42–48. Citeseer (2014)
3. Bousbahi, F., Chorfi, H.: MOOC-Rec: a case based recommender system for MOOCs. Procedia Soc. Behav. Sci. **195**, 1813–1822 (2015)
4. Bull, S., Greer, J., McCalla, G., Kettel, L., Bowes, J.: User modelling in i-help: what, why, when and how. In: Bauer, M., Gmytrasiewicz, P.J., Vassileva, J. (eds.) UM 2001. LNCS (LNAI), vol. 2109, pp. 117–126. Springer, Heidelberg (2001). doi:10.1007/3-540-44566-8_12

5. Freeman, S., Eddy, S.L., McDonough, M., Smith, M.K., Okoroafor, N., Jordt, H., Wenderoth, M.P.: Active learning increases student performance in science, engineering, and mathematics. Proc. Natl. Acad. Sci. **111**(23), 8410–8415 (2014)

6. Ho, A.D., Chuang, I., Reich, J., Coleman, C.A., Whitehill, J., Northcutt, C.G., Williams, J.J., Hansen, J.D., Lopez, G., Petersen, R.: HarvardX and MITx: two years of open online courses fall 2012-summer 2014 (2015). SSRN 2586847

7. Järvelin, K., Kekäläinen, J.: Cumulated gain-based evaluation of IR techniques. ACM Trans. Inf. Syst. (TOIS) **20**(4), 422–446 (2002)

8. Koprinska, I., Yacef, K.: People-to-people reciprocal recommenders. In: Ricci, F., Rokach, L., Shapira, B. (eds.) Recommender Systems Handbook, pp. 545–567. Springer, Boston (2015). doi:10.1007/978-1-4899-7637-6_16

9. Miller, G.A.: Wordnet: a lexical database for English. Commun. ACM **38**(11), 39–41 (1995)

10. MITx and HarvardX: Harvardx-mitx person-course academic year 2013 de-identified dataset, version 2.0 (2014)

11. Onah, D.F.O., Sinclair, J., Boyatt, R.: Dropout rates of massive open online courses: behavioural patterns. In: Proceedings of EDULEARN 2014, pp. 5825–5834 (2014)

12. Pizzato, L., Rej, T., Chung, T., Koprinska, I., Kay, J.: RECON: a reciprocal recommender for online dating. In: Proceedings of the Fourth ACM Conference on Recommender Systems, pp. 207–214. ACM (2010)

13. Shani, G., Gunawardana, A.: Evaluating recommendation systems. In: Ricci, F., Rokach, L., Shapira, B., Kantor, P. (eds.) Recommender Systems Handbook, pp. 257–297. Springer, Boston (2011). doi:10.1007/978-0-387-85820-3_8

14. Wu, Z., Palmer, M.: Verbs semantics and lexical selection. In: Proceedings of the 32nd Annual Meeting on Association for Computational Linguistics, pp. 133–138. Association for Computational Linguistics (1994)

15. Zepke, N., Leach, L.: Improving student engagement: ten proposals for action. Act. Learn. High. Educ. **11**(3), 167–177 (2010)

Co-evaluation, to Scaffold the Creation of Open Educational Resources

Silvia Baldiris[1(✉)], Laura Mancera[2], Gloria Liliana Velez Saldarriaga[3], and Jutta Treviranus[4]

[1] Direction of Research, Innovation and Social Projection,
Fundación Universitaria Tecnológico Comfenalco, Cartagena, Colombia
sbaldiris@tecnologicocomfenalco.edu.co
[2] Universidad de la Sabana, Chía, Colombia
laura.mancera@unisabana.edu.co
[3] Universidad Pontificia Bolivariana, Medellín, Colombia
gloria.velez@upb.edu.co
[4] Inclusive Design Research Centre, OCAD University, Toronto, Canada
jtreviranus@ocadu.ca

Abstract. Open Educational Resources (OER) has been recognized by UNESCO not only as a possibility to offer open access to educational content to people under long-life learning but to ensure inclusion of people on education. However, the achievement of high quality OER that address the diversity is still a challenge due to many factors such as teachers training or availability of accessible creation tools and methodologies. In this context, the CO-CREARIA model to support the co-creation of inclusive and accessible OER was proposed. Specifically, in this paper the Co-Evaluation component of CO-CREARIA model is presented and evaluated. The sample consisted of 9 co-creators teachers from a Master Program of the Universidad Pontificia Bolivariana. Results show co-evaluation as an important strategy to scaffold the creation of inclusive, accessible and high quality OER.

Keywords: Open educational resources · Inclusion · Accessibility · Co-creation

1 Introduction and Related Work

Open Educational Resource is a term coined at UNESCO's 2002 Forum on Open Courseware (UNESCO 2002) and designates "teaching, learning and research materials in any medium, digital or otherwise, that reside in the public domain or have been released under an open license that permits no-cost access, use, adaptation and redistribution by others with no or limited restrictions. Open licensing is built within the existing framework of intellectual property rights as defined by relevant international conventions and respects the authorship of the work".

UNESCO in Paris Declaration (UNESCO 2012) encourages governments to promote OER adoption and many projects have been funded with this aim. Different initiatives have been carried out for offering models to support OER

© Springer International Publishing AG 2017
H. Xie et al. (Eds.): ICWL 2017, LNCS 10473, pp. 168–176, 2017.
DOI: 10.1007/978-3-319-66733-1_18

creation (Arimoto et al. 2016; Menon 2014) an others to support OER evaluation. However, there is still a gap in OER movement development because as mentioned by Vladoiu (2011) "there is no articulated set of quality criteria to be used for the development, use, modification, evaluation, and comparison of such resources, though, there is concern about this subject".

In this context, CO-CREARIA was presented as an alternative to support the OER movement development by offering a model of collaborative Creation of Inclusive and Accessible OER (Baldiris et al. 2015) promoting the active participation of teachers, but also from the different actors in the learning process - including students and several experts – to identify and address the educational needs that have to be attended through the co-created resources. In this paper, the OER Co-Evaluation Model of Co-CREARIA is introduced. The model facilitates the comparison of the generated OER but also scaffolds the work of co-creators when they create OER. The paper is organized as follow. Section 2 introduces CO-CREARIA as an OER co-creation model. Section 3 presents the Co-Evaluation model of CO-CREARIA followed by its evaluation in the Sect. 4. Finally, Sect. 5 remarks conclusions and future work.

2   CO-CREARIA

The CO-CREARIA model has the following characteristics: (1) It is a systematic process that involves several activities organized into stages. Some of the outputs of these stages are used as input in the subsequent stages of the process; (2) It is a collaborative process in which different actors of different disciplines contributing to achieve a high quality OER; (3) It is a dynamic process that allows actors to retake and improve the OER when deemed necessary. This dynamism permeates the OER "open" character, openness to adoption, reuse, review, redistribution and the possibility to mix it up with other OER (Wiley et al. 2014). Finally, (4) It is a creative process in which the attention to the needs and preferences of students becomes a challenge around which ideas and solutions are generated.

The bases that guide CO-CREARIA model are: (1) Diversity must be considered a value in the educational process; as well as (2) The openness taking into account the UNESCO call for an equalitarian and inclusive society; (3) The vision of technology as a way that facilitates the attention to the needs and preferences of actors in the educational process; and (4) The web accessibility is a chance to break potential barriers in the web contents associated to the OER.

The systematic sequence of actions used by CO-CREARIA are based on ADDIE model (Analysis, Design, Development, Implementation and Evaluation) (Branch 2009) which together with the aforementioned bases allow the co-creators to advance in the creation of an OER attending the diversity of the educational system.

In the **Analysis** phase, the teacher identifies the development team and the member's roles in the OER. Collaboratively, this team defines: (a) the educational purposes that guide the didactic process offered in the OER and can be expressed in terms of competencies, objectives and/or achievements; (b) the educational needs and preferences of the target population in terms of the UDL principles (Rose and Meyer 2002); and (c) the previous required competencies. With all this information, the teacher gets a first approximation of the learning units that they will offer to their students through the OER. The outputs of this phase are: an initial description of the OER and the profile of the target population according to UDL (Fig. 1).

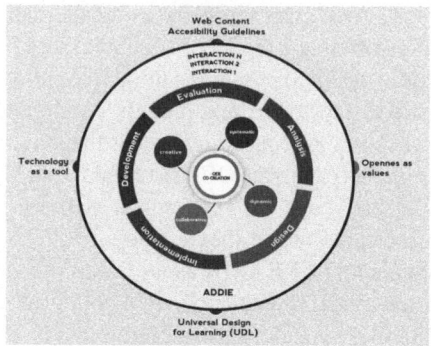

Fig. 1. CO-CREARIA model conceptual outline

In the **Design** phase, detailed scripts and prototypes for the OER are created. According to the UDL guidelines the methods and materials defined are susceptible of presenting potential barriers for learning, for these reason those barriers are analysed and addressed. This phase advances the graphic design of the learning resources, the user interfaces and the contents, choosing the right delivery platforms (video, animation, sounds, text, etc.). The outputs of this phase are: the methods and materials designed for the OER, indicating the digital resources that will be used in their construction; and the Analysis of the barriers of the methods and materials of the OER according to UDL.

In the **Development** phase, the learning materials are created. It is very important to select adequately the authoring tools for the creation of contents in a way that they be accessible. The outputs of this phase are: the Open Educational Resource co-created and a descriptive document of the OER development.

The **Evaluation** phase defined by ADDIE is not a single moment in CO-CREARIA. Evaluation consists of a set of evaluations moments that will be described in detail in next section.

The **Deployment** is referred to the real delivery of the OER to the target population. It implies an Evaluation Moment that involves the final user. The objective in this phase is to ease the students to attain the proposed learning purposes. The outputs of this phase are: a description of the deployment scenarios of the OER, a report of the results of the deployment process of the OER.

These stages are developed recursively in a dynamic co-creation process where the various moments of evaluation play an important role in the continuous improvement of the OER and the process that, in turn, improves with practice. These improvements are done in continued interactions throughout time.

3   OER Co-evaluation Model of CO-CREARIA

Co-Evaluation Model of CO-CREARIA is a collaborative and systematic process that ensures at least three features in the created OER: inclusiveness, accessibility and quality. The Co-Evaluation is perfectly integrated into the co-creation process carry out by the co-creators, it is not an independent or external process, it is part of the co-creation because it generates inputs that support the OER improvement over the creation timeline. Next sub-sections Evaluation Moments defined.

3.1   Co-evaluation Moment 1: UDL Principles Evaluation

Analysis and Design phases permit to co-creators define learning purposes to be address by the OER, the OER structure as Unit of Learning, the target group to be attended by the OER, the materials identifying possible futures barriers and finally giving solutions to such barriers taking specially care of the accessibility. Definitions should be aligned to the UDL principles in order to guarantee the attention to all students considering the three UDL principles: to provide multiple means of engagement, to provide multiple means of action and to provide multiple means of representation. So, Co-Evaluation Moment 1 ensures the OER curriculum addresses the principles of UDL. Curriculum is judged by its capacity to support and accommodate the diversity and variability of learners (Inclusiveness) providing genuine learning opportunities for all students (Meyer et al. 2014). For doing so, a rubric designed by an expert team (diversity, psychologist, pedagogues and web content creators) to evaluate OER Inclusiveness of the curriculum in terms of: set clear goals as a foundation of any effective curriculum, provides multiple means of methods and materials, was defined. Co-Evaluation team receives the OER specification, Analysis and Design Documents and carry out the evaluation collaboratively.

3.2   Co-evaluation Moment 2: Accessibility Evaluation

The co-created OER is the input to the Accessibility Evaluation. It is important to highlight co-creation process considers the development of continuous automatic accessibility evaluation. Accessibility Evaluation Rubric include manual and automatic evaluation over the most used web content elements such as Headings, Images, Tables, Links, Lists, Videos, Color Contrast, Videos, List definitions, and Abbreviations and acronyms. The Accessibility Evaluation Rubric was defined by technical experts on web content accessibility guidelines (WCAG) W3C Web Accessibility Initiative (WAI 2008) and it permits to eliminate barriers in the created web content by considering WCAG and achieving a perceptible, operable, robust and compressible web content. Co-Evaluation team received the OER to be evaluated.

3.3 Co-evaluation Moment 3: Quality Evaluation

Quality evaluation judges the OER in terms of several dimensions that ensure tecnical and pedagogical requirements. The instrument used to evaluate OER quality is Learning Object Review Instrument (LORI) (Nesbit et al. 2005). LORI structure the OER evaluation over 9 evaluation dimension: Content Quality, Learning Goal Alignment, Feedback and Adaptation, Motivation, Presentation Design, Interaction Usability, Accessibility, Reusability and Standards Compliance. Accessibility dimension was eliminated to the quality evaluation since Co-Evaluation moment 2 included it. Co-Evaluation team received the OER to be evaluated as well as the associated documents of Analysis and Design phases.

3.4 Co-evaluation Moment 4: OER Implementation

OER implementation is the natural space to evaluate the OER impact over students learning. Although, a sample of students can participate in the creation process, OER implementation in the classroom permits to co-creators having a real input from a natural and real learning scenario. OER implementation can consider qualitative, quantitative or mixed methods to measure students behaviour before and after the OER usage and in this way corroborate the state of the OER dimensions previously evaluated, Inclusiveness, Accessibility or Quality from the perspective of the students results.

4 Evaluation

The main objective of the evaluation was identifying the perception of co-creators about the co-evaluation model to scaffold the OER creation. Scaffold means in this context how the model support co-creators teams to improve the OER been co-created.

4.1 Sample

OER Evaluation model of CO-CREARIA was qualitative evaluated by 9 co-creation teams lead by 9 teachers that teach in several educational institutions in Colombia. They come from diverse knowledge areas and different educational levels. Teachers were enrolled in the MSc programme on ICT hosted by the Universidad Pontificia Bolivariana in Medellín (Colombia).

4.2 Method

During the MSc programme on ICT, in-service teachers received training about the creation of OER including CO-CREARIA Model. Each teacher individually defined a co-creation team with professionals experts from their educational institutions and together follow the Phases of CO-CREARIA to co-create a OER that give a solution to an education need identified by each co-creation team. Each co-creation team evaluated an OER been created by other co-creation team (Peer Review) in each Co-Evaluation

Moment. After the training, a survey was presented to teachers as leaders of the co-creation team and they invited the co-creation teams to discuses about the survey and fill it out.

Evaluation was oriented to identify how the Co-Evaluation impacted the OER creation and also to perceive the opinion of the co-creation team about the instrument used in each Co-evaluation Moment.

4.3   Instrument

Research instrument was a survey divided in three parts, one for each Evaluation Moment. The scope of the MSc courses permitted to evaluate just three Evaluation Moments; the co-creation teams did not evaluate Evaluation Moment 4 because Implementation Phase was not carried out as part of the courses. Survey consists of a set of Open Questions that co-creation teams should answer about each Evaluation Moment. Table 1 presents the questions for each moment. Finally, an additional question about the co-evaluation as a whole was included: Do you consider OER co-evaluation as a good idea?

Table 1. Evaluation surveys

Evaluation Moment 1	Evaluation Moment 2	Evaluation Moment 3
1. Did the instrument seem appropriate for evaluating the inclusion capacity of an Open Educational Resource? Why?	1. Did the instrument seem appropriate for evaluating the accessibility of an Educational Resource? Why?	1. Did the instrument seem appropriate for evaluating the quality of an Educational Resource? Why?
2. Is the instrument easy to use for a teacher?	2. Is the instrument easy to use for a teacher?	2. Is the instrument easy to use for a teacher?
3. List how the instrument helped you improve the definition (analysis and design) of your OER?	3. List how the instrument helped you to improve your OER?	3. List how the instrument helped you to improve your OER?
4. Would you add any category of evaluation to the instrument?	4. Would you add any category of evaluation to the instrument?	4. Would you add any category of evaluation to the instrument?
5. Would you change anything of the format of the instrument?	5. Would you change anything of the format of the instrument?	5. Would you change anything of the format of the instrument?

4.4   Results

Results of the responses provide by co-creation teams are presented on Table 2.

Table 2. Evaluation results

%	Descriptions
Moment 1. UDL Principles Evaluation	
100%	The instrument is appropriate for evaluating the OER'inclusiveness; The instrument is easy to use; The co-creation team consider the instrument is adequate, they not should add any additional category.
77.78%	The instrument gives detail information about criteria to evaluate the UDL principles implementation.
11,11%	The instrument offers additional and not obvious information that could be useful to improve the OER inclusiveness; The instrument improves the OER design; The instrument was too long; It is important to add examples to explain the category according with the scenario of application; Some parts of the instrument are confuses.
44,44%	Some words used in the instrument should be explain in more detail using examples; The instrument helps to improve the assessment; the instruments helps to improve the means of representation by considering other means.
22,22%	The instrument is a guide to improve the OER during the co-creation; The instrument helps to improve the course profile.
55,56%	The co-creation teams were agreeing on the instrument helps to identify elements not considered initially in the OER analysis or/and design to address students' variability in the classroom.
33,33%	The instrument helps to improve the objectives; The instrument helps to improve the means of action by considering other means.
77,78%	The co-creation teams consider the instrument format is adequate.
22%	It is necessary to change the format to one oriented to selection, least descriptive.
Moment 2. Exhaustive Accessibility Evaluation	
100%	The co-creation teams consider the instrument is adequate to evaluate the OER accessibility; The instrument is easy to use; The co-creation teams consider the instrument as completely adequate.
33,33%	The instrument presents a simple language, which is adequate for non-expert users; The instrument helps to improve the accessibility of the images.
22%	The instrument could be used for a not accessibility expert.
11,11%	The language of some parts of the instrument should be improve for non expert users; The instrument supports the improvement of text quality; It is necessary to permit to add comments for each category and improve the graphical design.
22,2%	The instrument permits to improve the OER structure; The instrument permits to improve the accessibility of tables and links.
77,78%	The instrument improves the web content accessibility in general.
Moment 3. Quality Evaluation	
88,89%	The co-creation teams consider the quality instrument is adequate and easy to use.
11,11%	The categories should be better described using examples.
22,22%	The instrument supports the improvement of OER usability and OER reusability and help to improve feedback.
33,33%	The instrument helps to improve the capacity of OER to motivate students.
66%	Improve the OER content quality and improve the standards adoption.
88,89%	The co-creation teams argue the instrument do not need more categories.
77,78	The format is adequate
100%	The co-creation teams coincided on it is important to consider different points of view and the experience of diverse people to improve the OER.

Evaluation of the Co-Evaluation Model of CO-CREARIA showed Co-Evaluation Moments scaffold co-creation teams when they co-create OER, helping them to improve the OER in each moment. Different, differentiated and specific Evaluation Moments are important to improve the considered OER dimensions, Inclusiveness, Accessibility and Quality. Each Evaluation Moment gave to co-creators important and invaluable information, which contributed to the achievement of an inclusive, accessible and high quality OER.

5 Conclusions and Future Work

Open Educational Resources has a great potential to support learning for all students. However, methods and tools to support high quality, inclusive and accessible OER are necessary. CO-CREARIA is a new model to support the creations of OER with mentioned important features. Co-Evaluation model of CO-CREARIA has been described in detail in this paper, as a mechanism to scaffold co-creation teams when they co-create OER. Model support teams in the identification of possible inclusion barriers to the students learning but also technical problems in the web content been created that reduce the accessibility. The model also evaluate diverse quality dimension of the OER and assume the OER Implementation Phase as an important evaluation moment that support the OER continues improvement over the time. Results show each Evaluation Moments offer important feedback that teams used to improve the co-created OER. In this sense, co-evaluation becomes a great scaffold strategy to support de creation of a more inclusive, accessible and high quality OER.

References

Arimoto, M., Barroca, L., Barbosa, E.F.: Developing Open Educational Resources through Learning Design and Agile Practices, (Cbie), 240 (2016). http://doi.org/10.5753/cbie.sbie.2016.240

Baldiris, S., Avila, C., Fabregat, R., Potes, E., Cuesta, J., Muñoz, T., Cardona, S.: CO-CREARIA: Modelo de Co-Creación de REA Inclusivos y Accesibles. La experiencia de la maestría en TIC de la Universidad Pontificia Bolivariana. Revista Ingeniería E Innovación 3(2), 37–47 (2015)

Branch, R.M.: Instructional Design: The ADDIE Approach. Springer, Boston, MA (2009). doi: 10.1007/978-0-387-09506-6

Menon, M.B.: Wawasan Open University – Developing a Fully OER-based Course. In: Naidu, S., Mishra, S. (eds.) Case studies on OER-based e-Learning, p. 56. Commonwealth Educational Media Centre for Asia, New Delhi (2014)

Meyer, A., Rose, D.H., Gordon, D.: Universal Design for Learning, Theory and Practice. CAST Professional Publishing, Wakefield (2014)

Nesbit, J., Belfer, K., Leacock, T.: Learning Object Review Instrument (LORI) (2005)

Rose, D.H., Meyer, A.: Teaching every estudent in the digital age. Universal Design for Learning (2002)

UNESCO: Forum on the Impact of Open Courseware for Higher Education in Developing Countries Final report UNESCO (Vol. CI-2002/CO), Paris, France (2002)

UNESCO: 2012 World Open Educational Resources (OER) Congress, 2012 Paris OER declaration 1–2 (2012)

Vladoiu, M.: Towards a Quality Model for Open Courseware and Open Educational Resources Motivation for Research (2011)

W3C Web Accessibility Initiative (WAI): Web Content Accessibility Guidelines (WCAG) 2.0 (2008). http://www.w3.org/TR/WCAG20/

Wiley, D., Bliss, T.J., McEwen, M.: Open educational resources: a review of the literature. In: Handbook of Research on Educational Communications and Technology, pp. 781–789 (2014)

Organizing Online Computation for Adaptive Micro Open Education Resource Recommendation

Geng Sun[1(✉)], Tingru Cui[1], Ghassan Beydoun[2], Shiping Chen[3], Dongming Xu[4], and Jun Shen[1]

[1] School of Computing and Information Technology, University of Wollongong, Wollongong, Australia
gs147@uowmail.edu.au, {tingru,jshen}@uow.edu.au
[2] School of Systems, Management and Leadership, University of Technology Sydney, Ultimo, Australia
Ghassan.Beydoun@uts.edu.au
[3] CSIRO Data61, Marsfield, Australia
Shiping.Chen@data61.csiro.au
[4] UQ Business School, The University of Queensland, Brisbane, Australia
D.Xu@business.uq.edu.au

Abstract. Our previous work, Micro Learning as a Service (MLaaS), aimed to deliver adaptive micro open education resources (OERs). However, relying solely on the offline computation, the recommendation lacks rationality and timeliness. It is also difficult to make the first recommendation to a new learner. In this paper we introduce the organization of the online computation of the MLaaS. It targets at solving the cold start problem due to the shortage of learner information and real-time updates of the learner-micro OER profile.

Keywords: Micro learning · Cold start · Open education resource recommendation · Real-time computation

1 Introduction

The increasingly frequent use of mobile devices and fast-approaching life paces make micro learning possible [1]. Micro learning through open education resources (namely, micro open learning) is becoming a mainstream for next generation learners, who learn on the move, with easy access to the 'cloud' or Internet of Things [2].

In this paper we will focus on organizing the online computation of a smart micro open education resources (OERs) adaptation system, namely Micro Learning as a Service (MLaaS) [3]. This work aims to tackle the shortage of learner information and realize fast reaction on real-time learner interactions.

© Springer International Publishing AG 2017
H. Xie et al. (Eds.): ICWL 2017, LNCS 10473, pp. 177–182, 2017.
DOI: 10.1007/978-3-319-66733-1_19

2   Research Challenges

2.1   Online Computation and Cold Start Problem

Micro learning is defined as learning activities that are carried out within fragmented time pieces, preferably, 15 min [4]. The conjunction of micro learning and OER brings much more opportunities to make use of spare time, learn on-demand, learn informally and participate in the virtual class of leading universities [2].

Successful e/m-learning systems normally takes 'day' as the finest granularity in their only offline computation. Their time effectiveness is deficient by failing to keep user information up-to-date, and also the learning resource adaption process may suffer from the sparsity of data [5]. The experience and outcome of micro open learning highly depend on the educational settings, learners' personal learning styles, and, specifically, variable environment and fragmented time frames [6]. New OERs, in micro or non-micro modes, are rapidly released and updated day by day. Fast reaction mechanisms are needed to add incoming micro OERs into candidate lists for recommendation.

In addition, in micro open learning, the accumulation and attenuation of user interests and demands can be periodical and vary in different patterns than other online activities, for example, e-business and e-entertainment [7, 8]. Both open learning and micro learning are comparatively new terms in the e-society. A fresh learner can be at his/her wits end to choose the starting line of micro open learning given that the available resources are massive, meanwhile, the system faces difficulty to make recommendation because little is known about the learner [5, 9]. Carelessly treated cold start problem might cause the loss of learners whose satisfactions became lowered due to the unreasonable recommendations based on sparse data, as a result it could further affect the user acceptance of the new open learning mode [9].

2.2   Previous Works and Our Research Aim

In our previous works [3, 10], we have introduced a service-oriented recommender system, MLaaS, which aims to deliver adaptive micro OERs to learning in terms of their difference. It consists of online and offline computation components, where the offline computation is equipped with educational data mining and learning analytics mechanisms to process 'big data', and employs artificial intelligence based approaches to realize resource adaptation.

On the other hand, as discussed in Sect. 2.2, MLaaS's online computation is necessary to be facilitated because it not only serves as a complementary strategy to guarantee the rationality and timeliness of recommendations, but also targets on covering current gaps by relying solely on historical data. Basically, it deals with the 'new user' cold start problem from which a fresh learner in the micro open learning environment suffers. Meanwhile, the online computation compensates the limitation of offline computation by keeping the learner profile up-to-date (Fig. 1).

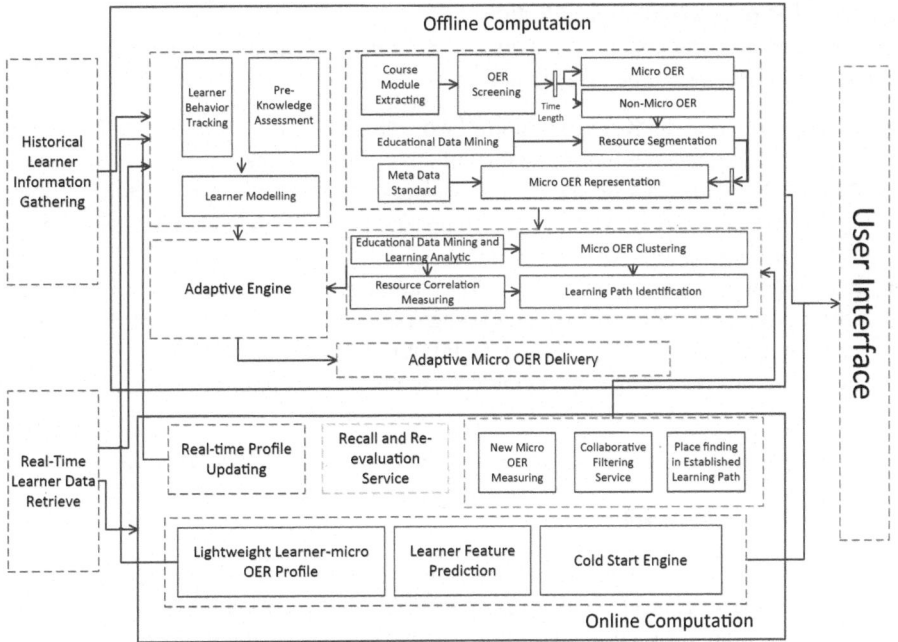

Fig. 1. Architecture of online and offline computation in MLaaS

3 Online Computation of MLaaS

3.1 Micro OER and Learner Profiling

Lightweight Learner-micro OER Profile for Cold Start Recommendation

In [10] we proposed a comprehensive learner model for micro open learning. From the user perspective, it is unlikely to have that sophisticated information in hand especially with a null history for a fresh learner. This cold start condition motivated us to simplify this comprehensive learner model to a lightweight version, which merely contains necessary information for decision making in order to act on the initialization agilely.

The lightweight profile consists of a static component and a dynamic component. The static component is represented by a vector, containing demographic and educational information. By matching the instances of both augmented ontologies, a user-item (learner-micro OER) matrix is generated, with the learners in rows and micro OERs in columns. In each three-dimensional element in this matrix (i.e. the dynamic component), three typical attributes are selected in respect to the 'micro' time piece and 'learn in mobile' spatial condition. They include a learner's preference to a micro OER, instant time availability, and the level of distraction in terms of the given learning environment and surroundings, respectively.

Micro OER measurement and Relation Extraction

For fast response and also for comparison purposes, the semantic relationships among each micro OER should be investigated:

- ConsistsOf is an inclusion relation. Two items with this relation are located in different hierarchies of the augmented micro OER ontology.
- RequiredSequence is a strong order between two items (OER or micro OER), where the former micro OER is necessarily to be learnt before the latter one, due to course setting and educational consideration.
- RecommendedSequence is a weak order relation between two items (OER and micro OER), where the former micro OER is suggestively to be learnt before the latter one, according to the instructors' guidance, but it is not mandatory.
- Both relations regarding sequencing can be inherited by entities' descendants.

3.2   Hybrid Approach for Cold Start in Micro OER Recommendation

Prediction for Sparse Data

Learner Preference Propagation.   A fresh learner is required to rate any micro OER available at the beginning of computation. This seed preference rate is propagated through a spreading activation algorithm. An upwards propagation is executed firstly to predict the preference rates for its ancestors, and then a downwards propagation follows up to spread up the predicted preference rates to every descendant. Innovatively a decay factor and a normalization factor are used in the propagation process, so that the predicted value takes into consideration the accumulation and attenuation of learning preference and demands.

Learner Distraction Prediction.   The distraction rate in the real-time environment is predicted by a demographic-based approach. This value also depends on the location data sensed from the mobile device. It runs in a three-phase manner: classifying users based on static information (demographic and educational data), calculating the users' similarities with their neighbors and foreseeing their distraction rates afterwards [11]. This follows the expectation that the learners who have similar general situation (i.e. social factors) and surroundings (i.e. environmental factors) are in high probability to have similar degree of distraction.

Heuristic Rule-based Optimization: In a generated list of recommended micro OERs, those ones with higher learners' interests are placed at the top. For two micro OERs MR_u and MR_w, their sequence is determined according to heuristic rules, which are defined in accordance with the extraction of three kinds of relations. These rules are executed sequentially with priority.

1. If there is a RequiredSequence relation between these two micro OERs, the prerequisite one is placed above (refer to the previous section).
2. If the preferences regarding these two OERs, MR_u's is higher than MR_w's, then the MR_u is above MR_w

3. If, in the absolute terms, MR_u's preference has high confidence degree, then the MR_u is above MR_w, and vice versa.
4. If there is a RecommendedSequence relation between these two micro OERs, the one which is suggested to be accessed first is placed above.
5. The micro OER, which is more related to the learners' education background, or falls in the relevant disciplines or inter-disciplines is placed with priority if the disciplinary difference between these two candidate micro OERs is obvious.
6. Otherwise the recommended micro OER list is randomly ordered if none of the above rules applies

To initiate the constrained multi-objective optimization, candidate solutions (chromosomes) are randomly generated, each of which is a learning path with a series of micro OERs. For a chromosome, its violation degree is investigated by examining the relations between each contiguously prior/posterior micro OER pair against the first 5 rules, and then summing up. The higher the violation degree is, the more serious the candidate learning path violates the rules. An evolutionary algorithm is applied to reach the decision of first recommendation in micro OER delivery.

4 Comprehensive User Profile Updating

The online computation copes with users' near-term and real-time activities which have not been sorted in historical data repository. In addition to solving the 'new user' cold start problem, it also holds a real-time algorithm in 'second' granularity, from the item perspective. This comes with two considerations, the first is to improve the recommendation performance for the micro OERs newly added in the same day, and also the most recent interactions on a micro OER can better reflect the its value of recommendation.

Redundant offline algorithms need to be simplified as the it should respond in seconds. The simplified online algorithm for profile updating is realized by a row extension in the learner-micro OER matrix. The online computation inquires and retrieves a specific learner's recent micro OER usage and complement the 'item' column in the matrix. This can eliminate the gap between new and old micro OERs, and solve the problem that the breadth of relations among micro OERs cannot be split. It also removes the impacts of the offline computation results caused by the connections among old micro OERs, which haven't been accessed by the specific learner in the real-time.

5 Conclusion

In this paper we introduced a solution to organize online computation for a recommender system oriented to adaptive micro OER delivery. It addresses the cold start problem in micro OER recommendation, and improves the performance of recommendation with higher timeliness and rationality.

References

1. Kovachev, D., Cao, Y., Klamma, R., Jarke, M.: Learn-as-you-go: new ways of cloud-based micro-learning for the mobile web. In: Leung, H., Popescu, E., Cao, Y., Lau, R.W.H., Nejdl, W. (eds.) ICWL 2011. LNCS, vol. 7048, pp. 51–61. Springer, Heidelberg (2011). doi: 10.1007/978-3-642-25813-8_6
2. Souza, M.I., Amaral, S.F.D.: Educational micro content for mobile learning virtual environments. Creative Educ. **5**, 672–681 (2014)
3. Sun, G., Cui, T., Yong, J., Shen, J., Chen, S.: MLaaS: a cloud-based system for delivering adaptive micro learning in mobile MOOC learning. IEEE Trans. Serv. Comput. http://dx.doi.org/10.1109/TSC.2015.2473854
4. Hug, T., Lindner, M.: ML: emerging concepts, practices and technologies after e-Learning. In: Proceedings of Micro Learning 2005, Austria, pp. 8–11, June 2005
5. Bruck, P.A., Motiwalla, L., Foerster, F.: Mobile learning with micro-content: a framework and evaluation. In: 25th Bled eConference, Bled, Slovenia, pp. 527–542 (2012)
6. Sun, G., Shen, J.: Facilitating social collaboration in mobile cloud-based learning: a Teamwork as a Service (TaaS) approach. IEEE Trans. Learn. Technol. **7**(3), 207–220 (2014)
7. Nawrot, I., Doucet, A.: Building engagement for MOOC students', introducing support for time management on online learning platforms. In: Proceeding of WWW 2014 Companion (2014)
8. Miranda, S., Mangione, G.R., Orciuoli, F., Gaeta, M., Loia, V.: Automatic generation of assessment objects and remedial works for MOOCs. In: 12th International Conference on Information Technology Based Higher Education and Training, Antalya, Turkey, Octorber 2013
9. Lika, B., Kolomvatsos, K., Hadjiefthymiades, S.: Facing the cold start problem in recommender systems. Expert Syst. Appl. **41**(4), 2065–2073 (2014)
10. Sun, G., Cui, T., Guo, W., Beydoun, G., Xu, D., Shen, J.: Micro learning adaptation in MOOC: a software as a service and a personalized learner model. In: Li, F.W.B., Klamma, R., Laanpere, M., Zhang, J., Manjón, B.F., Lau, R.W.H. (eds.) ICWL 2015. LNCS, vol. 9412, pp. 174–184. Springer, Cham (2015). doi:10.1007/978-3-319-25515-6_16
11. Sorour, S.E., Abd El Rahman, S., Kahouf, S.A., Mine, T.: Understandable prediction models of student performance using an attribute dictionary. In: Chiu, D.K.W., Marenzi, I., Nanni, U., Spaniol, M., Temperini, M. (eds.) ICWL 2016. LNCS, vol. 10013, pp. 161–171. Springer, Cham (2016). doi:10.1007/978-3-319-47440-3_18

Practice and Experience Sharing

What Children Really Contribute When Participating in the Design of Web-Based Learning Applications

Helene Gelderblom[✉]

Department of Informatics, University of Pretoria, Pretoria, South Africa
helene.gelderblom@up.ac.za

Abstract. Over the past 20 years a vast amount of research has been published on participatory design (PD) with children – especially in the field of educational technology design. The literature reveals many advantages (e.g. giving children voice in design), but also some challenges (e.g. overcoming the power distance between co-designers). What is difficult to find in published results on PD with children, is evidence that the children's design ideas are suitable for development into actual products. Serious educational games (SEGs) have to meet certain requirements. If children participate in the design of SEGs but their designs do not fulfil these requirements, are we still supposed to include them in the final product? Researchers often present examples and descriptions of the prototypes produced by child designers, but they do not always discuss to what extent these ideas are implementable. This paper reports on a study to assess children's contribution to the design of a web based educational application in the form of a SEG. Using a case study, children's prototypes were analysed using a valued framework for SEG design to determine if their designs satisfy the requirements of SEGs. The results demonstrate how children naturally include the elements of the SEG design framework. The findings confirm that involving children in the design of a web based educational game using well-tested techniques for doing PD with children, will result in design ideas that are in line with general requirements for SEGs and are thus implementable.

Keywords: Participatory design · Cooperative inquiry · Children · Serious educational games

1 Introduction

Interaction design and children is a noteworthy field of research within human-computer interaction (HCI). The ACM SIGCHI conference on Interaction Design and Children and Elsevier's International Journal on Child-Computer Interaction include participatory design (PD) with children as a recurring theme. PD actively involves the stakeholders (such as the users) in the design process [5]. Druin [2] is the 'PD with children' pioneer and introduced the Cooperative Design (CI) method. CI involves intergenerational design teams consisting of children (usually between the ages of 7 and 11) and adults designing interactive products for children together, using techniques such as brainstorming and low-tech prototyping.

© Springer International Publishing AG 2017
H. Xie et al. (Eds.): ICWL 2017, LNCS 10473, pp. 185–195, 2017.
DOI: 10.1007/978-3-319-66733-1_20

Academic literature on designing with children mostly reports on the *process* of designing with children rather than on the design *outcomes*. A clear impression of what children's actual contribution to real-world products could be is therefore elusive. The study reported here is an attempt at addressing this gap through a thorough investigation of one CI project during which a web based educational application was designed with the help of children. The designers intuitively interpreted the intended outcome to be a serious educational game (SEG). I analysed the children's design prototypes to establish to what extent they satisfy the requirements of educational game design. Mapping the elements of their designs to the elements included in Annetta's [1] framework for SEG design, revealed which aspects they intuitively incorporate and through what mechanisms.

The paper is organized as follows: The next section introduces related literature focusing on PD with children and SEG design. Section 3 presents the research process – how the PD sessions were conducted and how the outcomes were analysed for comparison with SEG design requirements. I then discuss the design outcomes and their assessment in terms of SEG requirements in Sect. 4 and conclude the paper in Sect. 5.

2   Related Work

2.1   Participatory Design with Children

In PD, the end-users of an organisational or technological system take part in the design and decision-making processes associated with that system. It originated in Scandinavia in the 1970s as a mechanism for workers to influence the design of new technologies for use in their workplace [5]. CI with children evolved from PD to make children part of the teams that design technologies aimed at improving their education and their lives in general [2].

Guha, Druin and Fails' [7] primary motivation for designing with children rather than with adults who are experts on children's technologies, is that no adult really knows what feels like to be a child 'today'. The assumption is then that the technology that results from CI will be more successful or appropriate for children than if it was designed by adults only. Kelly and colleagues [8] describe how the literature on designing for children displays a pattern 'of designing for no use or for local use'. They explain that much of the most cited research on the topic reports on design experiments from which no built product would result or where the product was just for use within a small, closed user group. There is thus a discrepancy – on the one hand we are encouraged to design technology for children with the help of children, but on the other hand, when children had been involved as design partners, it seems that widely used technologies seldom emerged.

KidPad is an example of an implemented result of CI [3]. It seems however that the outcome of CI need not be complete, built products. They can also be ideas that inspire adult designers towards better or more innovative solutions implement [11]. Nickelodeon's 'do-not-touch button' is an example of a design element that emerged in a prototype designed by two nine-year-olds and became a prominent feature of the Nick App (www.nick.com) in 2013.

The advantages of CI include giving children voice in design [6, 7] and approaching the design of children's technology from a child's point of view. The challenges include overcoming the power distance between adult and child designers and that children's creative ideas may be impossible to realise [11].

CI traditionally involves children from ages 7 to 11 working with adults. However, Gelderblom [6] reports on CI with young children and teenagers and Yip et al. [12] describe successful child led CI sessions. In the project reported here, I used a combination of child led and teenager facilitated CI.

2.2   The Design of Serious Educational Games (SEGs)

Different frameworks, models and guidelines exist for the design of SEGs. For example, Moreno-Ger et al. [10] propose integration, adaptation and assessment as high level pedagogical requirements for online educational games. Mitgutsch and Alvarado's [9] SEG assessment framework includes six criteria that respectively relate to purpose, aesthetics, narrative, game mechanics, framing and content.

Annetta's [1] well-cited framework for designing SEGs includes six elements. This hierarchical framework has 'identity' as the core element. Annetta's comprehensive explanation of each element makes it an appropriate tool to evaluate early prototypes of a SEG. The six elements are:

- Identity: A SEG should convince players that they are unique individuals in the game environment. This is best achieved through unique avatars that user select themselves.
- Immersion: This is achieved if players see themselves as the main character in the game and feel completely present in the virtual world. Good feedback supports immersion by giving players a clear sense of where they are in the narrative.
- Interactivity: This can be achieved through social communication with other players or non-player game characters. Immediacy is important– that is, the interaction must reduce the player's perceived distance from other players or game characters.
- Increased complexity: There must be multiple levels of complexity. Players must continuously progress and be rewarded for performance or in-game decisions. The aim must be to maintain 'pleasurable frustration'.
- Informed teaching: Data about the player's progress and achievement in the game must be recorded over time to assess student understanding.
- Instructional: A SEG should foster learning. There should be clear opportunity for mental development to occur during game play. Designers should understand cognitive information processing and use it as a guide. Scaffolding must be available at the right time and in the correct form.

In the study reported here, children's prototypes of a web based educational game were analysed to determine to what extent they adhere to the above, generally accepted requirements for SEG design.

3   Research Methods

Case studies allow a researcher to obtain a rich analysis of a phenomenon. A case study was suitable to identify the contribution that child designers make to real world products when they participate in the design thereof. Using one CI design case, I studied all the design ideas generated by children in depth and then assessed these ideas according to the requirements of a SEG design framework.

3.1   The Case

The case I investigated was the design of a web based platform for the Edublox reading and learning clinics [4]. Edublox is a South African company that specialises in cognitive training, reading, spelling, comprehension and mathematics [4]. Edublox programs, in the form of face-to-face sessions as well as computer based exercises, develop skills that underlie reading, spelling, writing and mathematics. Many of the Edublox exercises involve a set of coloured blocks that children have to manipulate and organise to improve their memory capacity and logical thinking skills.

In 2016, Edublox decided to develop a comprehensive web based platform that will allow them to expand their client base. I was approached to assist with the design of the web application that would incorporate their existing computer based exercises as well as additional aspects that had previously only been offered through face-to-face sessions. The new web based interface was designed over a period of three months with the help of an intergenerational design team.

3.2   The Participating Designers

The design team included seven children, two teenage facilitators and a professional graphic artist. The children and teenagers were divided into three groups for the design task (see Table 1). Group 1 consisted of three boys, one of whom had previously designed with me and since they seemed comfortable in the context, I decided they could lead their own design. The other groups each included one designer with previous design

Table 1. The participating designers.

	Participant	Age	Gender	Role
Group 1	P1	10	Male	Novice designer
	P2	12	Male	Novice designer
	P3	12	Male	Designer
Group 2	P4	10	Female	Designer
	P5	10	Female	Novice designer
	P6	18	Female	Facilitator/Designer
Group 3	P7	9	Female	Designer
	P8	10	Male	Novice designer
	P9	15	Female	Facilitator/Designer

experience, one novice designer and a teenage facilitator. The facilitators had been involved in several CI projects, some conducted at the University of Maryland's Kidsteam with Allison Druin – the originator of CI.

3.3 The Design Task, Materials and Procedure

The design sessions were conducted in a university based design lab with ample space for children to sit on the carpet to build their prototypes. Following Druin's [2] CI process, we started with everybody sitting in a circle on the floor. We went round the circle for introductions and to answer the question 'What is the brain?'. The 'question of the day' is meant to direct the focus of activities to the design task and stimulate ideas related to the task.

Next, I explained who our client was and what the design task entailed. A representative of Edublox who was present then described in detail what their different programs involve. For the next 30 min she put volunteers from the team through some Edublox exercises while everybody else observed. This familiarised them with what they were about to design.

After a quick snack, each group received a large 'bag of stuff' [7] to be used for prototyping. Different sized sheets of board and paper were available on a communal table. Figure 1 shows part of a group's 'bag of stuff' content.

Fig. 1. Prototyping materials (i.e. 'bags of stuff')

They had an hour to work on their prototypes with no interference from the adults. Each group then presented their designs to the whole team. We recorded the presentations and the questions and discussion that followed.

To conclude the session we sat in a circle again and reflected on the design experience. I thanked them and we played games and enjoyed more snacks until their parents arrived to collect them. The complete session lasted almost three hours.

Prior to the design session parents were given detailed information on the project and they had to sign a consent form that allowed us to record the activities for the purposes of design only. No video or audio material by which any child could be identified may be published or even made available to Edublox, and all reports refer to the children as P1, P2, et cetera.

3.4 Data Collection and Analysis

The data consisted of the low fidelity prototypes created by the designers; recordings of the group presentations; recordings of the discussions and questions that followed the presentations; and detailed notes of all design elements and ideas that emerged from the prototypes and discussions.

I used the above data sources to compare the design outcomes to the six elements of Annetta's [1] SEG design framework. This involved considering the six elements one by one and for each going through all the data sources and noting down any related design idea or feature. I carefully studied these notes to determine which the SEG requirements are fulfilled (and how) and which not.

4 Design Outcomes and Their Relation to SEG Requirements

The results are discussed by describing the children's design prototypes and then relating these designs to Annetta's [1] six elements.

4.1 The Design Prototypes

Design Group 1: This group planned a five week program with three 15 min challenges per day. In the first week players escape from the enemy's castle and then have to find their way home. Levels are unlocked once a day only so that 'you don't rush through everything and forget it'. Depending on how many challenges you complete in 15 min, you gain points that represent cash units.

The challenges take the form of the Edublox exercises recreated within the fantasy world. One designer created a 3D implementation of an Edublox exercise as a physical add-on (Fig. 2, right). It communicates with the game, so when the challenge calls for

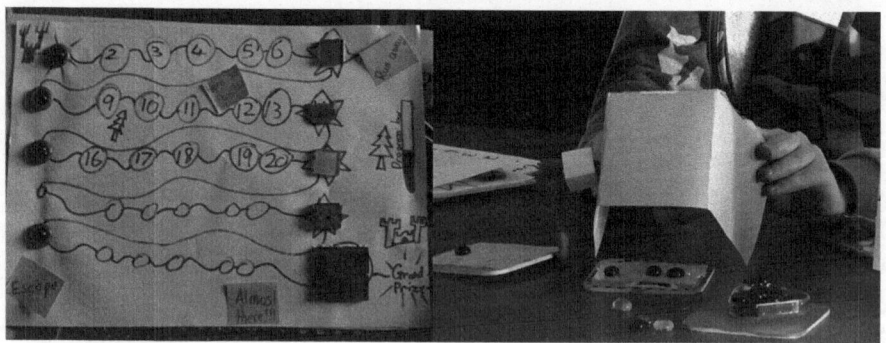

Fig. 2. Part of Group 1's prototype.

that particular exercise, the player can play the physical game and the results will be transferred into the online game.

They have a progress map that serves to keep track of the players' progress (Fig. 2, left). As they complete levels the circles change colour and messages of encouragement pop up.

Players are represented by unique avatars that they design themselves and they can use cash units accumulated to 'buy' accessories for their avatar.

Design Group 2: They created a 'story game' that takes place in a fantasy forest (or any other fantasy setting). They placed a lot of emphasis on the reward system and on viewing progress. Players complete a 45 min exercise session per day to qualify for rewards. Timing was a prominent feature here. Rewards include time to play games, prizes and coins that can be used to accessorize 'Ed' – an in-game character that guides players through the game and provides help when required.

Like Group 1, they have a progress map (Fig. 3, right) that indicates the levels reached. Every time you go a level up you get 100 coins. This is the 'fun' progress map for children. There is also a 'serious page' for parents that shows the child's progress in the form of charts.

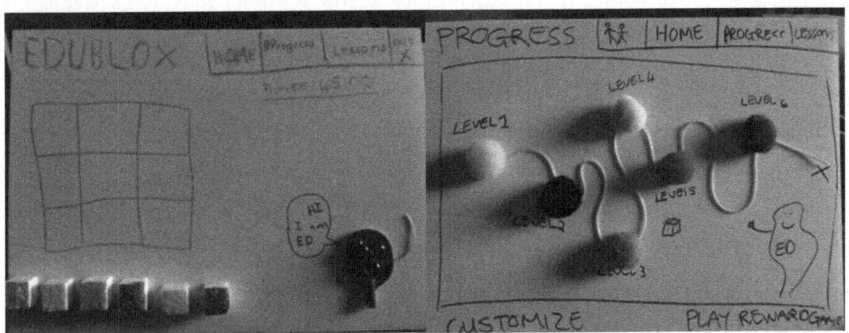

Fig. 3. Part of Group 2's prototype.

A webcam records the child while playing so that the parent need not be with the child to see if they cheat. When parents note that children lose motivation, they can send little mystery prizes that will appear as additional rewards.

The Edublox exercises (e.g. Figure 3, left) are separate from the fantasy world, but performance in the exercises determine what children can do in the fantasy world. They appear like on-screen replicas of the face-to-face versions.

Design Group 3: Figure 4 shows parts of their design. They immersed the games in a social media-like environment rather than a game world. On the Home screen players choose a name and an icon that represents them, as well as a language. Once logged in, a screen with four parts appear: Games, Progress, Time, Instructions. The Games link takes a player to the Edublox exercises that they designed as on-screen replicas of the face-to-face versions. There is an 'Earth' icon that will connect a player with other players. Play can happen in three ways: 1. Race other kids; 2. Time yourself; 3. Normal (no timer).

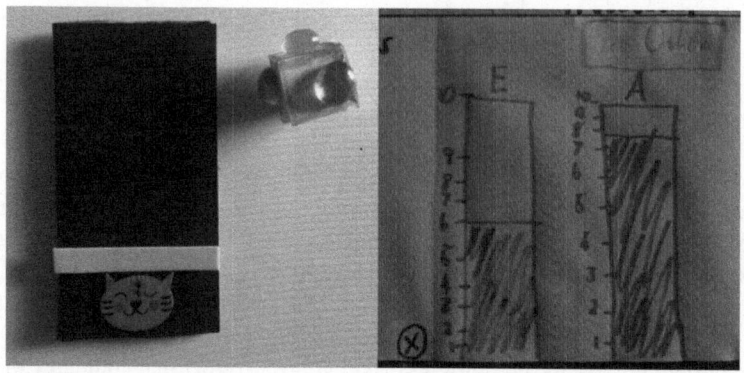

Fig. 4. Part of Group 3's prototype.

The Progress link brings up a screen with a bar chart-like visualization that indicates the player's progress against that of other players (Fig. 4, right). Players have the choice to hide their progress from other players.

A Help button appears in the form of a golden block (Fig. 4, left) that moves around on the screen. Clicking it will 'call a parent for help' on a phone-like device through which parents can also observe what the child is doing. A Time screen shows how much time you have left and a Feedback link will tell players where they did things wrong.

4.2   Mapping the Children's Design Ideas to the SEG Design Model

The features included in the children's designs were mapped onto the six elements of Annetta's [1] framework. Table 2 summarises the results. Besides the absence of *interactivity* in Group 1's design, every element is present in all three designs. *Identity* and *increasing complexity* are thoroughly represented in all three designs. Two groups guarantee *immersion* with interesting fantasy worlds, a story line and elaborate, immediate feedback mechanisms. Group 3's social media-like, competitive environment is also likely to support *immersion,* and scores high on *interactivity*. Group 2 also does well in terms of *interactivity*. With regard to *informed teaching*, all groups keep track of progress through the game in ways that would make it possible for parents or educators to analyse their performance. Group 1's design lacks scaffolding elements, which means they did not fulfil the requirements related to *instruction*.

Table 2. Mapping the design elements onto Annetta's [1] desired SEG elements

	Group 1	Group 2	Group 3
Identity	Player creates own avatar and points earned in the game can be used to accessorize the avatar	The design is set in a fantasy forest. A 'persona' can be adapted using 'money' earned	The player chooses an 'icon', a name and a language. No fantasy world was used
Immersion	All activities are performed within fantasy narrative. Constant feedback and encouragement appears on a progress map that clearly communicates the player's progress in the game	Players can change the fantasy game setting. Ed guides players. He can be customized using money earned, so each player's Ed is unique. Progress maps provide clear feedback on progress	A social media-like platform where players interact and compete. Their character represents their real selves rather than an in-game avatar. Parents can provide feedback/help at any time
Interactivity	No social interaction with other players or any indication of communication with in-game characters	Ed is always there to interact and help. There is indirect interaction with parents who can plant mystery prizes and follow play through webcam	Parents have a mobile device that connects with the game to observe child's play from afar. A floating button will get help from the parent
Increasing complexity	Very clear instructions on how levels of difficulty are unlocked (one a day) at the correct pace to support real learning	Progress maps indicate different levels achieved. Rewards can be games, prizes or money if certain goals are achieved	On the progress screen, bar charts show players' level of achievement compared to other players'. Timing is used to increase difficulty
Informed teaching	Data about players' progress are collected and displayed in the form of a progress map, levels completed and points earned	There a 'serious' progress page where adults can see how children are progressing. All game play is recorded for parents to view later	Progress is recorded per exercise and can be viewed in the form of a bar-chart like visualization
Instructional	Four of the first five elements are included in the design. They did not mention any specific scaffolding mechanisms in their design	The first five elements appear in the design. Players must play 45 min to get any reward. Ed provides scaffolding	The first five elements appear in the game but some in limited form. A Feedback link is available where players can see where they went wrong in the exercises

5   Conclusions

The aim of this study was to determine whether the designs produced by children when they participate in the design of web based games for learning, can make a real contribution towards the implemented application. Through a CI case study I showed that the six elements of Annetta's [1] framework for SEG design all appear in at least two of the three prototypes and that three of the four most important elements (identity, immersion and increasing complexity) are prominent in all the prototypes.

The children received no guidance from adults in this design task, only a demonstration the face-to-face Edublox exercises. We expected their prototypes to be representations of these exercises, but they offered more – they intuitively designed web based SEGs. Two groups focused on immersing the exercises in a game world with a storyline and reward system that would motivate users to do the exercises as a means to thrive in the fantasy world. The third group embedded the exercises in a social media-like environment where interactivity is the main feature, but they also used interaction and competition with other users (elements of SEGs) as motivators.

Without any formal knowledge of, or training in the design of SEGs, these young designers displayed a natural ability to design an online game that incorporates what design experts have established as requirements of SEGs. The application was released in March 2017. In continuation of the research reported here we will now investigate the final, implemented application to determine to what extent the children's designs determined the final product.

References

1. Annetta, L.A.: The "I"s have it: a framework for serious educational game design. Rev. Gen. Psychol. 14(2), 105–112 (2010)
2. Druin, A.: The role of children in the design of new technology. Behav. Inform. Technol. 21(1), 1–25 (2002)
3. Druin, A., Stewart, J., Proft, D., Bederson, B., Hollan, J.: KidPad: a design collaboration between children, technologists, and educators. In: Proceedings of the ACM SIGCHI Conference on Human Factors in Computing Systems, pp. 463–470. ACM (1997)
4. Edublox (2017). https://www.edubloxsa.co.za/. Accessed 30 Apr 2017
5. Ehn, P.: Scandinavian design: on participation and skill. In: Participatory Design: Principles and Practices, pp. 41–77 (1993)
6. Gelderblom, H.: Giving children voice in the design of technology for education in the developing world. S. Afr. Comput. J. 54(2), 34–42 (2014)
7. Guha, M.L., Druin, A., Fails, J.A.: Cooperative inquiry revisited: reflections of the past and guidelines for the future of intergenerational co-design. Int. J. Child-Comput. Interact. 1(1), 14–23 (2013)
8. Kelly, S.R., Mazzone, E., Horton, M., Read, J.C.: Bluebells: a design method for child-centred product development. In Proceedings of the 4th Nordic Conference on Human-Computer Interaction: Changing Roles, pp. 361–368. ACM (2006)
9. Mitgutsch, K., Alvarado, N.: Purposeful by design?: A serious game design assessment framework. In: Proceedings of the International Conference on the Foundations of Digital Games, pp. 121–128. ACM (2012)

10. Moreno-Ger, P., Burgos, D., Martínez-Ortiz, I., Sierra, J.L., Fernández-Manjón, B.: Educational game design for online education. Comput. Hum. Behav. **24**(6), 2530–2540 (2008)

11. Nesset, V., Large, A.: Children in the information technology design process: a review of theories and their applications. Libr. Inform. Sci. Res. **26**(2), 140–161 (2004)

12. Yip, J.C., Foss, E., Bonsignore, E., Guha, M.L., Norooz, L., Rhodes, E., McNally, B., Papadatos, P., Golub, E., Druin, A.: Children initiating and leading cooperative inquiry sessions. In: Proceedings of the 12th International Conference on Interaction Design and Children, pp. 293–296. ACM (2013)

DNR and the Use of Blended Learning Methodology in German Police Education

Melanie Brand and Kirsten Mahlke[✉]

University of Konstanz, Konstanz, Germany
Kontakt-dnr@uni-konstanz.de

Abstract. The article purposes to examine the opportunities and challenges of introducing blended learning modules for the facilitation of reflexive learning within the police. It will discuss the conceptualization of 'DNR' (Death Notification with Responsibility), a blended learning course for police students in Germany which focuses on the administering of death notifications according to both professional and legal requirements, reacting flexibly and compassionately to the needs of the bereaved. DNR has two main aims: (1) the imparting of crucial factual knowledge, and (2) the creation of opportunities for intensified reflexive and participatory learning. The concept combines classroom-based learning with e-learning modules. E-learning components allow students to engage with the sensitive issue of death notification at their own pace; when and where they feel comfortable. The overall course objectives are complicated by the police's hierarchical organizational structure, as well as the preference of experience-based, on-the-job learning, and a general mistrust towards 'academization' of police education in Germany.

Keywords: Blended learning · Death notification · Police education

1 Introduction

Imparting news of a death to next of kin is a stressful and delicate task falling to medical and law-enforcement professions. Research indicates the need for further training on death notification as a form of professionalization (Douglas et al. 2013; Nordström 2011). Despite classroom-based training, availability of best-practice recommendations and step-by-step guidelines on the process of death notification, police officers in Germany still feel ill-prepared for delivering notifications (cf. Fresen 2016). Currently, no standardized police training for such procedure is available in Germany.

The experiences of bereaved individuals who have received a death notification add urgency to the need for deeper engagement with death-related grief in police education. A study conducted by the German police with the local chaplaincy revealed that the bereaved felt excluded from legal process and police procedure pertaining to the death

This paper is part of the ERC-financed Proof of Concept Death Notification with Responsibility. A Blended Learning Course for Police (DNR 754949).

H. Xie et al. (Eds.): ICWL 2017, LNCS 10473, pp. 196–201, 2017.
DOI: 10.1007/978-3-319-66733-1_21

of their loved one, many complaining about a lack of information and support (Trappe 2001). These impressions were substantiated through exploratory conversations with both police officers and bereaved parents during the planning phase of DNR. These demonstrated the still-pressing need of adequate death notification training.

Reflecting on the challenges of communicating an unexpected and often violent death, the article discusses the blended learning module 'DNR – Death Notification with Responsibility'. Funded by the European Research Council (ERC), the training module is currently being developed by a team of cultural scientists and social anthropologists at the University of Konstanz in partnership with the police. Given the delicacy of the issue, how can death notification be formally taught?

Put simply, ideal training should encompass both 'hard facts' and 'soft skills' (cf. De Leo et al. 2015; Trappe 2001). The concept of DNR follows the notion that new educational approaches are necessary to facilitate experience-based learning and reflexive learning within the peer group, whereby communicative competencies in work-based emotional engagement may be strengthened. The blended learning course will enable police to prepare for death notification delivery through a multi-layered approach, integrating classroom education and group-work as well as inter-active e-learning components on a range of topics related to death and communication in sensitive situations.

2   Death Notification and Police in Germany

2.1   Telling the Untellable

In Germany, no specific law or regulation exists that clearly identifies the delivery of death notifications as a responsibility of law enforcement. In terms of prevention, the protection of individual or public safety and the protection of victims' rights, death notifications clearly fall into the realm of police duty (see Fresen 2016; Trappe 2001). The importance of victims' rights has recently been emphasized on EU-level through Directive 2012/29 that specifically highlights victims' rights to information.

There is literary consensus indicating that the way a death notification is conveyed drastically impacts the grieving process (cf. De Leo et al. 2015; Trappe 2001). Psychological disorders such as depression, listlessness and phobia are among the long-lasting effects which may in turn contribute to likelihoods such as suicide if the delicate initial bereavement is handled with careless or uninformed communication. At the same time, bearing the news which causes a person's world to collapse, and witnessing the emotional aftermath, has the potential to result in psychological complications. By communicating a death, even the death of a stranger, one's own mortality is implicated. Confronting one's feelings about death and mortality seems likely to reduce a general discomfort in facing the sensitive subject. Incorporating questions concerning 'emotion work' (Szymenderski 2012) into the blended learning module provides an impulse to scrutinize the meaning and importance of processes that may seem at first to belong to the realm of tacit knowledge and informal learning in the workplace.

2.2 Police Education in Germany

It is most important to note that police education in Germany is organized federally with the respective curricula of the sixteen federal states varying widely. Today, due to the educational reform known as the Bologna process, higher law-enforcement students graduate with a Bachelor of Arts diploma. The content of the three-year study is manifold. However, the proliferation of more 'theoretical' topics is often met with skepticism, even evoking fears of an academization of the otherwise hands-on police training (see Kersten 2013: 57).

At university-level, death notification training usually forms a feature of ethics, psychology or communication training. Death notification training is most often provided by chaplains, but in some federal states may fall to ethics professors. In Baden-Württemberg, students of the Bachelor program preparing them for positions in higher law-enforcement receive six hours of training on death notification as part of a module on ethics. This includes two hours on psychological aspects of grief, two hours of group work including roleplays, one hour's reflection on the experiences simulated by the roleplays and one hour on intercultural aspects of death and grief.

We understand DNR as a tool that may be fully or partly integrated into the existing learning environment. Preference for 'learning on the job' over theoretical discussion indicates the need for adequate educational methodologies. For example, DNR includes a roleplaying unit during which students gain valuable experience through simulation. By outsourcing knowledge dissemination to the course's online component, the relatively limited classroom-based learning can be productively devoted to participatory and experienced-based forms of learning.

To summarize: Death notifications present a highly sensitive and challenging task for police officers which requires specific factual, legal and bureaucratic knowledge as well as interpersonal skills, reflective abilities and self-care competencies. If ill-prepared to deliver appropriately, notifications result in negative consequences for the bereaved by drastically complicating the grieving process. Additionally, the task presents a risk to the emotional and psychological wellbeing of officers.

3 Death Notifications: Preparing Police Students

Relevant literature on death notification, trauma elicited by death encounters, and the needs of next of kin in cases of sudden, violent death is readily available. However, there remains a lack of comprehensively informed, systematically established and didactically tailored teaching material on the subject, and on how it may be applied in practice. Police students in the second decade of the 21st century are digital natives and require educational material corresponding to their learning habitats. Blending face-to-face classroom training with e-learning allows for flexibility in modalities and multi-faceted medial representation of diverse learning content. Blended learning provides students with both the possibility to reflect on sensitive issues at their own pace and in their preferred environment, and the opportunity to interact with peers and facilitators in a group setting.

The blended learning course follows the idea of the 'flipped classroom' meaning that classroom sessions are used for interactive and participatory, experienced-based and dialogical learning instead of teacher-centered knowledge dissemination. Lectures and sharing of factual knowledge is outsourced to DNR's e-learning components. In this way, the blended learning module makes the most of the limited time and space available. Furthermore, blended learning enables a "community of inquiry" that, according to Garrison and Kanuka (2004: 97), consists of cognitive and social elements as well as teaching presence. Such communities of inquiry strengthen students' commitment to the joint learning project (ibid.: 99). In order to encourage the community building process, DNR follows Garrison and Kanuka's suggestion to start with a face-to-face session and proceed with e-learning modules afterwards.

Before the first session, students will be able to log into the e-learning platform in order to familiarize themselves with the medium. A video will inform them about the importance of death notification training and the responsibility that comes with the task. In another sequence, the overall structure of the e-learning component is explained. The sequential structure of the e-learning component follows the typical course of police action, leading students through several phases of the notification process. Already implicated by the structure, a thought-cue is given: death notifications are not a 'once-off' but must be understood as the beginning of a process that continues long after the doorbell is rung and the death message is conveyed.

In order to prepare for the first face-to-face session, participants watch a comical video of a worst-case notification scenario and are encouraged to reflect and discuss. The aim of the first session is to engage in team- and trust-building activities. Through various exercises, participants reflect on their own experiences with death, discuss society's view of death and the role of death communication in a police officer's profession. Questions encouraging intense reflection will be posed, for example: "If something tragic was to happen to you, how would you like your next of kin to be informed?" Ideally, a person who has received a death notification in the past is invited to the session. This would allow students to engage with a 'survivor', ask questions and listen to first-hand accounts, enabling the essential change of perspective. After the first face-to-face session, DNR's e-learning phase will commence. The following outlines the basic content of each of the six chapters:

Coordination of Police Operation. During first contact via an emergency call, basic information about what has happened, where and to whom is transmitted to police. On this basis, deployment is coordinated and officers sent to the location. Already at this stage, information can be identified that might become important during notification, i.e. Who placed the emergency call? Are there witnesses to the incident?

Arrival at the Scene and First Investigations. Officers' responsibilities and involvement is defined and the chain of information coordinated. During first investigations and collection of data, officers must be aware that information not relevant to criminal investigations may still be crucial to notification. These must be noted.

Collecting Background Information. Officers responsible for notifying next of kin must collect detailed information about the incident, who was involved and who needs to be notified. If available, information about family structures must be considered. In the case of divorced parents, for example, cooperation with another police district might be necessary to ensure a personal notification of next of kin through appropriate local authorities.

Preparing the Notification. As notifications are always handled by two officers, roles must be delegated. Based on the specific details of the situation and availability, chaplains or crisis intervention experts must be consulted. Officers must engage in emotion work and attune to the imminent notification.

Conveying the Death Notification As early as possible, the message must be conveyed in clear, concise language. Officers need to react to the specifics of the situation, answer questions, provide basic emotional support and provide crucial information such as contact details. In terms of prevention, and the protection of victims, officers must wait until a third party is present. Emotion work and debriefing ensues.

Follow up and Completion. Police officers function as gatekeepers and are in a position to provide the bereaved with access to (a) further information about the incident, (b) ongoing procedure, (c) possessions carried by their loved one at the time of death, (d) prosecution, (e) other parties involved such as witnesses and first-aiders.

All chapters are structured following the same logic. Eight categories, visually represented as tiles, organize the learning contents: *Chapter Introduction* (overview of contents, learning objectives, duration), *Knowledge Dissemination* (lectures, texts, animations), *Spheres of Responsibility* (legal aspects, policies, discretionary powers), *Video Element* (interview, film), *Voices* (perspectives of bereaved, first-aid responders, chaplains), *Further Material* (database including relevant songs, books, movies, articles), *Tools* (brochures, check lists) and *Test/Quiz* (checking learning progress via multiple-choice questions).

One of DNR's most important features constitutes the category *Voices*. Here, students are provided with first-hand accounts from individuals who have received a death notification, willing to share their experience. The students will also find expert accounts from people engaged in 'death work'. This includes chaplains, medical doctors, nurses, police officers, pathologists and morticians. Depending on interviewees' preferences, their accounts are given as text, audio or video allowing different degrees of anonymization. *Voices* offers students a change of perspective, an opportunity for intense reflection on the meanings and consequences of death in context. The e-learning component also features an FAQ section and forum in which students may engage and share.

After the completion of the e-learning phase, a second classroom-based session will follow during which the online modules are discussed. The session will include experience-based learning via roleplaying. Course facilitators will receive scripts providing the basis for learning activity. The role of next of kin may be played by professional actors, but if not possible, by the course facilitator or students themselves. The benefit of simulation exercises in death notification training has been highlighted in different contexts (cf. Nordström et al. 2011).

DNR will be prototyped in the police academy of Duisburg/Germany where it will be integrated into a semester-based course on ethics and social communication skills.

Students as well as facilitators will receive evaluation forms in which to rate each course component by comprehensibility, usability, relevance and sophistication.

4 Conclusion

Put simply, blended learning is "the thoughtful integration of classroom face-to-face learning experiences with online learning experiences" (Garrison and Kanuka 2004: 96). In DNR, contents of classroom-based learning and e-learning are geared to each other. During roleplays, students get to apply and to reflect upon their acquired knowledge in a concrete experiential situation. DNR draws on a student-centered methodology with the learning process being supported by the teacher and peers. In contrast to Cope and Kalantzis (2017: 1) who state that "technology is pedagogically neutral", Garrison and Kanuka (2004: 97) assume specific pedagogical qualities implicated in online learning like encouraging reflection and precision of expression. By implementing a moderated forum in which facilitators give impulses for reflection, DNR encourages students to formulate their thoughts and attitudes and to share them with other participants.

As the conceptual review has shown, blended learning methodologies offer promising opportunities to integrate reflexive, experiential and participatory learning into the environment of police education. In the face of various challenges, it is the aim of DNR to train police officers for professional death notification delivery and, in so doing, prevent both the re-victimization of the bereaved and potential trauma suffered by the officers themselves.

References

Cope, B., Kalantzis, M.: E-learning Ecologies. Principles for New Learning and Assessment. Routledge, New York (2017)

Douglas, L., Cheskes, S., Feldman, M., Ratnapalan, S.: Death notification education for paramedics. Past, present and future directions. J. Paramedic Pract. 5(3), 152–159 (2013)

De Leo, D., Anile, C., Ziliotto, A.: Violent deaths and traumatic bereavement: the importance of appropriate death notification. Humanities 4(4), 702–713 (2015)

Fresen, L.: Überbringen von Todesnachrichten als Herausforderung und kulturübergreifende Aufgabe für die Polizei. BA Thesis, Police Academy Niedersachsen (2016)

Garrison, D.R., Kanuka, H.: Blended learning: uncovering its transformative potential in higher education. Internet High. Educ. 7(2), 95–105 (2004)

Nordström, A., Fjellman-Wiklund, A., Grysell, T.: Drama as a pedagogical tool for practicing death notification-experiences from swedish medical students. BMC Med. Educ. 11(1), 74 (2011)

Szymenderski, P.: Gefühlsarbeit im Polizeidienst. Wie Polizeibedienstete die emotionalen Anforderungen ihres Berufs bewältigen. transcript, Bielefeld (2012)

Trappe, T.: Die Unwirklichkeit des Todes Erfahrungen und Überlegungen bei der Begleitung von Verkehrsunfallopfern und ihren Angehörigen. Psychotraumatologie 2(3), 17 (2001)

Kersten, J., Ansgar, B.: Police science in Germany. History and new perspectives. J. Police Stud./ Cahiers Politiestudies 1, 1 (2013)

The Perception of South African Parents on the Use of Technology in Schools

Machdel Matthee[✉], Marié Hattingh, and Lizette Weilbach

Department of Informatics, University of Pretoria, Pretoria, South Africa
{machdel.matthee,marie.hattingh,lizette.weilbach}@up.ac.za

Abstract. Parents are recognized as an important group of stakeholders to take into account when implementing technology in schools. However, very little research has considered the parent's view in the learning development of his/her child, when introducing technology. This paper addresses this gap by presenting the findings of an inductive study to improve the understanding of parents' perception on the adoption of technology in their child's learning environment. A qualitative study was done with data gathered through an online anonymous questionnaire containing open-ended questions. The questionnaire was distributed on parents' communication platforms. The data indicated that the introduction of technology has caused concern amongst parents. The parents sensed that their children's (inter alia) academic goals, neurological development, competency in computer usage and health, are affected by the introduction of technology. They experienced an increase in difficulty to monitor learning; some children find it more difficult to study and that children are easily distracted. The parents managed these interferences by amongst others acquiring hard copy textbooks; adjusting the way they monitor homework and agreeing to trust their children rather than attempting to monitor everything. The findings illustrate the importance of involving parents in the technology implementation process because of their close involvement in the academic development of their children (especially primary school children).

Keywords: Parents · Technology implementation in schools · Learning environment · e-Textbook

1 Introduction

Educational technology is increasingly introduced in South African schools - albeit with mixed results. The resistance of especially teachers to accept this technology has been well documented [1, 2]. The implementation of technology in schools provokes change and the success of such an implementation according to Lim et al. [3], depends to a large extend on its compatibility with the learning and teaching environment. Several authors emphasise the importance of understanding and managing these changes. Ng and Nicholas [4] call for a people-centred framework when implementing mobile technology in schools to accommodate both the technical and the people-related aspects involved. These include management, teachers, learners, technicians and the wider community.

© Springer International Publishing AG 2017
H. Xie et al. (Eds.): ICWL 2017, LNCS 10473, pp. 202–207, 2017.
DOI: 10.1007/978-3-319-66733-1_22

The 2010 US National Science Foundation's (NSF) Roadmap for Education Technology [5] advises that employers, parents, administrators, teachers and students should be consulted regularly to build their confidence in systems implemented in schools. Parents are considered important stakeholders, but despite this, there is a lack of research that takes into account the role of parents in the implementation of technology in education.

The authors of this paper had some informal discussions with the teachers, learners and parents of a local school, where information technology was implemented. Chrome books were rolled out to grade 4 to 12 learners, with a blended learning platform aimed at making the creation, distribution and grading of learner assignments paperless, together with an interactive e-textbook reader – all printed textbooks were replaced with e-textbooks. This implementation created quite a stir amongst some parents and we subsequently decided to investigate the concerns.

This paper consequently aims at reporting on the perceptions of South African parents regarding their children's learning environment and their role in it when technology is integrated into it. The research is intended to assist principals and other decision makers with ways to approach parents during the decision making process to implement technology in schools.

2   The Use of Educational Technology in Schools

Educational technology refers to the use of a wide variety of technologies aimed at the facilitation of educational practices [6]. It has become synonymous with the terms computer based learning and online education. The New Media Consortium's 2010 Horizons report highlights electronic books and mobile devices as two technologies to observe in the 'near future (one year or less)' category. These technologies are indicated as well-known technologies that have already made their way into the educational context as is the case in the school we investigated.

An e-textbook is a subset of the e-book category and comprises of educational material in an electronic environment [7]. Learners are able to underline important aspects, write notes and lookup new and unfamiliar words or definitions. Other advantages include the portability on light mobile devices and an extensive search facility [8, 9]. However, Embong et al. [10] report that learners will only use e-books if their teachers and their school establish a suitable e-book environment.

To successfully implement technology in schools, such as e-book readers and a Learning Management System (LMS), all stakeholders (school board members; the principal; teachers; technologists; parents; and policy makers) have a specific role to play in the successful adoption of and adaption to the new technology. LMS's combines a range of subject administrative management tools, as well as instructional tools which allow educators to design, build and deliver online learning environments [11].

While the school board members may consider the role the technology could play to help them attain the school's mission, the teachers will focus on adapting to the usage of the new technology when performing their teaching task and the support they would need to implement it successfully. The school principal has to deal with how the implementation will affect the school's administration, schedules and technology infra-structure, while the parents will have to consider the implications of this new close connection their children will now have with the technology on their educational outcome, as well as the intended and unintended costs associated with implementing the new technology [12].

3   Research Design

A qualitative study was done with data gathered through an online anonymous ques-tionnaire containing open-ended questions. Convenience sampling was used by making the questionnaire available on the school's official communication platforms. Parents of grade 4 to 12 learners, who have been on the receiving end of the revolutionary implementation of technology in their child(ren)'s school, were invited to participate in the study. Only thirty-nine parents out of a possible 500 households participated. 80% of the respondents had children under 12 years old. The questionnaire included seven questions dealing with (1) parents' attitude towards technology in general, (2) their opinion regarding the use of technology in schools, (3) what they consider as risks asso-ciated with the use of technology in schools, (4) to what extent the technology meets their expectations, (5) to what extent the technology makes them vulnerable, (6) how dependent they are on technology to help their children meet their educational needs and (7) what the school can do to help them with this transformation process. These responses were analysed (see Sect. 4) and the findings and some recommendations have consequently been communicated to the school principal and management in a written report format.

4   Data Analysis and Findings

Thematic Analysis (TA) was used to analyse the data. As TA is typically used to analyse written, verbal or visual messages it was ideally suited to analyse the qualitative responses obtained through the online questionnaire used to obtain the data. Clarke and Braun [13] describe TA as a theoretically independent method to identify and analyse patterns in qualitative data. The responses to the questions were coded after which themes were identified from the codes. The focus of the analysis was on the negative responses. The emerging themes can be explained as: the integration of technology in their children's learning environment results in parents with *concerns* accompanied by *negative emotions*. This leads to parents taking *corrective actions* or *wanting corrective actions to be taken* by the school. Positive parents (the minority), felt excited about their children being prepared for the technological age.

Table 1 below summarises the **concerns** expressed by parents.

The concerns listed in Table 1 led to **negative emotions** such as loss of control and helplessness. *"I feel out of control as I do not have something physical in my hand because I cannot print etc."; "My authority as parent is undermined", "I am a very concerned and worried parent. Above all, with very little say in what I think is good and not good for my child. That is distressing!"; "All control that the parent did have, based*

Table 1. Concerns caused by technology emerging from the data

Concerns	Examples of remarks
Concern about over-emphasis of IT	"Technology should not be overused. There is no replacement for an involved teacher"
Concern about studying using e-textbooks (going paperless)	"I think they are way too young to go completely paperless and are expected to study without textbooks. It is extremely difficult to study directly from a computer screen." "Worldwide trends go back to books". "Children have to keep referring to different pages in different sections causing some information to be missed! NOTHING is printed for parents nor children to review what's being learnt. My opinion: it has resulted in such a steep learning curve for our children resulting in poorer marks, no typing skills so time consuming so overall not something I would recommend"
Concern about neurological and other fundamental development of child	"Physical writing however should still take priority over electronics" "Children are not playing before school!!!"
Concern about health of child	"Too much screen time impact on concentration and the child's ability to stay focused as it influences their alertness levels" "Movement is medicine and screentime hampers that." "I also think it is bad for their eyes"
Concern that child is too young for full implementation	"I think it is beneficial for older children"
Concern about cyber safety	"I have found that the googling search functionality is not as secure as I would like and depending how the kids word a search, some undesirable search results inevitably get through" "If not monitored, our kids may be exposed to cyber bullying and access to inappropriate content"
Concern about distractions	"Playing games as you can't monitor what they are doing"
Concern that child is given too much responsibility	"It is our belief that there are more gaps in the education framework with the use of ICT in education taking the control and centralization of the education away from the parents and educators, placing this management and control into the hands of the child/student who, in our opinion, is ill-equipped to handle this level of responsibility and accountability"
Concern about extra costs	"I see this as a cost saver and convenience to the school, at the detriment of the pupil. The printing costs have just been passed to the parents. Lots of parents are complaining that it takes longer to find the work to be done, than doing the actual work. Also, some parents are buying the text books anyway, because the pupils struggle to read the screens"

on a full or partial paper based learning framework, has, literally, overnight been removed and placed in the hands of the student (child) who is ill-equipped to take on this responsibility."

Parents expressed their need for **the school to take corrective actions** by providing training and improved communication with parents: *"Parents should have been informed what the benefits are of using Chromebooks, based on extensive research conducted by the school. I am not convinced that such research was actually done. It seems to me that the school simply wanted to follow the latest trend. Trends, unfortunately, cannot be trusted as good indicators of what is beneficial for our kids."* They also expressed their wish for a more gradual implementation, rules regarding the use of chrome books during breaks and before school, limiting the implementation only to secondary school learners, the availability of a helpline and training in cyber safety.

The parents themselves took **corrective actions** by obtaining information from other parents via social media, monitoring the application all the time since *"teachers seemingly post work at random times"*, monitoring their child's computer use to protect them from cyberbullying and access to inappropriate content, acquiring the hard copy textbooks, printing out study material, consulting educational psychologists regarding health and neurological developmental concerns and monitoring eye deterioration. Some parents simply decided to trust their children more.

5   Discussion

Only a small percentage of the school's parents responded to the questionnaire. A possible interpretation could be that only a few of the parents are concerned. However, we believe that only a small percentage felt determined enough to participate in the survey. Other parents might have felt that technology integration is inevitable and unstoppable and they therefore saw no point in participating in such a survey. Should these concerns then be ignored? We believe that it should be heard and addressed – threats to cyber safety for example is a real danger and parents should be made aware of the dangers and how to protect their children against it.

Although most respondents expressed negative feelings towards the technology integration, a small number of respondents were decidedly positive: *"The world is moving and our kids must be exposed and assisted to adapt to the changing world. I am super exited"*. Some pointed out the improved communication between school and parent. Other advantages mentioned were the fact that all information was in one place and that *"information can be accessed anytime"*; the positive effect on his/her child's self-reliance; the useful app on his/her phone making it easy to see which homework or assessments are due; and a lighter school bag.

The findings described above indicate that parents felt that they lost control over fulfilling their responsibility with regards to their children's educational needs. Future research could include a deeper theoretical understanding of this phenomenon by using a theory such as the Perceptual Control Theory (PCT). The Perceptual Control Theory (PCT) is a theory of behaviour derived from control theory, with the core principle being that "all behaviour is the control of perception" [14]. It could be used to explain the perceptual control parents have over their children's educational development using the technology implemented by the school.

6 Conclusion

The findings illustrate the important role played by parents in the educational development of their children (especially children in the primary school). The change management process, when implementing technology in schools, should therefore recognise, apart from teachers and learners, the parents as key stakeholders. The negative attitudes of parents towards technology implementation in schools might have an influence on their children's adoption of the technology in the classroom. On the other hand, parents can give valuable feedback on the practicalities and difficulties experienced because of the technology integration. Although the use of technology alters the interaction between stakeholders, communication between parents, teachers and learners should be encouraged and facilitated. This triad remains at the heart of successful education.

References

1. Weilbach, L., Matthee, M.: Understanding change from a socio-technical perspective: the case of an e-Textbook implementation. Int. J. Syst. Soc. **3**(1), 80–93 (2016)
2. Zhao, Y., Cziko, G.A.: Teacher adoption of technology: a perceptual control theory perspective. J. Technol. Teach. Educ. **9**(1), 5–30 (2001)
3. Lim, C.-P., Zhao, Y., Chai, C.-S., Tsai, C.-C.: Bridging the gap: technology trends and use of technology in schools. Educ. Technol. Soc. **16**(2), 59–68 (2013)
4. Ng, W., Nicholas, H.: A framework for sustainable mobile learning in schools. Br. J. Educ. Technol. **44**(5), 695–715 (2013)
5. Spector, J.M.: Emerging educational technologies and research directions. Educ. Technol. Soc. **16**(2), 21–30 (2013)
6. Kinshuk, H.W.H., Sampson, D., Chen, N.S.: Trends in educational technology through the lens of the highly cites articles published in the journal of educational technology and society. Educ. Technol. Soc. **16**(2), 3–20 (2013)
7. Landoni, M., Wilson, R., Gibb, F.: From the visual book to the web book: the importance of design. Electron. Libr. **18**(6), 407–419 (2000)
8. Cavanaugh, T.: EBooks and accommodations: is this the future of print accommodations? Teach. Except. Child. **35**(2), 56–61 (2002)
9. Lam, P., Lam, S.L., Lam, J., McNaught, C.: Usability and usefulness of eBooks on PPCs: how students' opinions vary over time. Aust. J. Educ. Technol. **25**(1), 30–44 (2009)
10. Embong, A., Noor, A., Rafek, M., Othman, H., Zarina, P., Khalid, M.: What do teachers and pupils say about using e-books in the classrooms? Int. J. Soc. Sci. Humanit. **4**(6), 451–457 (2014)
11. Coates, H., James, R., Baldwin, G.: A critical examination of the efects of learning management systems on university teaching and learning. Tert. Educ. Manag. **11**, 19–36 (2005)
12. Windschitl, M., Sahl, K.: Tracing teachers' use of technology in a laptop computer school: the interplay of teacher beliefs, social dynamics, and institutional culture. Am. Educ. Res. J. **39**(1), 165–205 (2002)
13. Clarke, V., Braun, V.: Teaching thematic analysis: over- coming challenges and developing strategies for effective learning. Psychologist **26**(2), 120–123 (2013)
14. Farrell, P., Hollands, J., Taylor, M., Gamble, H.: Perceptual control and layered protocols in interface design: I. Fundamental concepts. Int. J. Hum. Comput. Stud. **50**, 489–520 (1999)

Visual Computational Thinking Using *Patch*

Hasan M. Jamil[(✉)]

Department of Computer Science, University of Idaho, Moscow, USA
jamil@uidaho.edu

Abstract. With the future likely to see even more pervasive computation, "computational thinking" is now being recognized as a fundamental skill needed by all students. Computational thinking is conceptualizing as opposed to programming, promotes natural human thinking style than algorithmic reasoning, complements and combines mathematical and engineering thinking, and it emphasizes ideas, not artifacts. In this paper, we outline a new visual language, called *Patch*, using which students are able to express their solutions to eScience computational problems in abstract visual tools. Patch is closer to high level procedural languages such as C++ or Java than Scratch or Snap! but similar to them in ease of use and combines simplicity and expressive power in one single platform.

Keywords: Conceptual modeling · Visual programming · Web interface · Computational thinking · eLearning · eScience · STEM · High level languages

1 Introduction

The differences between computing and computational thinking (problem-solving skills incorporating computing knowledge) are significant and can be explained in a number of ways. According to Jeannette Wing [12], "computational thinking confronts the riddle of machine intelligence: What can humans do better than computers, and what can computers do better than humans? Most fundamentally, it addresses the question: What is computable? Today, we know only parts of the answers to such questions." In particular, we believe computational thinking is (1) conceptualizing, not programming, (2) a way that humans, not computers, think, (3) complements and combines mathematical and engineering thinking, and (4) it is ideas, not artifacts.

Supporting facets of computational thinking have been an area of intense research for decades under the banners such as visual programming [4], block based programming [11], programming by example [8] and natural language programming [5] which have witnessed only limited success. In a recent research, we have introduced the Mind*Reader* [7] integrated assessment and tutoring system for computational thinking STEM assignments following the "logic first, syntax later" principle in its three abstraction layers – example based, visual, and

© Springer International Publishing AG 2017
H. Xie et al. (Eds.): ICWL 2017, LNCS 10473, pp. 208–214, 2017.
DOI: 10.1007/978-3-319-66733-1_23

textual programming. A distinctive aspect of Mind*Reader* is that it extends automated online tutoring and authentic assessment support to students differently
and in more powerful manner than the recently proposed Java tutor [9] that intel-
ligently selects predefined templates to explain errors and how to correct them.
Nonetheless, keeping in mind the experiences thus far of the various approaches
to computational thinking programming support, in this paper, we embark upon
describing and illustrating the contours of a customizable high level programming environment called *Patch* using a well-known sorting example. Patch is
planned to be embedded within the online Mind*Reader* self-learning system. In
this paper, we only discuss the visual programming component of Patch.

2   Patch Highlights Using an Example

High school and freshman CS students learn several fundamental algorithms to
use them as building blocks in more complex algorithms by combining them in
some fashion eventually. These algorithms are language independent and can be
understood at various levels of abstractions. For example, decades of research
helped develop numerous sorting algorithms that are vital to computing in general and all computer scientists are expected to master them. One of them, a
bubble sorting algorithm, arranges the values of objects in a collection (a list) in
order of their significance – size of their values, shades of their color, or scale of
the sounds. The way the bubble sort algorithm works, i.e., its principal mechanism, is depicted visually in Fig. 1 on a list of six values $29, -4, 2, 17, 45$, and 9,
as presented to the system, say, by a student. However, while the idea of sorting is simple, developing an algorithm or writing a computer program for them
often is not. Yet, given a few elements, students can usually rearrange them in
the expected order by hand or by visual inspection.

There are many online sorting algorithm visualization tools such as Toptal
[3] and David Galles' data structure visualization library [6]. These tools offer an
intuitive understanding of the underlying working principles of the algorithms
and even show the differences how they accomplish identical goals possibly with
different performance overheads and under the conditions they do so. Nevertheless, these tools do not necessarily help the students develop the abstraction or
the algorithm to perform the sorting. Needless to say that the distance from
gleaning the sorting idea from these viz tools to developing the corresponding
C++, Java or Python code is still significant.

2.1   Lowest Level of Abstraction

Let us assume that we ask a student to develop an algorithm to rearrange a list
of values a_i satisfying the condition that for all i, $1 \leq i \leq (n-1)$, $a_i \leq a_{i+1}$
(or, $a_i \geq a_{i+1}$) holds. We can then contemplate three levels of abstractions - the
lowest level is a C++/Java/Python interface in which she can directly enter a
code fragment, execute it and see the results, and possibly use a visualization
tool to see generated objects rearranged using her code. This is the lowest level of

abstraction in Mind*Reader*. At this layer, learners have various tool support for finding correct syntax, locating libraries, linking modular programs, compiling and executing, testing and visualizing their results where appropriate, in ways similar to the viz tool Toptal. As an alternative, learners are also able to drill down to this lowest level from the two upper programming levels, i.e., example based and visual language levels of programming, described next. Programs written in the upper two levels can be mapped to a code snippets at the lowest level for execution and review at the click of a button.

2.2   Abstract Thinking

Instead, learners can choose to use the topmost abstraction layer to visually code the algorithm using programming by example approach. Patch supports a graphical tool in which learners are able to generate a set of n values that they can also visualize in size proportional to the values, and manually and graphically rearrange the objects online. At this level, it is largely conceptual, and the actions will reflect how humans think. For example, one might choose to select the visually largest element at location j to swap position with the one at the nth location, or simply bump all the elements up one location up to j to make room at location n. If one continues to do so for the next largest, and then the next largest, a pattern will emerge. There are many ways this exercise can be modeled visually and some may be more sophisticated than the others. Regardless, it is possible to settle for one. For example, one of the visual implementations of the well known bubble sort algorithm is shown in Fig. 1.

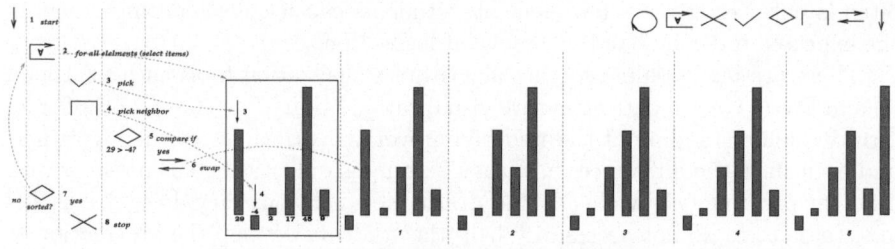

Fig. 1. Bubble sort using patch (first iteration).

In this example, a student used iconized predefined operations on a grid to explain her procedure (numbered 1 through 8) to the computer to help the computer write the code for her in a language of choice. Icons in this figure represent conceptual actions, and further explained using forms, and they are used in a hierarchy – one to the right on the grid expands the icon immediately on the left, giving it a tree structure. Objects can be selected, highlighted, dragged and dropped to indicate actions. The diagram shows the module begins at step 1, which consists of the remaining steps to the right. She then created a random list of six animated values. In step 2, she selected all the elements to signify that the operations to the right of step 2 apply to all the elements starting with the first one in step 3. She selected the neighbor element in the list, and then compared in step 5, swapped them in step 6, the first being larger than its neighbor. The process can be animated with the push of a button at any point, and be visualized. She noticed that at the end of the animation, the largest element was placed in the sixth position. She then repeated the process in step 2 deciding that it wasn't sorted. When she noticed at some point, the list was sorted, she added the stop icon at step 8, completing the algorithm. It easy to see that in many ways this abstraction level closely follows the programming by example approach to computational thinking.

2.3   Conceptual Thinking

To bridge these two levels of abstractions, we envision an intermediate or middle layer, which is still conceptual but uses constructs closer to programming languages such as assignments, loops and decision, and is language and syntax agnostic. Closest analogy to this abstraction layer is a computational biology querying system called VisFlow [10]. In VisFlow, users express their computational procedures visually using high-level conceptual icons, and connecting them in meaningful ways. While the objectives and functionalities of VisFlow are significantly different from the Patch interface we are proposing, the look and feel, and the approach to expressing algorithms are similar.

3   Conceptual Programming in Patch

The design of Patch is based on the principle of simplicity, clarity and naturalness of computational thinking toward programming with support for modularity and extensibility. These choices roughly means simpler scope rules, structured concept generation and incremental programming, and automatic concept matching for module identification between modules. At the level of language, it also means Patch supports both name independence (similar to C++, Prolog), and position independence (similar to SQL) so that the order or the naming of parameters of a module will have almost no relevance to its appropriateness when called from or used in another module. All a user will have to know what a module conceptually requires as inputs to generate a desired output. In this sense, Patch is more declarative than procedural in design but procedural in its execution.

Broadly, the interface has three panels, one icon bank to the left (blue ellipse) and one command and folder bank at the top (cyan box). The left panel (red box) is a canvas where users express their computational solutions, and right panel (green box) serves as the display and input console while the bottom panel (blue box) is reserved for diagnostics and system messages. Users draw a tree involving the icons in the icon bank, the root of which is the module icon. The solid arrows represent downward flow of control or sequence of actions, and the dashed arrows represent membership of actions in another action or step.

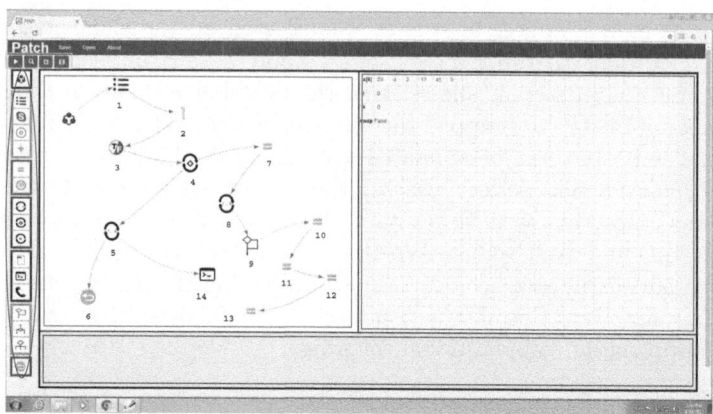

Fig. 2. Patch visual interface showing bubble sort procedure in Fig. 1. (Color figure online)

For example, the dashed arrow from the top module icon means the remaining subtree is contained within the module, and the same way the subtree rooted in 7 is contained within node 4. The Patch tree shown in Fig. 2, is the bubble sort algorithm as designed by a user and Patch is showing the state after step 3.

Technically, every Patch program is a set of named modules each with a (possibly empty) set of input data objects, and a set of data objects it returns when called. Any subset of the data objects in its I/O sets can be from/to the console, a stored repository or another module that uses it. Naturally, I/O from/to console and stored repository takes place inside the module. A module is a pair $\langle D, S \rangle$ where D is a set of data objects it uses, and S is a sequence of logical steps it follows to manipulate the data objects. The basic and complex data types Patch supports can be used to declare the I/O data objects. Users are able to execute the tree on the canvas at any point and see the results on the green panel. The interface is interactive and actually shows what could be expected on the green panel as the drawing continues. The qualitative details of each node is entered using appropriate forms that can be opened with right clicks of the mouse. The drawing rules ensure all graphs are trees and each node has no more than one solid or one dashed arrow.

4   Related Research

The emergence of Scratch and Snap!, and online tools such as Khan Academy [1] or PythonTutor [2] are relatively new. The focus of each of these systems are different and thus often are hard to compare on identical grounds. But we believe in functionality, Patch shares its execution style and some of its features with PythonTutor, and it is conceptually similar to Scratch and Snap! But Patch combines the power of Mind*Reader*'s tutoring and assessment that no other system currently has. We believe the ability to build programs visually, incrementally and interactively with active tutoring support is a powerful combination. Research is, however, outstanding on the effectiveness of the approach adopted in Patch and Mind*Reader* in real life classrooms.

5 Summary

Patch is an experimental prototype with limited but emerging set of functionalities and support for multiple abstraction layers for diverse student groups and multiple STEM disciplines. Patch supports exploration and self-learning naturally. It is currently being implemented and tested to validate the hypothesis that all three abstraction layers can be seamlessly supported in a single platform and augmented with an active tutoring and assessment component. Initial experimental results are promising though more research is needed. Patch aims to guarantee generating functionally equivalent code segments at all three of these layers if the solutions specified are indeed identical. Generated and written codes can be compared at the click of a button. Currently, a set of basic programming features for entry level programming course is being identified and abstracted, and methods are being devised to make the system incremental and hierarchical so that complex features can be designed and added using the basic features. A community based approach to incremental design is being contemplated.

References

1. Khan Academy. https://www.khanacademy.org/. Accessed 19 June 2017
2. Python Tutor. http://pythontutor.com/. Accessed 19 June 2017
3. Toptal. https://www.toptal.com/developers/sorting-algorithms. Accessed 19 Apr 2017
4. Broll, B., Lédeczi, Á., Völgyesi, P., Sallai, J., Maroti, M., Carrillo, A., Weeden-Wright, S.L., Vanags, C., Swartz, J. D., Lu, M.: A visual programming environment for learning distributed programming. In: SIGCSE, pp. 81–86. ACM (2017)
5. Ernst, M.D.: Natural language is a programming language: applying natural language processing to software development. In: SNAPL. LIPIcs, vol. 71, pp. 4:1–4:14 (2017). Schloss Dagstuhl - Leibniz-Zentrum fuer Informatik
6. Galles, D.: Data structure visualization library. https://www.cs.usfca.edu/~galles/visualization/Algorithms.html. Accessed 19 Apr 2017
7. Jamil, H.M.: Automated personalized assessment of computational thinking MOOC assignments. In: Proceedings of the 17th IEEE International Conference on Advanced Learning Technologies, ICALT 2017, Timisoara, Romania, 3–7 July, pp. 261–263 (2017)
8. Jin, Z., Anderson, M.R., Cafarella, M.J., Jagadish, H.V.: Foofah: a programming-by-example system for synthesizing data transformation programs. In: SIGMOD Conference, pp. 1607–1610. ACM (2017)
9. Martin, V.J., Pereira, S., Sridharan, T., Rivero, C.R.: Automated personalized feedback in introductory Java programming MOOCs. In: IEEE ICDE, California, 19–22 April, pp. 1259–1270 (2017)
10. Mou, X., Jamil, H.M., Rinker, R.: Visual orchestration and autonomous execution of distributed and heterogeneous computational biology pipelines. In: IEEE BIBM, Shenzhen, 15–18 December, pp. 752–757 (2016)

11. Turchi, T., Malizia, A.: Fostering computational thinking skills with a tangible blocks programming environment. In: IEEE VL/HCC, UK, pp. 232–233 (2016)
12. Wing, J.M.: Computational thinking. Commun. ACM **49**(3), 33–35 (2006)

A Framework for Integrating Pedagogy and Technology in Context-Aware Learning Environment

Betty Mayeku[1(✉)] and Dieter Hogrefe[2]

[1] Kibabii University, Bungoma, Kenya
bmayeku@kibu.ac.ke
[2] Georg-August University, Geottingen, Germany

Abstract. Context-aware technologies promise great potential in Technology Enhanced Learning (TEL). They are transforming the learning environment in a way that we are now frequently surrounded and immersed in learning experiences. However, as transformation arises in TEL as a result of these technologies, so does the challenge of understanding and applying a sound pedagogical foundation when utilizing these technologies for effective learning. It is clear that a comprehensive and inclusive framework is needed for ensuring sound pedagogy when applying these technologies. This paper presents a framework for the integration of pedagogy and technology in a Context-Aware Learning Environment (CALE). The elements identified as critical in guiding the development of this framework include: ensuring sound pedagogical foundation; addressing the uniqueness of distance learning environment and the social aspect of learning; considering context in which learning occurs and providing adaptive and/or personalized learning in order to ensure that learning is tailored to learners' needs based on the context in which learning occurs. The CALE framework may be significant to designers, developers of CALEs and instructors because it provides a guideline on how CALE can be rooted best in a sound pedagogical foundation.

Keywords: Context · Context-aware technology · Pedagogy

1 Introduction

Context-awareness is proposed as an essential component of pervasive and ubiquitous computing. Context as defined by [1] is any information that can be used to characterize the situation of an entity. An entity in this case is a person, place, or object that is considered relevant to the interaction between the users and application [1]. In the field of Technology Enhanced Learning (TEL), context has been defined as the current situation of a person related to a learning activity [2]. The ability for the applications and services to use context information is what is referred to as context-awareness.

The use of context-aware technologies for learning and teaching brings optimism and opportunity for education since they promise vast potential to offer great innovations in TEL. Just to mention a few of these potentials; they provide possibilities to adapt the learning spaces to different contexts of use hence capable to cater for different learners' needs. They also hold the potential to provide learners with personalized learning

© Springer International Publishing AG 2017
H. Xie et al. (Eds.): ICWL 2017, LNCS 10473, pp. 215–220, 2017.
DOI: 10.1007/978-3-319-66733-1_24

experiences in real-world situations [2]. This is because context-aware learning environment has the capability to integrate real and virtual learning environments.

2 Problem Overview

The mobility, heterogeneity and dynamism attributes that normally characterize context-aware technologies are transforming the learning environment in a way that we are now frequently surrounded and immersed in learning experiences. However as transformation arises in TEL as a result of these technologies, so does the challenge of understanding and applying sound pedagogical foundation in utilizing these technologies for effective learning. It is imperative as noted in [3] that pedagogy (thus the collected practices, processes, strategies, procedures and methods of teaching and learning [3]) continues to transform and evolve as technology changes. One major issue faced by emerging TEL environments as pointed out by Park [4] is the lack of a solid theoretical framework which can guide effective instructional design and evaluate the quality of programs that rely significantly on the technologies used. Furthermore, addressing the social aspect of learning in applying these technologies in creating new models of TEL also poses a challenge because of insufficient understanding of pedagogical application outside the classroom. Therefore it is clear that there is a need for a comprehensive and inclusive framework that provides a guideline on how these emerging technologies can be rooted best in a sound pedagogical foundation. This study specifically focused on context-aware technologies.

3 Integrating Pedagogy and Technology in CALE

Pedagogy is the cornerstone of effective learning in any learning environment. Considering the best possible uses of context-aware technology for pedagogical advantage is critical in achieving effective learning in a Context-Aware Learning Environment (CALE). In order to achieve quality education while tapping into the full potential context-aware technology offers, there is need for these two components thus technology and pedagogy to be properly integrated. To explore how CALE can be rooted best in a sound pedagogical foundation, this study attempted to formulate a framework that offers a platform for the integration of pedagogy and technology in CALE. Existing literature was extensively reviewed to guide the formulation of the framework. Four elements were identified as critical in providing a platform for proper integration of pedagogy and technology in CALE. These elements were in turn used as building blocks in the formulation of CALE framework. The elements include: (a) ensuring sound pedagogical foundation, (b) addressing the uniqueness of Distance Learning (DL) (in the case of DL environment) and social aspects of learning, (c) considering context in which learning occurs, and (d) adapting and/or personalizing learning to ensure that learning is tailored to learners' needs based on the context in which learning occurs. These elements are discussed in details below.

3.1 Sound Pedagogical Foundation

No matter the learning environment, understanding of how people can learn as revealed in several studies is key in offering guidelines for a solid pedagogical foundation. Over the years, a huge effort has been made to understand how people can learn resulting into the formulation of learning theories. The most dominant theories to learning include behaviorist, cognitivist, constructivist, and connectivist. Each of these learning theories has been noted to play an important role in learning. This study therefore argues that a good instructional designer in a CALE should not strictly apply only one theory when designing, rather, it is important to consider the specific learning task in relation to the approaches. Therefore, there is need for a framework comprising of well integrated learning theories. To capture and achieve a well-balanced synthesis of these learning theories, this study adopted the instructional framework by Saskatchewan Education [5]. The framework is heavily influenced by learning theories. It also provides a guideline on the integration of interrelated levels of approaches. These levels of approaches include: instructional models (which reflect learning theories), instructional strategies, instructional methods and instructional skills.

3.2 Uniqueness of Distance Learning and Social Aspects of Learning

Distance learning (DL) environment comes along with its uniqueness like the separation of the teacher and learner and learner diversity among others. Furthermore, in a CALE, the diversity aspect is even further broadened due the mobility, dynamism and heterogeneity characteristics of context-aware technologies. Another unique feature of DL is its evolving nature. DL has been described as a changing paradigm [6]. However, as DL evolve alongside technological changes, there exist theories and frameworks that have been developed over the years to offer guidance in achieving effective DL in their respective technological eras. In attempt to develop a comprehensive framework, this study explored the existing theories and frameworks with elements which, if properly integrated offer guidance in addressing the uniqueness of DL in CALE extensively. This study adopted Park's pedagogical framework (PPF) [4] which integrates some of the Activity theory [7, 8] elements into Transaction Distance theory [9] to support both individual and social aspects. In order to consider the importance of the social aspects of learning, PPF has an individual versus collective (or socialized) activities dimension. This dimension that indicates the range of individualized to socialized activity can be a useful lens for reviewing diverse learning activities which is a key feature of CALE.

3.3 Considering Context in Which Learning Occurs

Learning always occurs in context [10]. This is because learning is interwoven with other activities as part of everyday life. Context situates the learner within an environment from which the senses continually receive data that is interpreted as meaningful information and employed to construct understanding [11]. Context in which learning occurs varies from learner to learner. Therefore, taking context into consideration is crucial in generating appropriately designed learning experiences that are tailored to learners' unique needs. Furthermore, with learning taking place in a rich environment, there exist overwhelming resources available for learners to choose from. In order to identify and retrieve suitable resources for individual learners based on their needs, there is a need to take the context of the learner into account.

3.4 Adaptive and Personalized Learning

The key to the success of accessing learning resources in using context-aware technologies as argued in [12] is adaption and personalization. Adaption deals with taking learners' situation, educational needs and personal characteristics into consideration in generating appropriately designed learning experiences. The adaptability of the learning environment to different contexts during the learning process promotes greatly effective learning since it tailors learning to individual learner's needs. Personalization on the other hand, in addition to responding to the learners' needs and interests, learner involvement is its key attribute. Learners manage their own learning as stated in [13]. It allows them to control their own academic experiences as well as be involved in the creation of learning activities. As a result, it satisfies learners' needs and it creates an engaged learner. Context-aware technology promises great potential in providing adaptive and personalized services due to its context-aware capability.

4 Context-Aware Learning Environment Framework

The elements discussed above thus: ensuring sound pedagogical foundation; addressing the uniqueness of DL (in case of DL environment) and social aspect of learning;

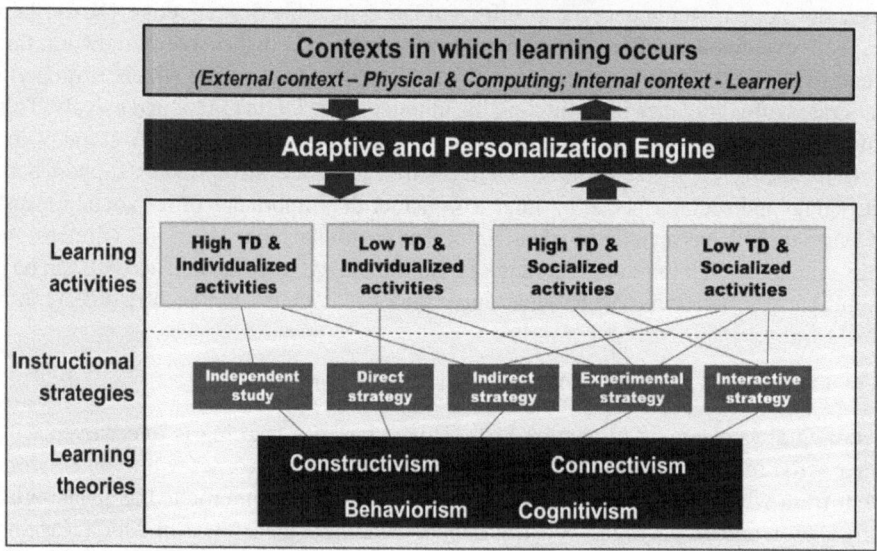

Key - TD: Transactional Distance

Fig. 1. CALE pedagogical framework

considering the context in which learning occurs and providing adaptive/and personalized learning were used as building blocks in formulating a CALE pedagogical framework. The framework as presented in Fig. 1 comprises of three layers: the bottom layer (pedagogical layer), the middle layer (adaption and personalization engine) and the top layer (contextual layer).

The bottom layer which offers the pedagogical foundation integrates learning theories which serve as the foundation block of the framework. The theories are linked with instructional strategies as adopted from the Saskatchewan instructional framework [5]. The layer also links different context-aware learning activities with their possible instructional strategies. The utilization of different context-aware learning activities supports different forms of transactional distance (i.e. the psychological and communication space between the learner and the teacher [9]) hence addressing the uniqueness of DL. It also addresses the social aspects of learning through a range of individualized to socialized activities. Applying PPF in CALE, the four types of learning activities that can be generated in DL environment mediated by context-aware (CA) technologies include (a) high transactional distance socialized CA learning, (b) high transactional distance individualized CA learning, (c) low transactional distance socialized CA learning, and (d) low transactional distance individualized CA learning. The middle layer i.e. the adaption and/or personalization engine acts as the mediator between the pedagogical layer and the contextual layer. This middle layer ensures that learning is tailored to learners' individual needs based on the contextual information received from the context layer. Based on the contextual information, the ideal learning activities, instructional strategy, methods among others are also determined through this layer.

The top layer presents context in which learning occurs. This is where the learner is situated. The layer is responsible for offering contextual information of which the adaptive and/personalization engine will use to communicate with the bottom layer in order to determine the ideal pedagogical approach. Since context is an open concept, this study classified its context dimensions into two major categories thus the external context (which comprises of physical context and computing context) and internal context (which mainly comprises of learner context). In this study, physical context refers to the surroundings which are peripheral to the learning activities but affect the learner's behavior or influence the learning process. Computing context refers to the artifacts i.e. the technology used to mediate learning. The learner context reflects learner profile and the cognitive state of the learner. It refers to aspects about the learner like the learner's preferences, goals, tasks, emotional state among others.

5   Conclusion

Context-aware technology promises great potential in TEL. However, understanding and applying sound pedagogical foundation for effective learning when utilizing these technologies still poses a challenge. This has been attributed to the lack of a solid theoretical framework which can guide effective instructional design as well as properly integrate the social aspect in applying these technologies. In attempt to address these challenges, this paper presented a CALE Framework whose aim was to provide a platform that offers proper integration of pedagogy and technology when applying context-aware technology. The CALE framework may be of significant importance to designers, developers of CALEs and instructors because it provides a guideline on how CALE can be rooted best in a sound pedagogical foundation.

6 Work in Progress and Future Work

The formulated framework has been used to guide the development of a Personalized and Engaging CALE (PECALE) software prototype. PECALE, which is still under study is aimed at addressing the learner diversity and learner engagement challenges in collaborative online learning environment.

References

1. Dey, A.K., Salber, D., Abowd, G.D.: A conceptual framework and a toolkit for supporting the rapid prototyping of context-aware applications. Hum. Comput. Interact. **16**(2), 97–166 (2001)
2. Sampson, D.G., Zervas, P.: Context aware adaptive and personalized mobile learning. In: International Conference for E-learning and Distance Education, Riyadh (2013)
3. Naidoo, L.: Integrating pedagogy, cognition and technology in higher/distance education. In: Distance Education Conference, Pilsen (2010)
4. Park, Y.: A pedagogical framework for mobile learning: categorizing educational applications of mobile technologies into four types. Int. Rev. Res. Open Distance Learn. **12**(2), 78–102 (2011)
5. Saskatchewan, E.: Instructional Approaches: A Framework for Professional Practice. Saskatchewan Education, Saskatchewan (1991)
6. Moore, M., Kearsely, G.: Distance Education: A Systems View, 2nd edn. Thomson/ Wadsworth, Belmont (2005)
7. Vygotsky, L.: Interaction between Learning and Development. Mind and Society, pp. 79–91. Harvard University Press, Cambridge (1978)
8. Engeström, Y.: Activity theory and individual and social transformation. Multidiscip. Newsl. Activity Theor. **7**(8), 14–15 (1991)
9. Moore, M.: The Theory of Transactional Distance. Handbook of Distance Education, pp. 89–105. Lawrence Erlbaum Associates, Mahwah (2007)
10. Uden, L.: Activity theory for designing mobile learning. Int. J. Mob. Learn. Organ. **1**(1), 81–102 (2007)
11. Sharples, M., Taylor, J., Vavoula, G.: A Theory of Learning for the Mobile Age. The Sage Handbook of E-learning, pp. 221–247. Sage, London (2007)
12. Sharples, M., Taylor, J., Vavoula, G.: A Theory of Learning for the Mobile Age. The Sage Handbook of E-learning, pp. 221–247. Sage, London (2007)
13. Basye, D.: Personalized vs. differentiated vs. individualized learning. https://www.iste.org

ICT-Enabled Open and Distance Learning - Its Influence on Career Development and Employability in Least Developed Countries: Case of Malawi

Dimson Kalelo-Phiri[✉] and Irwin Brown

University of Cape Town, Cape Town, South Africa
dkphiri@yahoo.com

Abstract. This article proposes a study that will explain how open and distance learning facilitated through the use of information and communication technologies influences career development of learners and employability of graduates in least developed countries. The study will adopt interpretive research methods due to the nature of the data to be collected. The paper proposes a conceptual framework which will be tested empirically in the proposed study and can also be adopted in research studies similar to the one proposed. Data will be collected through semi-structured interviews with national-level policy makers, higher-education institutions and leaders in various industries a part from learners and teachers. The study will make an explanatory contribution to theory in the field of distance education especially in open and distance learning facilitated through the use of information and communication technologies.

Keywords: Open and distance learning · Career development · Employability · Community of inquiry · Social cognitive career theory · Employability theory

1 Introduction

Open and Distance Learning (ODL) in the form of print, radio/audio or video helps to reach out to learners having geographical and time barriers (Ally 2004). Since its first introduction in 1994, Information and Communication Technology (ICT) enabled ODL has been accepted in societies and is increasingly gaining popularity (Bhuasiri et al. 2012; Tarus et al. 2015) in response to the popularity of the growth of the Internet (Muilenburg and Berge 2005). The concept of ICT-enabled ODL is well researched and research trends in the broad field of distance education well established (Zawacki-Richter 2009; Bozkurt et al. 2015). Using Sherry (1996) categorization system, research in distance education conducted from 1990 to the present time has mainly focused on instructional design issues (design, development, evaluation and revision), learner characteristics (behaviour patterns and learning styles) and strategies for increasing inter-activity and active learning In contrast, professional development and faculty support (learner competences and how they can be developed) has persistently been identified as one of the areas that deserve further attention (Berge and Mrozowski 2001; Zawacki-Richter et al. 2009; Bozkurt et al. 2015).

© Springer International Publishing AG 2017
H. Xie et al. (Eds.): ICWL 2017, LNCS 10473, pp. 221–226, 2017.
DOI: 10.1007/978-3-319-66733-1_25

Professional development relates to career development and it is defined as activities aimed at enhancing an individual's knowledge and skills in order to stay current or advance in a particular industry. Career development refers to a process of managing learning, work, leisure, and transitions in order to move toward a personally determined and evolving preferred future. Studies which explain ICT-enabled ODL with particular focus to professional development and career development and further how career development contributes to employability of graduates are arguably limited and in some cases lacking altogether.

Secondly recognized research in the field of distance education is mainly that conducted in developed countries despite disparities in ODL motives between developed and least developed countries. While ODL in developed countries aims at developing knowledge economies (Zhang 2005), ODL in least developed countries is aimed at providing access to higher education to individuals living in remote and rural areas (Mahmud 2010). Thirdly research in distance education also identifies learners and teachers as main actors in ICT-enabled ODL (Bozkurt et al. 2015). However actors such as national-level policy makers, higher-education institutions and leaders in various industries are also suggested as important players in ICT-enabled ODL (Bhuasiri et al. 2012).

The proposed study will explain how ICT-enabled ODL influences career development of learners and how career development contributes to employability of graduates. The study will be conducted in Malawi which United Nations Development Programme (2016) classifies as one of the least developed countries having a Human Development Index (HDI) of 0.476. Malawi adopted its National ICT Policy in 2013. Among others, the ICT Policy aims at modernizing education systems in Malawi through ICT use and promotes ICT-enabled ODL to complement face-to-face campus based education systems. The National ICT Policy also recognises higher-education institutions as key players in ICT-enabled ODL (Gombachika and Kanjo 2014) hence making Malawi empirically sound for the study.

Three theories; Community of Inquiry (CoI) Framework, Social Cognitive Career Theory (SCCT) and Employability Theory are identified as relatively sound in talking to the data to be collected following interpretive research methods. The study will make an explanatory theoretical contribution in the field of distance education. Higher-education institutions and policy makers will find the study useful when making decisions concerning ICT-enabled ODL. The study will also be useful to scholars when structuring future research in related areas.

1.1 Problem Statement

Three areas can be noted from the literature overview to be problematic. Firstly, research that explains how ICT-enabled ODL influences career development and how career development contributes to employability of learners are lacking. Secondly, published research in distance education is mainly that conducted in developed countries despite differences in ODL motives between developed and least developed countries. Thirdly, research recognises learners and instructors as main actors in ICT-enabled ODL while perspectives from players such as national-level policy makers, higher-education institutions and leaders in various industries may provide more insight that can help to understand the ICT-enabled ODL concept.

1.2 Research Question

The proposed study will be guided by the research question: *How does ICT-enabled ODL influence career development of learners and how does that contribute to employability of graduates in least developed countries?*

2 Literature Review

An ICT-enabled ODL class was first offered in 1994 (Daniel 1997). Since then, ICT enabled ODL has increasingly been gaining popularity (Bhuasiri et al. 2012; Tarus et al. 2015). The concept of ICT-enabled ODL is well-researched as evident in a series of literature reviews (Berge and Mrozowski 2001; Zawacki-Richter 2009; Bozkurt et al. 2015). The focus areas are mostly associated with "interaction and communication in learning communities, learner characteristics and instructional design" (Bozkurt et al. 2015, p. 355). Individual learners (58%) and teachers (10%) are identified as the main studied groups in ODL research. This is in line with what prominent researchers in the field of ODL (Randy Garrison, Terry Anderson and Walter Archer) consider as main participants in ICT-enabled ODL (Berge and Mrozowski 2001). Out of the reviewed 861 research articles, only 2% of the articles focused on educational institutions (Bozkurt et al. 2015).

While individual learners and teachers form the main participants for most research in distance education (Bozkurt et al. 2015), other participants such as policy makers, higher-education institutions and leaders in various industries are equally important (Bhuasiri et al. 2012). Policies provide a rational for ICT-enabled education systems (Kozma 2008) and motivate, change, and bring together dissimilar efforts in order to advance nation's overall educational goal (Jones and Kozma 2003). Related to policy formulation is planning which is performed at institutional level hence the importance to solicit perspectives from higher-education institutions.

Research that is considered as representative in the field of distance education is mainly that conducted in developed countries (Bozkurt et al. 2015). This is against varying ODL motives between developed and least developed countries. While ODL in developed countries aim at building knowledge economies, ODL in least developed countries is aimed at providing basic and literacy education (Zhang 2005). Findings for research conducted in developed countries may therefore not be applicable to situations that are particular to least developed countries. This calls for research in premised on ODL motives that are specific to least developed countries.

3   Theoretical Background

Three theories will form the lenses for examining the empirical data. First, the CoI Framework will be used to explain how learning experiences are achieved in ICT-enabled ODL. Secondly, the SCCT will be used to explain the career development process and lastly the employability theory will be used to advance the concept of career development to employability. The three theories are preferred over many others since, as Grover and Lyytinen (2015) recommend, they all seem to interact well with the data to be collected.

The notion in CoI framework is that any effective learning is a function of three interacting principle elements: teaching presence, social presence and cognitive presence (Arbaugh 2008) while a SCCT is more linked to cognitive mediators (career interests, choice goals, choice actions and performance domains) through which learning experiences guide career behaviour (Lent et al. 1994). It highlights three interlocking models that explain (a) how academic and career interests develop, (b) how career interests promote career-relevant choices and (c) how people attain varying levels of performance (Lent and Brown 1996). Lastly the Employability Theory identifies career development, experience, degree subject knowledge, generic skills and emotional intelligence as principal components of employability (Pool and Sewell 2007). These components influence self-efficacy, self-esteem and self-confidence whose interaction results in employability profile of an individual.

An integration of the three theories results in the framework presented in Fig. 1.

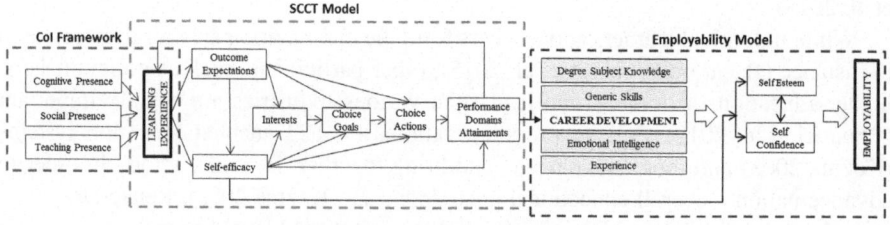

Fig. 1. Proposed conceptual framework for the study

The logic in the proposed study is that learning experiences which result from ICT-enabled ODL is explained through the CoI Framework. From the SCCT perspective, the learning experience influences learners' self-efficacy and outcome expectations which in turn shape career interests, choice goals, choice actions and performance domains which result in career development. Further, the Employability Model identifies career development as one element that contributes to employability.

4   Methodology

A qualitative research approach will be employed in the proposed study. Phenomenology which focuses on lived experiences (Monod et al. 2007) and recognizes human experience as essential in developing patterns and relationships among underlying concepts (Creswell 2013) will be adopted as a method of data collection. Secondly, hermeneutics will be employed as a data analysis method. Hermeneutics fosters understanding (as opposed to describing) in order to make sense of and comprehend a phenomena of interest (Bauman 1978) and assumes the world as created by people's subjective and intersubjective meanings (Orlikowski and Baroudi 1991).

5   Conclusion

This article is a concept paper that presents a proposal for a study which is aimed at understanding how career development of learners is influenced by ICT-enabled ODL and how that contributes to employability of graduates in least developed countries.

References

Arbaugh, J.B.: Does the community of inquiry framework predict outcomes in online MBA courses? Int. Rev. Res. Open Distance Learn. **9**(2), 1–21 (2008)

Ally, M.: Foundations of educational theory for online learning. Theor. Pract. Online Learn. **2**, 15–44 (2004)

Bauman, Z.: Hermeneutics and Social Science: Approaches to Understanding. Hutchinson and Son, London (1978)

Berge, Z.L., Mrozowski, S.: Review of research in distance education, 1990 to 1999. Am. J. Distance Educ. **15**(3), 5–19 (2001)

Bhuasiri, W., Xaymoungkhoun, O., Zo, H., Rho, J.J., Ciganek, A.P.: Critical success factors for e-learning in developing countries: a comparative analysis between ICT experts and faculty. Comput. Educ. **58**(2012), 843–855 (2012)

Bozkurt, A., Akgun-Ozbek, E., Yilmazel, S., Erdogdu, E., Ucar, H., Guler, E., et al.: Trends in distance education research: a content analysis of journals 2009–2013. Int. Rev. Res. Open Distrib. Learn. **16**(1), 330–363 (2015)

Creswell, J.W.: Research Design: Qualitative, Quantitative, and Mixed Methods Approaches. Sage Publications (2013)

Daniel, J.S.: Why universities need technology strategies. Change Mag. High. Learn. **29**(4), 10–17 (1997)

Grover, V., Lyytinen, K.: New state of play in information systems research: the push to the edges. MIS Q. **39**(2), 271–296 (2015)

Gombachika, H.S., Kanjo, C.: Use of ICT in science and engineering: a case of University of Malawi (2014)

Jones, R.M., Kozma, R.: Local and national ICT policies. In: Technology, Innovation, and Educational Change: A Global Perspective, pp. 163–194 (2003)

Kozma, R.B.: Comparative analysis of policies for ICT in education. In: Voogt, J., Knezek, G. (eds.) International Handbook of Information Technology in Primary and Secondary Education, vol. 20, pp. 1083–1096. Springer, Boston (2008). doi:10.1007/978-0-387-73315-9_68

Lent, R.W., Brown, S.D.: Social cognitive approach to career development: an overview. Career Dev. Q. **44**, 310–321 (1996)

Lent, R.W., Brown, S.D., Hackett, G.: Toward a unifying social cognitive theory of career and academic interest, choice, and performance. J. Vocat. Behav. **45**(1), 79–122 (1994)

Mahmud, K.: E-learning for tertiary level education in least developed countries: implementation obstacles and way outs for Bangladesh. Int. J. Comput. Theor. Eng. **2**(2), 150–155 (2010)

Monod, E., Pallud, J., Klein, H.: Heidegger's phenomenology still a 'preferred research approach' for user-driven research? The case of cultural organizations. In: Proceedings of AMCIS 2007, p. 356 (2007)

Muilenburg, L.Y., Berge, Z.L.: Student barriers to online learning: a factor analytic study. Distance Educ. 26(1), 29–48 (2005)

Orlikowski, W.J., Baroudi, J.J.: Studying information technology in organizations: research approaches and assumptions. Inf. Syst. Res. 2(1), 1–28 (1991)

Pool, D.L., Sewell, P.: The key to employability: developing a practical model of graduate employability. Education + Training 49(4), 277–289 (2007)

Sherry, L.: Issues in distance learning. Int. J. Educ. Telecommun. 1(4), 337–365 (1996)

Tarus, J.K., Gichoya, D., Muumbo, A.: Challenges of implementing e-learning in Kenya: a case of Kenyan public universities. Int. Rev. Res. Open Distrib. Learn. 16(1), 120–141 (2015)

UNDP: Human development for everyone (2016). http://hdr.undp.org/sites/all/themes/hdr_theme/country-notes/fr/MWI.pdf. Accessed 20 June 2017

Zawacki-Richter, O.: Research areas in distance education: a Delphi study. Int. Rev. Res. Open Distance Learn. 10(3), 1–17 (2009)

Zawacki-Richter, O., Bäcker, E.M., Vogt, S.: Review of distance education research (2000 to 2008): analysis of research areas, methods, and authorship patterns. Int. Rev. Res. Open Distrib. Learn. 10(6), 21–50 (2009)

Zhang, K.: China's online education: rhetoric and realities. In: Carr-Chellman, A.A. (ed.) Global Perspectives on E-learning: Rhetoric and Reality, pp. 21–32. Sage Publications, London (2005)

Author Index